Landscape

Traveled by Coyote and Crane

ى

The World of the Schitsu'umsh

(Coeur d'Alene Indians)

Landscape
Traveled by Coyote and Crane

꒖

The World of the Schitsu'umsh
(Coeur d'Alene Indians)

RODNEY FREY

in collaboration with

THE SCHITSU'UMSH

A McLellan Book

UNIVERSITY OF WASHINGTON PRESS

Seattle & London

Grateful acknowledgment to Harry and Colleen Magnuson

of Wallace, Idaho, and to the John Calhoun Smith Memorial Fund,

University of Idaho, for supporting the 2005 edition of this book.

This book is published with the assistance of a grant from

the McLellan Endowed Series Fund,

established through the generosity of

Mary McCleary McLellan and Mary McLellan Williams.

Library of Congress Cataloging-in-Publication Data

Frey, Rodney.
Landscape traveled by coyote and crane : the world of the Schitsu'umsh :
Coeur d'Alene Indians / Rodney Frey in collaboration with the Schitsu'umsh.
p. cm.
"A McLellan book."
Includes bibliographical references and index.
ISBN 0-295-98171-7 (cloth: alk. paper); ISBN 0-295-98162-8 (pbk.: alk paper)
1. Skitswish Indians.
E99.S63 F74   2001
977.7/00497—dc21   2001044281

In memory of

Lawrence Aripa, Lucy Finley, and Henry SiJohn,

whose wise counsel and love of the lake,

rivers, and mountains

helped inform and inspire the words of this book.

May their example continue

to guide and inspire future generations.

Contents

Stories

Foreword

There is a story in the title itself. *Landscape Traveled by Coyote and Crane* brings to life the culture, history, and traditions of the Coeur d'Alene Tribe. It brings to life the world our Creator gave us; it declares our commitment to this homeland and the lessons we have learned through the millennia.

Rodney Frey has studied it well. For some ten years, his research has included the traditional study of a scholar and it has included adopting an American Indian tradition of listening and, therefore, learning.

We share now and we have always shared our world with the animals of the forests and the birds in the air. Just as importantly, we learn from them. These classic lessons have and will always be the instruments of our education, taking us from childhoold through the journey of life and all the experiences and challenges it provides us.

There is a grand treasure of American history that has existed and survived since long before the coming of non-Indians. Millions of people lived and thrived on this continent for thousands of years and part of our treasure has been the oral tradition of handing from generation to generation the lessons of life and the stories that make the world.

In that world, we were wealthy Indians. The Schitsu'umsh homeland spans the western edge of the northern Rocky Mountains, from the Clark Fork River in Montana to Spokane Falls in Washington, including the vast forests, lakes, streams, and valleys of north Idaho. Nature's gifts in this homeland are endless and since time immemorial have provided everything we needed for life and for prosperity.

Our traditions include sharing this wealth. And we continue that tradition by sharing the knowledge and wisdom of our own Lawrence Aripa, Lucy Finley, and Henry SiJohn. We cherish their memories just as they cherished the memories and teachings of their own elders and ancestors. So we offer our treasure with the hope that more Americans will take ownership in it and understand the depth and value of their own history in the landscape we share across the continent.

As Henry SiJohn often said, we are here because this is where the Creator put us. This is our landscape of natural beauty and the people in its midst. This is where we have lived and grown with Coyote and Crane. You will understand our love for our Creator, this homeland, and for the wealth with which we are blessed.

Truly, our roots are here. They extend to the very center of the earth.

MX^w *Qin* (Snow on the Mountain)
Ernie Stensgar, Chairman, Coeur d'Alene Tribe

Acknowledgments

A project that seeks to convey something so cherished by a people must emanate from that people. I wish to give heartfelt thanks to the many Schitsu'umsh who opened up their lives and shared their stories with me. It is their voice I hope I have conveyed accurately and with "heart." Among those to whom I am particularly grateful are John Abraham, Felix Aripa, Lawrence Aripa, Lucy Finley, Mariane Hurley, Roberta Juneau, Marceline Kevis, David Matheson, Richard Mullen, Lawrence Nicodemus, Alfred Nomee, Henry SiJohn, Cliff SiJohn, Frenchy SiJohn, Skip Skanen, Dixie Stensgar, Ernie Stensgar, Marjorie Zarate, Jeannette Whitford, and Father Thomas Connolly. There can be no better teachers than those whom you have come to know as "elder brother," "elder sister," "father," and "grandmother."

Much of the research for this project is based upon materials gathered as part of the Coeur d'Alene Tribe's Natural Resource Damage Assessment. A special thanks goes to Phil Cernera, Project Director; to Ray Givens, Tribal Attorney; and to Ted Fortier of Seattle University and David Nugent of Colby College, fellow anthropologists and team members, whose encouragement was appreciated throughout. I also want to thank Robert McCarl of Boise State University and Gary Palmer of the University of Nevada, Las Vegas, for their thorough and insightful comments and suggestions on earlier drafts of this work, and to Rick Harmon for his invaluable editing assistance.

For permission to reprint copyrighted materials, I am grateful to the Jesuit Oregon Province Archives, Gonzaga University, for Morris Antelope's undated letter (retitled "Everything We Do a Sin") to the Commissioner of Indian Affairs; for Father Joset's letters (retitled "The Hunt"), from "The Coeur d'Alene," 1838–77:JP 36; and for "Somesh," from "A Quarter of a Century Among the Savages," 1838–77:JP 69; to Henry Holt and Company for Father Point's observations (retitled "A Medicine Lodge Ceremony Prior to the Hunt") from *Wilderness Kingdom,* 1967; and to the American

Anthropological Association for Susan Antelope's retitled "Camas Baking," from Gladys Reichard's "An Analysis of Coeur d'Alene Indian Myths," *Memoirs of the American Folk-Lore Society* 41, 1947. Unless otherwise noted, the photographs are by the author.

This manuscript was reviewed for its accuracy and appropriateness, and approved for public dissemination for educational purposes by the elders of the Schitsu'umsh and the Coeur d'Alene Tribal Council. The Council members were Lawrence Aripa, Norman Campbell, Norma Peone, Chuck Matheson, Henry SiJohn, Marjorie Zarate, and Ernie Stensgar, Chairman. While I am most appreciative of this review process for its ethnographic and ethical implications, and, as a result of the review, feel immensely honored by having been entrusted by the elders and Council with helping tell their story, I also take full responsibility for any errors or misconceptions that may have been inadvertently conveyed in *Landscape Traveled by Coyote and Crane.*

Royalties from the sale of this book go to the Schitsu'umsh Tribe.

Limlemtsh. Thank you.

R.F.
May 2001

Landscape

Traveled by Coyote and Crane

☙

The World of the Schi̱tsu'umsh

(Coeur d'Alene Indians)

Swift water on the St. Joe River, c. 1910
(courtesy Museum of North Idaho, Coeur d'Alene, acc. no. SJR-2-8)

✦

Introduction to the
Sch̲itsu'umsh Landscape

As the elders would remind us, the place to begin our understanding of the people who call themselves Sch̲itsu'umsh ("the ones that were found here"; pronounced schēts-ü'ümsh), and whom others often call "Coeur d'Alene," is in their oral traditions, in the accounts of the First Peoples. The following story tells of Crane and Coyote, who, along with the other First Peoples, created and transformed the world of the Sch̲itsu'umsh. Ingrained within the narrative are certain "teachings." These teachings go to the very heart of Sch̲itsu'umsh life. They have shown great resilience in the face of tremendous Euro-American pressures, and they continue to pervade much of Sch̲itsu'umsh society today.

Crane and Coyote[1]

Here is the village. There, far from it, lives Crane and his grandmother. He is a good hunter. He always has plenty of deer meat hanging from his lodge.

Then in this village the Chief asks his daughters to go to Crane's lodge. "He may share meat with you. The people in our village are hungry," he says. His daughters are Little Squirrel and Chipmunk.

Then the girls go to Crane's lodge. When they get to the door to his lodge, they see it is dotted with cooked camas. They pick some off, eat it. The girls think it must be meat. Then Crane comes out. "This is not what you are looking for." He invites the girls into his lodge here. Then he calls on his grandmother to cook some meat for them to eat.

Then his grandmother boils some meat, places it before the girls. She takes a piece of fat, cuts it in half, then in quarters. The grandmother then puts two quarters of the fat there on each of the girl's dishes.[2]

Then each morning Crane goes out to hunt deer. He gets two deer each time. Then he hangs one on each side of his belt. About two days later he goes out again. He never takes more than two. There is always plenty of

3

meat of all kinds hanging here in his lodge—fresh meat, smoked meat, dried meat.

Then one morning Crane says to his grandmother, "Get the meat ready. The girls are going back to their village." The grandmother makes huge bundles of meat. Then the older girl comes out. She says, "That's certainly plenty of meat. How can we carry it all?"

"I'll go with you. Just put the meat under my belt," Crane says. The bundle is made very tiny. Crane sticks it in his belt.[3]

Then they go to the village. It's the village of Crane's in-laws, the father of his wives. Crane throws the bundles down, goes into the Chief's lodge there. The two sisters who had been away so long are glad to see their mother.

"Get the bundle, for now we will eat well," the elder sister says to her mother. The mother goes out. "Take half for yourself, half for the rest of the village," the girl says to her. "It's such a small bundle," the mother says. The mother is just about to untie it. Her daughter stops her. "It must first be placed on a big mat," she says. Then the mother unties it. The tiny bundle spreads out, becomes a huge pile. The mother puts half away for her family, half she ties in a number of bundles for all her relatives. Then all the villagers come and eat the meat.[4]

One day Crane announces that they should get fresh meat. They prepare for the hunt and moccasins are readied. Crane asks if everyone is ready. The Coyote comes along.

Then Crane and the others go off. Having gone not too far, he says, "Now, we'll stop to make a fire and warm up." Coyote says, "What must it be that is tame enough for you to shoot?" Here is a rotten tree. Crane kicks it. It cracks and begins to burn. Coyote says, "Oh, you know that trick too. My father's father's father used to do it." This Coyote goes to that tree, but when he kicks it, it doesn't burn, and he falls on his back over there. He says, "It wet!" So he looks for another. Then again he kicks it, and again falls. Then Crane says, "You burnt-eye of a Coyote there, come warm your hands."

Then Crane tells the people to drive the deer toward him here. The people scattered to their positions and Crane prepares himself. The people drive the deer up. As they come near, Crane directs the men not to kill more than two each, and to get ready to shoot. The Coyote did not get ready, but keeps his arrows tied up. Coyote says, "Why should I get ready when there is nothing to shoot."

Then Crane calls, "*hi . . . . . . hi . . . . . . ,*" and immediately the deer run up. No one shoots more than two. Then Coyote is leaning against a tree when he hears a noise in the snow. He sees it is a deer. He reaches for his quiver but cannot untie it. So he tears the quiver trying to get the arrows out. He aims at the biggest deer and shoots it. He shoots another and then there are no more deer. Then the Coyote tracks the deer he had shot. He goes only a little way and there lays a small fawn. He goes farther and there lays another, smaller than the first.

Then the people come and look. Coyote says, "This is not my game. I had shot two big ones." But the people see that it is Coyote's arrow in the small fawn. Coyote says, "Someone must have substituted his deer for mine." Then he keeps quiet.

Crane asks if each hunter got just two deer and how Coyote did. All got just two, but Coyote took two fawns. Crane tells them to skin the deer now and then go on.

Then Crane hangs one of his deer on each side of his belt. The Coyote sees Crane do this. He says, "Oh, you know that too; my father's father's father used to do it." So Coyote tries the same thing. But as he goes along, his game drags on the ground, even though he has only very small fawns. He ties it up more firmly and fastens his deer again, but it breaks. Crane says, "Coyote, you burnt-eye, take the meat to your children." It takes all of Coyote's strength to get home. He is thirsty.

Then, the end of the trail.

For the Schitsu'umsh, the oral traditions—such as in the stories of Crane and Coyote and the other First Peoples—have had an essential role in defining, bringing forth, and maintaining their entire world. As prominent figures in the oral literature, Crane and Coyote not only provide teachings— models for behaving in the world—but they also contribute to the making of that world. For example, Crane's character traits, and the corresponding model they provide for behaving, are manifested throughout Schitsu'umsh society—from the behavior of "designated hunters" to the rituals associated with the digging and distributing of camas and water potato, from the Jump Dance and Sweat House ceremonies to the Memorial Giveaway. And as the story of Crane and Coyote is told, the lessons and values embedded in the narrative are also intrinsically and unequivocally interwoven into the surrounding landscape—the mountains, rivers, and lakes. It is a landscape traveled by Crane and Coyote, and endowed with their teachings. Crane and Coyote will serve us well as guides into the territory of the Schitsu'umsh.

THE INTENT

This work provides a glimpse into the Schitsu'umsh's view of their world. Throughout my involvement with them, two questions have been preeminent: What does the surrounding landscape mean to the Schitsu'umsh? And, what effect does that understanding have on how the Schitsu'umsh relate to their landscape and to each other? I have been concerned not only with the significance of the mountains, rivers, and lakes within the landscape but also with the meaning held by the Schitsu'umsh of such specific phenomena as camas (or, in the Schitsu'umsh language, *sqha'wlutqhwe'*), white-tail deer (*ts'i*), huckleberry (*st'shastq*), water potato (*sqigwts*), and lovage (*qhasqhs*).[5] What is the significance of a field of flowering camas or a lone deer at the edge of a thicket to a Schitsu'umsh who encounters it, and what are the implications of that camas or deer for the members of the Schitsu'umsh family? The implications are indeed pervasive, their threads extending from and into the oral traditions and ceremonial expressions, the subsistence activities, the economic exchange networks, the kinship orientations, and the aesthetic nuances of the Schitsu'umsh people.

In my attempt to understand and frame this presentation of the Schitsu'umsh view of their landscape, a number of pivotal conceptual and methodological questions arose, each of which bears on the intent of this project. A review of Appendix A, "Research Considerations," will greatly assist readers through many of these concerns. But in order to set the stage, let me introduce a few key questions here. The most straightforward question was: What geographical boundaries define the Schitsu'umsh landscape? By far the most challenging questions were: Could I convey to my readers the Schitsu'umsh perspective? And, in attempting to do so, what ethnographic information would best inform and convey that perspective? And closely aligned to those questions: In attempting to identify the specific parameters that define the Schitsu'umsh view of their landscape, would the terminology and constructs used be accessible and understandable to both Schitsu'umsh as well as non-Schitsu'umsh readers? Finally, could a case be made that the Schitsu'umsh world view has remained relatively consistent through time, and, if so, how would I distinguish between Schitsu'umsh continuity and the variation brought on by a myriad of historical influences?

THE BOUNDARIES AND TERRAIN OF THE LANDSCAPE

The aboriginal landscape of the Schitsu'umsh encompassed much of what would become the Panhandle region of Idaho, as well as parts of eastern

Washington and western Montana (see the map on page 8). The northern boundary was marked by the lower end of Lake Pend Oreille, with the Kalispel and Pend Oreille peoples occupying the country to the north. The easterly area of Schị̱tsu'umsh country extended into the Bitterroot Mountain Range of Montana, with passes ranging from 4,700 to 5,200 feet in elevation, and with the tallest peaks towering from 6,000 to nearly 8,000 feet above sea level. On the other side of these mountains the Flathead people made their homes.

The southern boundary followed the prairie region south of the Palouse River to the North Fork of the Clearwater River and the Clearwater Mountains. Across these rivers and mountains was the country of the Nez Perce. The western reaches of the Schị̱tsu'umsh landscape were set by Plante's Ferry, an early Indian crossing on the Spokane River just east of Spokane Falls, and then extended south along the Hangman (Latah) and Pine Creek drainages to Steptoe Butte.[6] To the northwest and west was the home of the Spokane people, and to the southwest lived the Palouse Indians. In all it was a landscape consisting of more than 4 million acres of fir-, ponderosa-, and cedar-forested mountains, freshwater rivers, lakes and marshlands, white pine stands, and perennial bunchgrass and fescue wheat-grass-covered rolling hills and prairies.

While these boundaries were recognized by both traditional neighbors and the Schị̱tsu'umsh themselves, they were fluid delineations rather than confining barriers. Before settlement on their reservation in the late nineteenth century, Schị̱tsu'umsh families traveled seasonally well into the Big Bend country, far to the west of Hangman Creek, to dig bitterroot; met with other Salish peoples at Kettle Falls on the Columbia to the northwest to fish and trade; gathered huckleberries with the Kalispel in berry patches to the north, around Lake Pend Oreille; and, after the arrival of the horse, accompanied by Spokane and Flathead families, traveled east into what would become Montana to hunt buffalo. Even today, some families pick huckleberries in late summer in the mountains enveloping Lake Pend Oreille and assemble at Spokane Falls with other regional tribes to share in song and dance and to renew kinship.

The Schị̱tsu'umsh consider their "home" to be located at the core of this vast landscape, "since time immemorial." This is the landscape that includes Coeur d'Alene, Hayden, and Liberty Lakes, the mouth of the Spokane River, and the entirety of the Coeur d'Alene and St. Joe River basins. And at the very heart is Lake Coeur d'Alene, some 23 miles long with more than 103 miles of lakeshore. Fed by numerous creeks and rivers, the largest of which

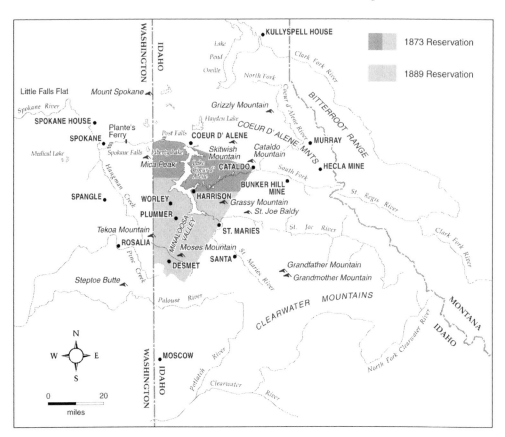

Landscape of the Schi̠tsu'umsh

are the St. Joe and Coeur d'Alene Rivers, the lake drains into the Spokane and eventually into the Columbia River. The term Schi̠tsu'umsh, which translates literally as "the ones that were found here," reiterates and affirms an identity anchored in a specific landscape.[7]

THE PERSPECTIVE AND TEACHINGS

For the Schi̠tsu'umsh, the world was "prepared" by the actions of the Creator, articulated linguistically as *Amo̠tqn*, or *K'u'lntsu̠tn*, and the First Peoples, such as Coyote, Chief Child of the Yellow Root, and Crane. In this time before the "coming of the Human Peoples," the First Peoples traveled the landscape, investing it with spiritually endowed "gifts," such as camas, deer, and *qhasqhs*, and setting forth certain teachings. It was a landscape given definition and meaning, "prepared for the coming of Human Peoples." And from that landscape the Human Peoples were brought forth. The teachings themselves were handed down from the beginning of time, conveyed through the oral literature of the Schitsu'umsh. In the act of telling the stories, the teachings continue to guide the behavior of the Human Peoples. The ritual behaviors, as expressed in the Memorial Giveaway or the Sweat House Ceremony, are thus a "bringing to life" of these teachings. A grand story has thus been told. The First Peoples have prepared the world for the "coming of the Human Peoples." Five fundamental teachings are set forth in this grand story and the landscape that embraces it.

The first teaching conveys the understanding that the landscape is spiritually created and endowed. Crane consistently demonstrates his *suumesh* powers, making "huge bundles of meat" small, kicking a tree and causing it to burn, calling in the deer during a hunt, and then carrying the two deer under his belt, all to the frustration of Coyote, who tries unsuccessfully to do the same. The world itself was created by spiritual beings, articulated by individual Schitsu'umsh as either the First Peoples, such as Coyote and Chief Child of the Yellow Root (as referred to in the oral literature), and/or the *Amotqn* or *K'u'lntsutn*, the Creator. It is the Creator who sent the First Peoples to prepare the world for the Human Peoples. The landscape is imbued with an abundance of "gifts" upon which the Human Peoples depend, such as camas, water potato, and deer (for food), *qhasqhs* (a healing root), and "*suumesh* songs" (spiritual power), all of which are understood as spiritually endowed.

The Spider

The Pest Control specialist stopped by that morning to offer his services to the school, a new facility that had just opened a few weeks before. Thinking that they must want to keep the facility pristine, he asked the school secretary, "Do you have any spiders or other insects, any pests? I can take care of them for you." She replied, "Yes, we have spiders here. Just the other day I had one on my typewriter stand. He crawled all around and then I watched as that spider crawled onto my typewriter. But why would I want to kill him?" And she went on to say, "I don't know why he came to me, but that Spider might have had a message for me, something to say to me. Why would I want to kill him?" (From participant observations at the Tribal School in October 1997.)

The second teaching conveys the understanding that the landscape is inhabited by a multitude of "Peoples," all of whom share in a common kinship. Among those in this all-inclusive kinship network is the Creator (as "father"), the Earth (as "mother"), the First Peoples (such as Crane, Coyote, and Chief Child of the Yellow Root), the Animal Peoples (such as Deer as "brothers and sisters" and Wolf as potentially a *suumęsh* guardian spirit—with the Animal Peoples, in fact, ultimately understood as synonymous with the First Peoples), the Mountains (as "father" or "grandmother"), the Sweat House and Sweat Rocks (as "grandmother" and "grandpas," respectively), the Ancestors (deceased relatives who have "crossed over"), and the Human Peoples (among them the Schịtsu'umsh). Even the antagonist Coyote is "related" to Crane, as is Spider to the school secretary. The Schịtsu'umsh family encompasses a vast landscape and the many Peoples within it.

Fire in the Housing Projects

I think sharing is a value that we all have. We just had a fire in the Housing Projects, and one of our lady's family lost their kitchen. So the girls just came, saying, "We were taking up a donation. We're going to find someplace for them to live until things get better." It's a value that we all have, we practice today, this sharing; the need to take care of each other. You see that all the time. Tragedy in the families, there's a death, almost immediately we have the tribe coming to them and being there, and the protecting way of just being with them. Helping them through that time of crisis; doing the cooking and taking care of the babies and the children. Just the value that I believe is really, really important to us as a tribe and as a family. In that way it's pretty unique. (From an interview conducted on February 12, 1997.)

Third, if kinship defines the structural relationship of the Peoples, the dynamic that helps bind them as members of the Schịtsu'umsh family is the ethic of sharing. Crane unselfishly feeds Little Squirrel and Chipmunk, as well as an entire village. The gifts bestowed on the landscape—the deer, camas, and *qhasqhs*, for instance—have been shared by the Creator and the First Peoples, shared by the Animal Peoples, for the welfare of the Human Peoples. In turn, the Human Peoples replicate those actions and share the gifts with those in need—the elders, children, and needy families. The act of sharing is done unselfishly. There is no expectation that what is given to another should be reciprocated.[8] Members of the Schịtsu'umsh

Camas prairie near the Palouse River
(from John Mix Stanley's lithographs in Stevens 1855, pl. LXI)

family are oriented toward not what can be personally acquired and possessed but toward the opportunity to share with and "give back" to all members of the family, including the landscape itself.

The Muskrat

We shared with the Animals, you know. Right after the Second World War, a few of us went to Rose Lake to get some water potatoes.[9] One of the guys seen a Muskrat, you know. He got all his water potatoes and stored them in there [pointing to the ground, the Muskrat's den]. This guy didn't feel like going to the lake to dig the water potatoes, so he's going to rob that there Muskrat. But his wife, when she found out what he's going to do, she called him and give him heck. "You leave that alone . . . That's the Animal's. You leave that alone." (From an interview conducted on March 10, 1998.)

Fourth, while the gifts are to be shared freely with those in need, the gifts are also to be respected and not abused. Crane hunts only two deer at a time, and, as a result, there is always plenty of meat hanging in his lodge. But when Coyote attempts to take more than what he needs, he manages only to lose it all. One hunts only the deer that are needed and can be used to feed the family, and never more. A "home" is open for all the relatives who need a place to stay, so long as they "leave it the way they found it." Above all, one is to show thanks for what is received. The gifts and kinsmen of the landscape—the camas, deer, and mountains—are to be respected as one respects his own grandmother or granddaughter. Not to respect the gifts is to lose one's right to them.

While the Schi̱tsu'umsh family is expansive, inclusive of humans and the phenomena of the landscape (animal, mountain, lake, and spirit), it is bounded. Not all humans are considered part of the Schi̱tsu'umsh family. At the geographic and social boundaries of the Schi̱tsu'umsh family can be found a world of competitively defined relations—the world of Coyote. The fifth and final teaching encompasses what I have come to term the ethic of competition.

This world of Coyote is inhabited by strangers, potential adversaries, and foes—formerly by the Blackfeet and Crow and, in more recent history, by many *Suuyapi* and "non-Indians."[10] It is a world in which the Schi̱tsu'umsh enter into competitive exchanges with others, to maximize gains and minimize losses. Instead of freely sharing the gifts of the landscape, the gifts are themselves items competed with and for. The means employed to accomplish these goals may include sharpened skills of calculation and negotiation, well-toned dexterity and physical prowess, or, occasionally, artifice and chicanery, to avoid "getting duped" by an opponent. In the character and actions of Coyote (that is, in those adventures in which he succeeds) are found the archetypal model for successfully traveling this world. Coyote's example is often manifested and well illustrated in the actions of those Schi̱tsu'umsh who compete in a "stick game" or football game against another tribe or rival high school, who are on "active duty" against the Blackfeet of the nineteenth century or the Viet Cong of the twentieth, or who negotiate with a federal governmental agency or a Fortune 500 company. It was the Coyote example manifested in the Schi̱tsu'umsh (in particular, their shrewd and aggressive trading skills) that so impressed the early fur traders, who soon began to call the Indians "Coeur d'Alene," or "heart of an awl." Nevertheless, whether engaged in sharing or competitive exchanges, the ultimate goal of the actions remains the same: sus-

tain and enhance the welfare of the Schitsu'umsh family. Thus a demar-
cation of kinship and nonkinship, and a defining of the boundaries of the
Schitsu'umsh family, are found in these competitively defined relations. A
contentious Coyote is seldom evident in the actions among and between
members of the family.[11]

My intention in identifying the ethic of competition is simply to acknowledge that the Schitsu'umsh family does have geographic and social boundaries. Our primary focus will be on the interrelations among the members
of the Schitsu'umsh family, on illustrating the first four teachings, and only
secondarily on nonkinship-based relations.

THE ETHNOGRAPHIC FRAMING

The research for this work, as well as the framing of the presentation of
that research, are based upon the oral, ceremonial, and social traditions of
the Schitsu'umsh. It will be through these traditions that we will access and
come to better understand the teachings. Six specific expressive traditions
are relied upon and described in this book. The first is storytelling and the
oral narrative accounts of Crane and Coyote and the other First Peoples.
In the act of storytelling, a landscape is perpetuated and the teachings of
the First Peoples disseminated. Appreciation of the oral tradition is a necessary prerequisite for understanding the other traditions.

The second tradition is the Powwow. As song and dance are essential to
many of the other traditions, the Powwow of the Schitsu'umsh is an exem-
plary and culminating expression of Schitsu'umsh vitality and identity. The
Powwow provides an opportunity, through song, dance, and regalia, to celebrate and renew one's kinship with the landscape.

The third tradition involves an assortment of rituals associated with gathering and hunting, and with the distribution of such foods as camas, huckleberries, and venison. The ceremonial acts accompanying a boy's first
successful deer hunt, the digging of water potatoes in the fall, and the distribution of elk meat by designated hunters at a meal served at a Powwow
or Memorial Giveaway exemplify such rituals. These rituals seek to give
thanks for what is received from the landscape and ensure that what is
received is then shared with those in need.

The Jump Dance and the Sweat House are the fourth and fifth traditions
described. They provide an opportunity to communicate the various needs
of the family, to heal their sufferings, and to help maintain the vitality of
the landscape.

The sixth tradition is the Memorial Giveaway. It allows the sorrow resulting from the death of a family member to be shared and to "fly away," and it prepares for the eventual reuniting of the entire family back into the landscape.

To accentuate the voice of those who tell the stories or sing in the Sweat House, I will cite specific excerpts from interviews I have conducted with various Schiṯsu'umsh, from archival material, or from conversations I had or from "talks" delivered. Segments of narrative text from the oral literature will also be presented. And I will provide descriptive accounts of events I witnessed in the course of my field research. These vignettes are distinguished typographically in the body of this work.[12]

It is upon an understanding of the "Crane and Coyote" narrative or of the ritual behavior of those participating in a Memorial Giveaway, for example, that this study is based. As such, for those Schiṯsu'umsh individuals, either past or present, who have told stories of Crane and Coyote, who have led as members of the Tribal Council, who have hunted deer and shared the venison, who have helped distribute the personal effects of a deceased loved one, or who have sung at a Jump Dance or in the Sweat House, the following account provides the model of how they view their landscape.

It is important to note that this presentation, while framing a Schiṯsu'umsh view of the landscape, is not a complete framing of Schiṯsu'umsh society. Contact with Euro-Americans has resulted in significant societal change. Certain economic, political, religious, and social-structural elements of Schiṯsu'umsh society, either adaptations to or assimilations from Euro-American society, have not been fully and ethnographically portrayed here. For example, discussion of "Indian Catholicism," the current tribal government, or employment and economic activities, while alluded to for their historical significance in the chapter "Winds of Change: Contact History," lies beyond my primary focus. My purpose has been to reveal those quintessential aspects of Schiṯsu'umsh culture, the teachings, that were originally brought forth by the First Peoples, maintained through time, and then carried forth and expressed in the contemporary lives of the Schiṯsu'umsh people and in a landscape.

CONTINUITY AND VARIATION

While the goal of this study is to enunciate expressions of culture that may be called "traditional," as in the stories of Crane and Coyote or in the ritual behavior in a Sweat House, and to identify in those expressions their

Father and son viewing the landscape from atop Steptoe Butte, May 1996

primary teachings, the Schitsu'umsh have obviously not existed in a temporal and spatial void. First, there have been significant societal changes primarily brought on by Euro-American contact. Among the most significant intercultural influences were the introduction of the horse as early as the mid-1700s; a series of smallpox epidemics, likely beginning in the 1770s; the arrival of Lewis and Clark in 1806, David Thompson in 1809, and the fur trade; the establishment of the Jesuit mission in 1842; military victory followed by defeat in 1858; confinement to a limited land base following the "Agreements" of 1873, 1887, and 1889, and the allotment of 1909; and the polluting of much of the landscape as a result of mining. Yet despite these substantive influences, the teachings of the First Peoples have shown amazing resilience and are as applicable to the Schitsu'umsh of the mid-nineteenth century as they are to those living today. In fact, ethnographic and historical sources indicate that the general description of the Schitsu'-umsh world view offered here can be extended to a baseline of 1850.

While the underlying teachings have shown astounding continuity through time and from family to family, the manner in which those teachings are expressed illustrates a certain degree of interfamily variation. This variability reflects Schitsu'umsh acceptance of individuality and the influences of intertribal trade and intermarriage, as well as Euro-American contact.

Certainly part of the variation between families today is the result of historic influences of the Jesuit mission, which gave rise to a syncretism of indigenous and Euro-American cultural practices. While our focus is on traditional Schitsu'umsh culture, we cannot neglect the important and integral role that "Indian Catholicism" has played, and continues to play, in the lives of the Schitsu'umsh people. It is certainly true that many of the "old ways" (e.g., Jump Dancing) have been inhibited or curtailed because of Church policies. But it is much more accurate to view traditional Indian and Catholic spirituality today as complementary rather than exclusive of each other. Schitsu'umsh people walk two paths—saying the Rosary in one activity, for example, and singing the "evening *suumesh* songs" in another—and can easily "jump over and jump back" between the two. The babies of Jump Dancers continue to be baptized, Jesuit Priests have "jumped" at the Jump Dances, and deceased Schitsu'umsh "cross over the creek" through an Indian Catholic wake-funeral. The term *Amotqn* can be understood as synonymous with both Christian and traditional notions of Creator. But a complete description of Coeur d'Alene Indian Catholicism is outside the scope of this work.

Variation in Schitsu'umsh culture is also a function of intertribal contact and intermarriage. From the earliest times, Schitsu'umsh families have regularly traveled to Spokane Falls and Kettle Falls to fish and trade for salmon with other Salish peoples. With the coming of the horse, some Schitsu'umsh families stayed among the Flathead for up to nine months of the year. Because of their proximity, regular contact with the Spokane was maintained by the Schitsu'umsh living around Liberty Lake and the north end of Lake Coeur d'Alene. The Agreement of 1887, in fact, brought several Spokane families onto the Coeur d'Alene Reservation. The automobile and interstate highway system further facilitated intertribal contact. Today we see many Schitsu'umsh who can trace part of their family heritage not only to Spokane but also to Colville, Flathead, or Kalispel families, for example. With this degree of communication and intermarriage with other tribes came variation among and between Schitsu'umsh families.

The many paths used by the Schitsu'umsh people to "jump over and jump back" are further enriched and diversified by the value they place on inclusivity. While they were certainly motivated by a variety of concerns, the Schitsu'umsh themselves welcomed the Black Robes and an additional "way to pray." Even before the Jesuits attempted to make farmers of the Schitsu'umsh, these hunters and gatherers had already incorporated potato cultivation into their way of life. Schitsu'umsh decisions resulted in their adoption of a Euro-American form of political governance. Rather than exclude, the Schitsu'umsh often elect to engage and even partner with the non-Schitsu'umsh community in education, environmental protection, healthcare delivery, and public safety. In these situations of shared advantage, it may be the "wise Coyote" (an astute competitor with foresight) in the Schitsu'umsh who recognizes that cooperation will serve him better than confrontation and exclusion. Or these may be partnerships in which kinship has been extended to certain individuals or even segments of the white community. In either instance, it is from this pattern of inclusivity that the Schitsu'umsh both tolerate difference and accept a certain degree of individuality. What may seem as mutually exclusive and inconsistent behavior to an outsider can be accommodated and even celebrated within and among Schitsu'umsh families.

For the Schitsu'umsh there is thus no inconsistency in being "successful farmers," as during the early reservation years, or "enterprising entrepreneurs" today, and also continuing to dig camas, gather huckleberries, and hunt deer. All are understood as complementary practices. The lives of contemporary Schitsu'umsh families include Sunday Masses, eight-to-five jobs, college education, golf, vacation trips to Reno or Seattle, voting on school levies and for presidents of the United States, as well as digging for camas and water potato, and attending Powwows, Jump Dances, and Memorial Giveaways. And among such families, differing cultural practices are also represented. For some families a "naming ceremony" might be incorporated into an evening's Jump Dance ritual, but for others it would not. One family might make a tobacco offering when digging camas; for others, *qhasqhs* would be offered. The details and specifics of a particular Coyote story may vary from family to family. For some families the story of Coyote is considered "true" and is told with regularity to their children. Yet for other families it is a story no longer told with regularity, or perhaps not at all. For them, the stories of the First Peoples may be understood simply as "stories" and "fairy tales." Cultural variance is today symbolically represented in the manner in which some Schitsu'umsh men wear their hair: "short and non-Indian in front" and "long and Indian in back."

Critically, while we may find specific instances of inter- and intrafamily variation in the expression of Schitsu'umsh culture, the underlying principles, the teachings that generate those behaviors, tend to be shared with consistency from family to family. For example, while there are differing terms used to refer to the Creator (those distinctions tending to follow along families lines), virtually all Schitsu'umsh I have interviewed hold to the belief in a supreme being, the Creator. Regardless of whether an offering of tobacco or *qhasqhs* is made, respect is still paid to the camas; and whether a "naming ceremony" is held or not, the evening's dancers still "jump" for the well-being of their respective families. The same moral lessons of Coyote are taught, despite the contrasting styles of storytelling of different raconteurs. The teaching that venison is to be shared with those in need continues regardless of whether deer is hunted with the sinew-backed wooden bow and arrow or by "spotlighting" from a pickup truck with a high-powered rifle. While rituals of the Catholic Church have replaced many eighteenth-century ceremonial expressions, both contemporary and ancient rituals include an ethic of sharing. It is thus important to note that while the specifics of a ritual activity or the comments of a particular interviewee included and cited in *Landscape Traveled by Coyote and Crane* may be singular and not shared by other families, those activities or comments express the same underlying teachings observed by other Schitsu'umsh families.

In helping me sort through this important distinction, one elder emphasized, "you have to distinguish between family traditions and tribal traditions." Individual family traditions are potentially unique and idiosyncratic, and, in fact, "this family may do something a certain way, and it may not even be acceptable to another family." Yet those family traditions can remain "tribal," based upon and reflective of the same teachings held in common by other Schitsu'umsh families. Or rephrased, the First Peoples have traveled many paths, some of which have grassed over and are no longer traveled, whereas others are only now being cleared, and still other paths are yet to be discovered. But the First Peoples still travel. While the Schitsu'-umsh tribal traditions—the teachings—have remained resilient, those teachings are continually reinventing and bringing forth new and varied societal expressions of themselves, often manifested in individual "family traditions."

Recognition as a traditional Schitsu'umsh is thus most likely to come from adherence to the teachings of the First Peoples. In turn, such recognition depends less on whether someone's consanguineal great grandmother was "Coeur d'Alene" or not, and thus whether there are discrepancies in the manner in which families express the teachings. To be Schitsu'umsh is to view Lake Coeur d'Alene and Grassy Mountain, for example, in terms of their spiritual and familial significance, and to share unselfishly and not abuse the gifts that emanate from that landscape.

The continuity of Schitsu'umsh teachings and the variety of their expression are thus not unlike a "tattered flag." The eagle-feather staff, the "Indian flag," of the Schitsu'umsh continues to fly in the face of the many winds of change. But clearly visible on that flag are the patches of stars and stripes, a crucifix, and the emblems of other tribes. And there are also a few holes evident. Nevertheless, the threads of the flag still hold true to their particular design, and the overall outline is distinctly Schitsu'umsh. Likewise, the underlying teachings (the "design" of the flag) have remained consistent even while some of the manifest expressions of Schitsu'umsh life (the "patches") have been altered. While the focus of this study is on the "design" of the Schitsu'umsh flag, we must also understand the various materials and fibers with which the flag is made if we are truly to comprehend its design. In viewing the variety and arrangement of the "patchwork," we can grasp the flag's underlying teachings. And in the process, what at first glance may have been seen as a "tattered flag" is later viewed as a richly patterned montage of integral insignia, indeed, the Indian flag.

Frenchy SiJohn holding the Indian flag on the Hngwsḭmn Memorial Ride, May 1996

The Water Potato

Earlier that morning, before we had arrived, he had sung his *suumesh* songs. The songs had asked the Creator for a good gathering of the water potato, and gave thanks. With the shovels in the back of the pickup, we drove to the shores of the lake. Each year in October, on the fourth Friday of the month, he and another man, often joined by other adults and children, dig the water potato. For these two men, they gather the water potatoes for their own families and, by extension, all the Schḭtsu'umsh families. Over the next couple of weeks, other Schḭtsu'umsh will also go to the lake's shore and dig for the water potato.

The elder pointed to a thick stand of cattails and mud, just along the shoreline, and we were instructed to begin to dig there. The shovels moved the mud out some eight to ten inches deep. Nothing on the surface of the mud marked that which we were looking for. Earlier that summer, the cattails intermingled with a "large-leafed" plant. Today there was no visible sign of the plant.

Almost right away, about six to eight inches down, the first water potato showed itself. It was a root about two inches long and three-quarters inch around, with a brown skin covering. As it was lifted and partially cleaned, all the others stopped their digging and briefly glanced at it in silence. With a second and third shovel, more water potatoes were soon revealed. Some were smaller, an inch or so, but most were larger, up to three and a half inches in length. Within a hour, all the water potatoes that were needed this year were gathered. Some years, more would be gathered. One of the men remembered how "gunny sacks full" of the water potatoes would be gathered, lasting through the winter.

The water potatoes were washed in the lake's water and placed in plastic and paper sacks. We were told that we can "prepare it just like a potato." As we were about ready to leave, the elder reiterated what he had mentioned as we dug: "Take at least one of these and give it to an elder, one who could not make it down here today, someone in need of this water potato." (From participant observations made on October 24, 1997, on the shores of Benewah Lake, at the southern end of Lake Coeur d'Alene.)

In order to better appreciate the continuity and resilience of the Schịtsu'umsh teachings, we must glimpse more fully some of the forces of intercultural contact and assimilation that have inadvertently or overtly sought their demise. Before proceeding with our consideration of the various contemporary expressions of the Schịtsu'umsh teachings, it would be instructive first to provide an outline of Schịtsu'umsh society prior to the coming of Euro-Americans. This discussion will be found in the chapter entitled "Since Time Immemorial: Precontact Society." We will then review the history of Euro-American influences on that society, presented in the chapter entitled "Winds of Change: Contact History." These discussions are not intended to be a complete history of the Schịtsu'umsh people, but rather a focus on the interrelationship of the landscape to precontact Schịtsu'umsh society and to events brought on by contact with Euro-American society. These next two chapters are an introductory history of the Schịtsu'umsh landscape.

✻

Since Time Immemorial: Precontact Society

"Since time immemorial," the Schitsu'umsh had traveled in a particular landscape, reliant upon its material and spiritual gifts.[1] Bordering this landscape were specific neighbors, both friends and foes. The language spoken by the Schitsu'umsh is classified as part of the Interior Salish family. Other peoples throughout the Plateau region who spoke an Interior Salish language included the Colville, Okanagan, Sanpoil, and Wenatchee.[2] The immediate Salish-speaking neighbors of the Schitsu'umsh were the Flathead to the east, the Pend Oreille to the northeast, the Kalispel to the north, and the Spokane to the west. Farther to the north were the Kootenai, who spoke a language unique to the region. To the southwest were the Palouse, and south of the Schitsu'umsh lived the Nez Perce, both peoples speaking Sahaptin languages. While classified as distinct Salish languages, Flathead, Kalispel, Pend Oreille, Spokane, and Schitsu'umsh were close enough linguistically to make them generally intelligible to one another's speakers. The categories "friend" and "foe"—certainly not fixed, but oscillating with changing circumstances—are fundamentally extensions and realizations of the designations "kinship" (with its ethic of sharing) and "nonkinship" (with its ethic of competition).

Among their Salish neighbors, especially the Spokane, the Schitsu'umsh entered into regular commodity exchanges and marriage partnerships. The Schitsu'umsh traveled to Spokane Falls to fish and trade with the Spokane. As deer were plentiful in Schitsu'umsh country, venison was given to the Spokane. Deer were relatively scarce in Spokane territory. In turn, the Spokane allowed the Schitsu'umsh to fish the Spokane River below the falls for salmon, or they entered into direct exchanges for dried salmon. Bitterroot was also sought from the Spokane, as it was scarce in Schitsu'umsh country but grew in abundance in the Spokane country. Given the proximity of some of the Schitsu'umsh families who lived around Liberty Lake and the mouth of the Spokane River on Coeur d'Alene Lake, these people may

Cascades of the Columbia River
(from John Mix Stanley's lithographs in Stevens 1855, pl. XLV)

have had relatively more interaction with various Spokane families than with some Schitsu'umsh families who lived up the St. Joe River. Extending beyond the Spokane, regular trade with tribes intermediary to the Pacific Coast peoples resulted, for example, in the acquisition of the dentalium and abalone shells used in making beads and other artistic ornaments.

When conflict arose, it was likely with one of the non–Salish-speaking tribes, though James Teit records a number of "occasional wars" with the Spokane, Flathead, and Kalispel (1930:119–29). With the Nez Perce, tensions could escalate upon encountering each other while hunting or gathering, especially in a context of unresolved past grievances. One area where such encounters likely occurred was the region south of the Palouse River extending to the Clearwater River. The Schitsu'umsh regularly hunted deer and gathered roots in this area. The name of the city of Moscow, in fact, likely derived from the Schitsu'umsh term *S'maqw'l*, used to designate the location (Palmer, Nicodemus, and Felsman 1987:39). This was an area frequented by Nez Perce hunters and gatherers as well. If tensions did erupt into hostilities, Schịtsu'umsh warriors, using sinew-backed, recurved wooden bows or bows made from a single mountain ram's horn, arrows, lances, and clubs, did not hesitate to use their fighting skills to resolve disputes. Before going into battle, a war dance would be held. The warriors sang their *suumẹsh* songs, seeking the assistance of their guardian spirits, and in their dance movements they portrayed the war deeds they were about to accomplish against their foes. In the following vignette, another approach to conflict resolution is illustrated.

Word Battle

There was a group of Kootenai warriors who came south into Coeur d'Alene territory.

There they came upon a beautiful Coeur d'Alene woman, alone, without men to protect her. Against her will, they decided to take her back to their camp, and traveled north. They violated one of our rules. In those days, we fought the Kootenais like we did with the Nez Perce. If someone came into our territory, or we theirs, we'd try to get him.

Upon hearing of the theft of the woman, the Coeur d'Alene war chief led a large group of warriors up to the Kootenai village to get her back. Five hundred Coeur d'Alene warriors headed north to Kootenai country. Word that the Coeur d'Alenes were coming reached the Kootenais, and 500 Kootenai warriors waited.

Not wanting a battle that would result in the death of many Kootenais and Coeur d'Alenes, the Kootenai chief asked to first meet with the Coeur d'Alene war chief and discuss the matter. He said that the warriors from each tribe should face-off. A line would be drawn between the two groups of warriors. With each side ready for battle, they would shame, and taunt, and verbally ridicule each other. They would battle with words. And the first man to take the dare, break down, and cross the line to the other side and strike an enemy, that side would lose.

So the warriors from the Kootenai and Coeur d'Alene faced-off. There were 500 Kootenais and 500 Coeur d'Alene warriors facing each other ready for battle. Faces were painted and weapons readied. And they started. Words and insults were sent and the battle was on. Warriors said all kinds of things, challenging the others. They jumped in place, and yelled at each other. Some took out their knives and pretended to attack the other warriors, without touching them. Even though they spoke different languages, each knew what the other was saying. But no one crossed the line. All day, under the hot sun, the word battle went on. Not a breeze in the air. The sun was hot and the warriors sweated hard. The dust rose in the air, as they jumped and yelled at each other. But no one crossed over. The painted faces were replaced with mud-covered bodies, as the sweat and dust mixed. But no one crossed. The day wore on. And when the sun set, the warriors dropped to the ground from exhaustion. But no one crossed the line.

So the Kootenai chief, recognizing the transgression his young men had made, had the Coeur d'Alene woman given back. He also showed the Coeur d'Alene a trail through the mountains and Blackfoot country that would take them safely to the buffalo country to the east. The trail could be used only by the Coeur d'Alene, as the Kootenai would keep it a secret from other tribes. The word battle occurred in the open fields, the flat, just north of the Kootenai River and east from the present village on the small Kootenai Reservation, near Bonners Ferry, Idaho. (Abbreviated, as told by Lawrence Aripa on April 15, 1995.)

SEASONAL ROUND

While travel into Spokane or Kootenai country to trade or battle occurred more or less regularly, travel within their own landscape was a prerequisite for successful Schitsu'umsh life. Theirs was not only a landscape that sustained the necessities for food, lodging, transportation, tools, and clothing; but it was a landscape *richly endowed* with roots, berries, fish, and game animals. And it was a landscape that offered spiritual guidance and healing powers. Addressing the Earth as mother and the Sun as father, this was a landscape that "watched over" and cared for the Schitsu'umsh people.

An Abundance of Game

Is there an abundance of game in the Coeur d'Alene country? Perhaps nowhere does so small an area contain such a variety. Next to the roe deer [white-tail deer], these are the most common: the deer [mule deer], the elk, the mountain lion, the carcajou [wolverine], the white sheep, the bighorn, the goat, the wolf, the fox, the wildcat [bobcat or lynx], the polecat [likely skunk], the hare, the otter, the weasel, the badger, the mink, the marten, the fisher, the beaver, the muskrat, a large variety of mouse-colored rats, squirrels, field mice, not to mention four or five varieties of bear.

Of the birds, there are the calumet bird [osprey] (which has the same importance as the eagle), the swan, the crane, the pelican, the bittern [heron],
the bustard, the snipe, the thrush, the duck, the teal, the magpie, the crow,
the swallow, the green woodpecker, the hawk, the turtledove, the fishing
bird, many varieties of aquatic birds, and others unknown in Europe.

Fish are abundant in lakes, rivers, and small streams. I will not speak here
of the mosquito or of the insects harmful to man. One is devoured by
them during certain seasons. Nor will I speak of the serpents which are
present in large numbers. In a single day I chased two out of my bed.
Fortunately, rattlesnakes are rare there.

What a vast collection of animals! And, sad to say, probably not one of
them has not at some time received homage from the Coeur d'Alenes.
The most celebrated ones in the history of their medicine are the bear,
the deer, and the calumet bird. The most curious of all is perhaps the wolver-
ine. This animal, which is only as large as an ordinary sheep, has many features in common with the bear. Like the bear, it climbs to the tops of the
tallest trees, [and has] such prodigious strength that it has been seen to
carry off whole deer and to climb, bearing animals larger than itself. Next
to the roe deer, the animals most hunted by the Coeur d'Alene are deer
and bear.

Bear hunting is seldom undertaken on a large scale because this animal
is rarely found in large numbers. It is naturally ferocious and very dangerous, but a good hunter does not fear it. I call a hunter good who combines
strength and courage with skill. I saw a Coeur d'Alene who possessed all
these qualifications to such degree that before he had reached the age of
forty he had killed more than 100 bears. A goodly number of these had
been of the most ferocious variety. (From Father Nicolas Point's 1842–43
observations, 1967:180–81.)

In order to access and benefit from the bounty, Schitsu'umsh families had
to be able to travel this landscape freely. In addition to an extensive network
of walking trails, curved-up and "sturgeon-nosed" pine and cedar-bark
canoes provided ease of movement over the navigable lakes and rivers that
connected the heartland of this area. Access and benefit also required
immense and sophisticated knowledge about the landscape in relation to
the seasons. Family members had to be able to interpret seasonal cycles as
well as idiosyncratic climatic changes, and know precisely when and where
to move as particular roots or game animals became available for digging
or hunting during the year. Felix Aripa remembered how young boys often

went to berrying areas and, noting the approximate elevation on the mountain slope, brought back branches from berry bushes. Upon inspecting such branches and noting their place of origin, a grandmother could tell with certainty when the berries would be ready for picking, and thus judge when the family should begin their movement to the berry patches.

Traveling

Before the advent of the horse, the Coeur d'Alene spent a good deal of time traveling, fishing, and hunting along the rivers and lakes of their country, although parties also went on distant hunting trips in the mountains during the fair season. At certain seasons considerable numbers of people congregated at the famous camas and other root-digging grounds. They also went to the Spokan for salmon fishing, trading, and sports. (Teit 1930:155.)

With the ease of movement provided by the vast network of trails and navigable waterways, and equipped with their extensive knowledge of the landscape, Schitsu'umsh families practiced a very successful transhumance pattern. During each of the five generally recognized seasons (Teit 1930:95)—*se'tqaps* (spring), *yalstk* (summer), *stsaq* (early fall), *stc'e'ed* (late fall), and *sitsîtk* (winter)—Schitsu'umsh families would, with deliberation, travel to the appropriate berrying, fishing, hunting, and root-digging regions. Each family's pattern of movement and associated subsistence activity, in turn, reflected a routinized, though consciously adjusted, pattern of year-to-year travel throughout the Schitsu'umsh landscape. It was anything but a random, nomadic existence, where chance encounters determined the success of a deer hunt or camas digging. Provided below is an outline of the seasonal cycle reflective of traditional, precontact transhumance. Variations resulting from changes in the weather and annual snowfall and rainfall, as well as the composition of the family groupings, could, of course, alter this pattern from season to season.

When the *smukwe'shn* (sunflower) blooms in the spring, the "fast was over" and root season would begin. This signaled the time to break the winter villages and camps, along the shores of Coeur d'Alene and Hayden lakes, and travel to the root areas. Some of the best root areas were found in the prairie country and the rolling hills west and south of Hangman Creek and Tekoa Mountain. Upon arriving, the Schitsu'umsh might be joined by families of Spokane, Kalispel, or even Nez Perce, who all engaged in digging, along with more competitive and recreation-oriented activities, such as stick games and footracing. Sixteen types of roots were dug, with camas, cous, and bitterroot among the most important. A curved digging stick, some three to four feet in length, called a *pitse'*, was used in gathering the roots. The *pitse'* was often made from the wood of the serviceberry bush, with the tip charred to harden it and the handle made from elk antler.

They Peeled It Off

There's a cedar basket that they made; it's about this time of year or a little earlier when the sap just begins to come up. They'll select a cedar and if they want to make a basket, they'll cut a strip about. . . . It all depends, after it's folded. They cut a certain section out of that tree. They'll peel it off. It's very easy to peel off that time of year and they can form it, the cedar basket. . . . They'll peel that off while it's all soft. . . . They'll put a ribbon around one inside. When it dries it keeps that shape. There are different shapes for different purposes. Some of them are made kind of long and narrow, because when you have a horse, . . . it gives you more room to get in between the trees. You still have the volume. But in some of the open countries they'll make it rounder.

I've seen my grandmother make some out of roots. She was getting blind but she was able to still, . . . by feeling. . . . It's almost a perfect specimen after she got it made and she's halfway blind, [laugh]. (From an interview conducted on May 20, 1996.)

The roots were often gathered in cedar-bark baskets. These temporary, easily constructed baskets were made from a single piece of bark folded and sewn up on each side, with a carrying strap attached. The camas was then simply dried or baked in pit ovens, along with black moss, and formed into cakes. To store these roots, and later the berries, well-made birch-bark baskets, twined round and flat bags made from knee-spun Indian hemp, or tightly woven, coiled baskets made of split red-cedar roots were assembled. Coarse grasses and porcupine quills dyed in yellows, greens, and reds (a technique of "false embroidery") were used to decorate the bags and baskets in geometric designs. The flexible twined bags were ideal for holding roots, and the rigidity of the coiled baskets protected the berries from being crushed. Both the coiled baskets and the twined bags kept their contents relatively secure from the elements throughout the seasons. In fact, the coiled baskets could be made watertight, and used, for example, for boiling foods by adding heated rocks to the water contained in them. The manufacture of the various bags and baskets, as well as the digging, storing, and preparation of the various roots, were typically activities of women, both married and unmarried, within the families.

Bags and baskets of dried berries, roots, fish, and meat were, in turn, placed in earthen-pit caches or occasionally on tree branches for later retrieval. The circular-pit caches were located in dry, well-drained locations. Anticipating the future needs of the family, use of these caches helped assure a diverse and balanced diet throughout the year, as well as provided a cushion against a lean year.

Bury Their Baskets

A lot of times they bury their baskets. Mostly they were made out of cedar. They get overloaded, or they kept too much to carry, or they have a lot of camas and they had extra baskets or something that they don't carry back. They dig it in the ground and bury it and they'd know where it's at. Next year when they come back, they dig it out. Of course, it would stay that way.

As a matter of fact, over here on the Moctelme Valley there's a farmer plowing up. There was an old Indian house or homestead; they knocked it all down and burned up the old lumber and they plowed it up. They uncovered one of those baskets. That's probably what they uncovered, some of those Indian women buried it. It was in pretty good shape. It must have been years. (From an interview conducted on May 20, 1996.)

Through the spring and into the early summer, some families also traveled to the lakes to fish lake trout and whitefish. The spring fish runs were at their height in April. Fishing was done using a variety of techniques, including wooden or bone hooks and lines of Indian hemp, and a three-pronged spear. In addition, dip nets of Indian hemp twine and willow-constructed traps and weirs were extensively used. Indian hemp grew in abundance and was gathered along the St. Joe and Coeur d'Alene rivers. Night fishing from canoes, with torches, was also practiced. Although there were no anadromous fish in either Coeur d'Alene or Hayden lakes, a limited number of salmon came up Hangman Creek into Schitsu'umsh country (as the creek drains into to the Spokane River just below the falls). Some families gathered along this creek during the salmon runs. To fish the salmon, weirs and spears of either a detachable, elk-bone harpoon or three-pronged type were employed. Construction of the fish weirs was under the direction of a shaman, who used prayer and ritual smoking to entice the fish into the weirs. Perhaps because of the year-round cycle of trout and whitefish fishing, in conjunction with the general lack of local access to seasonal salmon runs, the Schitsu'umsh did not practice the complex fishing ceremonials so characteristic of most other Plateau peoples. As with hunting, fishing was primarily, though not solely, the activity of men within the families.

Birch Canoes

Another thing that was really important was the canoe. My dad said they had big birch right around the rivers. They had selected certain birch where they make their canoes. He said they had made certain types of canoes for different purposes; hauling cargo or they can haul deer.

They used the canoe to sneak around the lake to get the deer when they came down to get water. They knew the trails where the deer would come down. But the canoe was their main transportation. (From an interview conducted on May 20, 1996.)

The Schitsu'umsh used a variety of canoe types to navigate the lakes and rivers of their territory. In addition to cedar and birch, the Schitsu'umsh were unique in their use of white-pine bark for their canoes. To fashion a canoe, long pieces of bark, sometimes a few feet wide and the length of the canoe, were peeled from the trees. "It was easy peeling [cedar bark] by mid-May when the sap comes up." The bark was then stretched out onto a framework, brought up, and sewed together at its ends. The seams were sealed with pitch. Besides the more common style of canoe, with prow and stern curved up, the Schitsu'umsh used the Kootenai-style, sturgeon-nosed canoe, with its prow and stern pointed down, under the water. In addition to bark-covered canoes, dugouts were also fashioned. Pine or cedar would be cut down and hollowed out by repeated burning and chiseling. Rafts made of tule reeds were also made. All types of canoes were rather easily constructed, since the materials to do so were readily available.

While the canoes facilitated fishing, hunting, and travel, they also brought the Schitsu'umsh into contact with the "Water Mysteries" (Teit 1930:181–82). Appearing as half fish and half human, or, as in two particular instances, a "huge buffalo" or a "huge fish," the Water Mysteries lived in the lakes and rivers, and traveled by underground, connected passages to "holes in the tops of mountains" or other bodies of water. One such well-known passageway linked Hayden Lake with Post Falls. In one incident, sisters were attacked and drowned by a Water Mystery as they gathered serviceberries along the St. Joe River. Shortly after, some hair from the sisters was discovered on the shores of a high mountain lake, the lake thus connected to the river.

Lake Coeur d'Alene itself was inhabited by a "water buffalo." Once a man was canoeing along the lake's shore after nightfall. Suddenly the man's paddling had no effect on his movement over the water, as he and his canoe were lifted out of the water. On each side of the canoe he felt the horns of some great animal holding his craft in place. The man immediately began to pray, beseeching the Water Mystery to set him free. Upon offering a gift, the Mystery allowed him to continue on his journey. From that time on, canoers would leave a gift under a particular bush located on the shore near where the incident took place.

Puberty Ritual

It used to be part of becoming a man. There was a puberty ritual that went along with it. When you were thirteen or fourteen, you had to go up there and do that before you could ride with the men and sweat with the men and smoke the peace pipe with the men. You had to go up and do that. And up there they received their spirit helper, their song, their vision, I guess, their medicine that they would have in their life to take care of and depend on.

And you know, they believe that the Creator never promised anybody a tomorrow. But there was a day reserved for everybody, when it would be their day. Until then, they had to be brave, they had to be strong. They had to be good horsemen. They couldn't be afraid of breaking horses or hunting buffalo. They might have to be a warrior and face the enemy. And they were supposed to be brave about it, not think, well, I need to get out of this because I might get hurt or I might get killed. They had to think, that's not going to happen until the Creator said, "This is your day. This is the day you're going to be called back." When that day comes, it doesn't matter. So they tried to live it.

And they began that by fasting in the hilltops. And there are some places between Cataldo and St. Joe, there's some hills up there, . . . up north of

Coeur d'Alene, . . . where our people did that traditionally. They didn't take weapons up there. They didn't hunt up there. That's all that they used those areas for.

And those places were the home for the Thunder and the Lightning. That's where they dwell, that's where they'd hang around. Even in the good whether they'd be up there living or whatever. So those places were deeply spiritual. . . . And there are rock formations up there when the old people over the years, they would build a pile of rocks and where they put down each rock, they would pray about what they did up there, what they saw, how they felt, what they're going to do. And there are hundreds, literally hundreds, on any hilltop of those formations from thousands of years of our people going up there and doing that. They're still there. . . . They're there from our people doing that.

And they would pray and then every morning at dawn, they'd go down to the water. And they'd pray there to the Creator. And they'd talk to the Water Spirits and they would ask the Great Spirit Creator through that water. They would absolve them, they would cleanse them again. They'd make them more ready, they'd give them life. But they couldn't drink it because they're fasting. But they would put themselves into the water to bathe themselves. That water would help them anyway, to let their life go on, to replenish them and to give them strength, cleanse their mind and their spirit and then they'd sing songs. And they'd leave some kind of an offering.

Then they'd come out of the water, go back up the hill, and they would stay up there all day and all night. And the following morning at dawn, before that sun came up, they'd go back down there to the water. So they did those things. . . . It's still deeply religious to our people. Big part of our life. (From an interview conducted on June 12, 1996.)

Also during the summer, while some families perhaps frequented the rivers and lakes to fish, and others continued to gather roots on the prairies, the younger members of those families might have traveled to the surrounding mountains to seek a *suumęsh*. Both men and women could quest for a vision. In spiritual preparation, a sweat bath would be taken prior to heading for the mountains. Constructed of willows and covered with mats, bark, or earth, the dome-shaped lodge could, depending on its size, accommodate from two to six adults. Typically sought in isolation from others, the vision quest required an individual to go without food and water for a prescribed number of days, or until his guardian spirit came to him.

In the vision, a particular animal spirit, such as the Elk or Wolf, or a bird spirit, such as the Eagle or Hawk, would appear and bestow the *suumesh*. Depending on the character of the guardian spirit, its power and benefits were applied by the beneficiary to such specific endeavors as hunting, gathering, or healing, in addition to a more general guiding of the life of the young man or woman. Prayer and song typically accompanied any request for and application of a *suumesh*. It was also common for the recipient of the *suumesh* to take on a "dream name," reflective of a characteristic or actual name of his or her associated animal spirit.

The following vignette conveys an exchange between Father Diomedi and his Schitsu'umsch interpreter and guide, Felician, occurring in 1876.

Make Friends with Some Spirit

"Do you believe in a supreme being?" "Our people believed in spirits a good deal, and thought they dwelt in everything, trees, stones, mountains and animals. When anyone went hunting, he would embrace whatever he met in his way, praying to the spirit and saying, 'let me find game.' Also each one tried to make friends with some spirit." "How could you do that, if you did not see, or hear them?" said I. "We would do it in this way. A girl, when she reached the age of about twelve years, would leave her home and go into the woods; boys would do the same at about fourteen years of age; they would walk on in search of the spirit and not drink water, nor taste fruit and roots until they found him. After a day or two they would fall asleep and then they would see the spirit who taught them a song and gave them something to keep sacred; then they would come home persuaded that they had found a friend who would always protect them during life." (Diomedi 1978:76–77)

In addition to *Amotqn* and the animal spirits, as well as huckleberries and deer, the mountains were inhabited by a host of other "beings" (Teit 1930:180–81). Among them were the "Dwarfs," who lived in the trees and along the cliffs and rocky places in the mountains. Generally, they looked like humans, though much smaller, and were either colored red or dressed in squirrel skins. They carried their babies upside down in cradle boards. Known not to have ever harmed anyone, the Dwarfs loved to play tricks on travelers, hiding their foodstuffs or calling out and confusing hunters. There were also the "Giants," who lived in mountain caves. As tall as a lodge, the Giants were able to look down the smoke hole of a tule-mat lodge.

They had a strong odor (that of burning horn), were painted black, and had a great appetite for fish. Though the Giants often stole the catch from weirs and traps, like the Dwarfs, they were not a serious menace to the Schitsu'umsh.

Not unlike the Water Mysteries, there were certain "Land Mysteries" who were to be feared. Appearing as half-human and half-animal, these beings lived in high trees or atop mountain peaks. At the summits of mountain trails, travelers often left special stones to placate them, the piles of such stones marking the abodes of the Land Mysteries. If a person failed to leave a stone, he or she would likely have bad luck; and if one of these beings was seen, death to the beholder typically followed a short time later.

By midsummer and into the early fall, the last of the camas was dug and the berry picking began. This was the time when families moved into the higher hills and along the mountain creeks to the berry patches. Twenty-two types of berries were gathered, including huckleberries, serviceberries, and chokecherries. "When the 'thimbleberries' ripen, the huckleberries would soon be ready." Huckleberries were plentiful along the creeks of the upper reaches of the St. Joe River, on St. Joe Baldy Mountain, and on Mica Peak, for instance. Medicines, such as *qhasqhs*, would also be collected by those picking berries.

At the moment when the first important berries, such as serviceberries, were gathered, but before any berries were actually consumed, an essential harvest ceremony took place. Among the families who had assembled for the gathering, a chief or headman of the group would come forward and offer a long prayer to *Amotqn*, thanking him for the berries. Facing the direction of the highest mountain in view, the chief would then hold out a basket of the berries as an offering to *Amotqn*. Song and dance generally followed, concluding with a feast of the berries. A similar prayer and dance also accompanied the digging of the first camas and bitterroot during the summer.

Throughout the summer and into the early fall, some family members traveled to Spokane Falls or, even farther, up the Columbia River to Kettle Falls. There the Schitsu'umsh would be joined by the Spokane, Colville, Kalispel, and Palouse to fish for salmon during their spawning runs, as well as to trade and recreate with one another. The Spokane area remains an important social meeting place, as a large intertribal Powwow is still held along the banks of the Spokane River toward the end of August each year. While some families traveled far, others remained closer to home to fish.

Kettle Falls on the Columbia River
(from John Mix Stanley's lithographs in Stevens 1855, pl. XLVII)

As with the spring spawning runs, whitefish would be trapped in fish weirs along the St. Joe River and at the mouth of the Spokane River, where it leaves Lake Coeur d'Alene.

Amo'tqɛn and the Bear Song

It seems that the chief deity prayed to was *Amo'tqɛn* [*Amǫtqn*], who is said to live on the highest mountains, whence he looked out over all the earth. He could see all lands, and understand what was required for the benefit of the Indians. He was supplicated to pity the people and to attend to their necessities. He was asked particularly for plenty of game, berries, and roots.

Before hunting, hunters often fasted and sweat-bathed; and in the sweat house they prayed to the animal they were to hunt and to other powers, such as the spirit of the sweathouse, that they might be successful in procuring game. When animals were killed they were often thanked.

Much respect was paid to bear and beaver, as these animals were thought to know, see and hear everything. They knew what people said and thought about them. If a man intended to hunt them they knew it. They allowed themselves to be killed only out of pity for the people. Skulls of bear and beaver were therefore always elevated on poles or put on trees. When a man killed a bear he blackened his face and sang the "Bear song," which had an air of its own and resembled a mourning song. He praised the bear in the song for giving himself up, and at the same time bewailed his death. (Teit 1930:184.)

With the coming of the late fall, a season of intense hunting for deer, elk, and bear began. One common method of deer hunting made use of dogs or designated men who acted as "drivers," herding the deer into a water crossing or a lake, where other men waited. The prayers of a shaman, invoking his *suumesh* to help ensure success, accompanied the hunt. From the shore or from canoes, the hunters would spear, club, drown, or shoot arrows at the oncoming animals. In addition to this collective form of hunting, individuals pursued deer and elk by use of blinds and individual tracking. During the summer and under the moonlight, hunters concealed themselves behind small screens of brush or behind trees, located near salt licks or watering places. When a deer came to drink or eat grass, it could be taken easily. In addition to deer, elk, and bear, moose and, as late as the 1820s, antelope were hunted by the Schitsu'umsh. As with fish, large quantities of meat was dried for later use. Dried fish and smoked venison was often stored in the earthen caches. Fresh meat was roasted, and dried meat was usually boiled.

The bows used in the hunts—rather short, sinewed-backed, recurved weapons of amazing strength—were often made of dogwood or syringa. Arrows were relatively long, up to three feet, and made of serviceberry wood. The arrow's fletching would consist of three hawk tail feathers. The Schitsu'umsh bow, short and not particularly accurate at long distances, was well adapted for hunting in the confines of forested hills and mountains.

The Schitsu'umsh were known throughout the region for their success in hunting deer and elk, having an abundance of deer and elk hides to trade with other peoples. In the 1840s or 1850s, Father Nicolas Point observed a single communal hunt in which 600 deer were killed (1967:178).

In the following vignette, Father Joseph Joset offers perhaps one of the earliest recorded accounts of a deer hunt, which likely occurred before 1850.[3]

The Hunt

Round the lake each family had their own exclusive part of the shore, to hunt with dogs in the fall: this was the way it was done: one would wait in his canoe while the other would lead the dogs: when they got the scent they pursued the animal until to escape them [the hunters] or to refresh himself he jumped in the water: the dogs would watch on shore until the canoe man came and killed the deer with his paddle: poor deer he comes to its death in so many ways: even the paddle is the death of many.

In a summer day, when the Indians were gone, one of our boys brought in the leg of a deer: what! who killed the deer? [asked Joset]. My Father [the boy responded]. It seems impossible the old man was a cripple who could move about only with crutches. How could your Father do it? He paddled to the lake and waited near a deer trail, under the cover of brushes: when the deer jumped in the water droven by the heat or by muskets, he moved between the animal and the shore behind and killed it with his paddle. . . .

One chief was chose who was thought to possess mysterious power over the deer, whose duty it was to determine the place for each day's work. Early in the morning he went out with a quantity of small rags which he tied them to bushes so as to form part of a line of a large circle. Then from the lodge, he started again to complete the circle with his fellows who were stationed at proper distance from one another. If a deer should pass the line of rags, as soon [as] it smelled them it would turn back and reenter the circle: so there was no escape.[4] (From the letters of Father Joset 1838–77, JP 36: "The Coeur d'Alene.")

The late fall also signaled the digging time for the last of the season's roots: the water potato. Water potatoes grew in the marshy areas along the shores of both Coeur d'Alene and Hayden lakes, often where creeks and streams entered the lakes. The water potato was unique to the Schitsu'umsh, not used by any of their immediate neighbors. Soon after the water potato had been gathered, the families began their journey to the winter villages and camps.

The winter traditionally saw the families congregate in several large, preestablished winter villages, as well as in a series of smaller camps along the shores of Coeur d'Alene, Hayden, and Liberty lakes, and on the banks of the lower Spokane, St. Joe, and Coeur d'Alene rivers. These were the sites of the "long communal houses" and, in the larger villages, supported populations of up to 300 individuals.

The primary Schitsu'umsh lodge, for both summer and winter use, was a conical-shaped structure, made of pine poles and covered with tule mats. Three poles were tied to form a tripod, which provided a foundation for the remaining poles. Growing in abundance and gathered along the lakes' shores and marshes, especially the southern end of Lake Coeur d'Alene, the tule reeds were sewn together in long, rectangular mats up to several feet in length. In addition to common tule, cattails were occasionally used in the construction of the mats.

Beginning at the base, a series of overlapping tule mats were wrapped around the pole foundation to form the conical lodge. Long poles were often laid over the mats to help secure them. The tule mats themselves were adaptable to the changing weather. During the heat of a summer's day, the poles of the lodge could be adjusted easily to aid the circulation of air.

In addition, air could flow between the sewn reeds of the mats to help provide ventilation. But if the mats became wet from rain or snow, the tules would swell, resulting in a more or less watertight covering. While a single layer of tule mats was used during the summer, the winter lodges generally employed several layers of matting. To add further protection from the winter's cold, cedar bark was used as an insulation between the layers of mats.

The lodge was either pitched on level ground or for more long-term camping and for winter sites, erected over a pit, dug as deep as a foot and a half. The removed earth was banked up around the base of the lodge to add further protection. The floor was covered with mats and beds of soft skins. These conical lodges ranged in size from fifteen to thirty feet in diameter and could accommodate from one to three related families. Interestingly, there seems to be no evidence of use of the semisubterranean pit houses so characteristic of other Plateau peoples. Since assemblage of materials and construction of the conical, tule-mat lodges were done by women, it is not surprising that the lodges themselves were considered the property of the women of the family.

For more temporary hunting or gathering camps, oblong-shaped lodges and simple lean-to structures, overlaid with tule mats, long strips of cedar bark, or brush, were constructed. In order to accommodate large gatherings for ceremonial, council, or recreational purposes, the lean-to lodges were sometimes built larger. Women's menstruation lodges (either coni-cal or lean-to) were located "at some distance" from the village.

The well-constructed, semipermanent long communal houses were made by aligning two large lean-to structures face to face. They ranged in size from fifteen to twenty-four feet wide and anywhere from fifty to ninety feet in length. Before putting the poles into place, the ground was exca-vated to a depth of twelve to thirty inches. In order to allow smoke from camp fires to escape easily, a narrow gap separated the ridgepoles of the two unconnected lean-tos. After fully securing the lean-to poles with long horizontal poles, the ends of the lean-tos were partially enclosed, leaving doorways at each end of the lodge. Layers of tule mats and cedar-bark insu-lation were then put into place, overlaid and secured by poles. If used for daily habitation, as many as "six fires" were placed lengthwise inside these lodges, each fire representing an individual family. Sometimes mat parti-tions attached to vertical poles anchored in the ground were erected to form separate "rooms" for families within the lodge. Unlike the conical lodges, the longhouses were the communal property of all those residing in a vil-lage, and were erected and maintained by common labor.

It was from inside the longhouses that much of villagers' winter life was conducted. Visitors were housed in them, and young men gathered there to receive instruction from elders. Stick games and other recreational activ-ities, the council meetings of elders and chiefs, and the Jump Dances all took place in these longhouses.

The stick game, also known as the "hand game" (Teit 1930:131), was a spirited competition in "guessing" that involved two teams. Teams could be based on kinship ties, as rival families would challenge one another. But when members of a visiting tribe were among the Schi̠tsu'umsh, tribal affiliation determined team composition, and competition was that much more intense. The teams alternated in concealing (in the palm of a team member's hand) two small "bones," one marked with sinew thread around its center. The other team attempted to guess which hand held the unmarked bone. To "guess," in fact, is something of a misnomer since it took "tremendous concentration and remembrance" to select the unmarked bone correctly.

During the guessing, special songs would be sung by the team hiding the bones, providing them with *suumesh* power. In an attempt to confuse the guesser, bodies would sway and arms wave to the rhythm of a song, beat with short sticks on a long pole in front of the players. To further conceal the bones, some players wore over their hands fringed "knuckle-covers"

*Tule mat longhouse, c. 1890s, from Nespelem, on the
Colville Reservation (courtesy Northwest Museum of Arts and Culture
and Eastern Washington State Historical Society, acc. no. L97–5.97)*

made of coyote, otter, or weasel skins. If successful in hiding the bones, a
counter "stick" was won from the guesser's team; but if unsuccessful, the
bones were forfeited to the guesser's team, which would then commence
hiding them. The team that won all twenty-two counter sticks won the game
and any bets made. With the ebb and flow of success and failure in hiding
the bones, a single game could last for hours.

During the extended winter nights, storytelling augmented with song
could also be heard from the longhouses. The stories recounted how
Coyote and the other First Peoples transformed the land, creating mountains and rivers, killing monsters of all types, providing salmon and camas,
and instructing the Human Peoples how to use fire and fish the salmon.

In addition to hearing of Coyote's adventures, accounts of particularly rewarding and challenging deer hunts, berry gatherings, or fishing endeavors were related in detail. In so doing, the vast and intricate knowledge associated with such activities—knowledge necessary to successfully travel on and live off the land—was imparted. As one elder recalled, "We learned from those stories."

The stories continued outside the longhouses. In addition to seeing results of the deeds of the First Peoples during the daylight hours, (a mountain ridge or a herd of deer, for example), during the long and brisk winter nights stars were most noticeable. "Most stars are considered to have been transformed people of the mythic period" (Teit 1930:78). The Big Dipper constellation, for example, tells the story of three brothers and their brother-in-law, Grizzly Bear, and the treachery perpetrated by the two eldest brothers against their brother-in-law. Upon attempting to kill their rival, Grizzly Bear was transformed into the four corner stars of the Dipper and the brothers into the three stars of the handle. Among the stars of the Pleiades is a small star, Coyote's Child, and a red star, Badger, who had attempted to abduct Coyote's favorite child and were transformed into these stars as a result. Another cluster of stars refers to the story of a group of women baking camas and the attempts of Skunk to spoil their cooking. The women appear in the night sky circling and protecting their camas oven, whereas Skunk looms a short distance away. Another cluster, Canoe, tells the story of five men who were constructing a canoe, each forming part of the outline of their canoe.

During the winter, ice fishing on the frozen sections of the lakes, as well as hunting from snowshoes, took place. Lying on a tule mat near a hole cut in the ice, a fisherman would use a line and lure to entice fish within reach of his three-pronged spear. Communal deer hunting also continued, with January the most active time for such hunting. With the addition of the stored roots and berries, as well as dried fish and meat kept on the pit and platform caches, and within the warmth of the tule-mat lodges, the winters were lived in relative comfort and health.

While arriving at an exact number is problematical, the Schitsu'umsh landscape likely supported a population of nearly 5,000 men, women, and children.[5] Approximately a third of the total Schitsu'umsh yearly diet consisted of roots and berries, another third came from fresh and dried deer and elk meat, and the other third was made up of fish taken from the local rivers and lakes, and obtained from trade. But to provide for the needs of this population, its members needed to travel the landscape fully. In a year's time, members of a family might have dug camas near Santa, hunted deer in the Minaloosa Valley, picked huckleberries on St. Joe Baldy, fished salmon at Spokane Falls, gathered water potatoes near Harrison, and finally wintered on the shores of Lake Coeur d'Alene near St. Maries. Using sturgeon-nosed, cedar-bark canoes on the lakes and rivers, and relying on well-walked trails through the hills and over the mountains, members of a family could easily establish and use as many as six different campsites. During a single year's seasonal round, a family might have transversed up to 300 miles through the Schitsu'umsh landscape.

THE BANDS AND FAMILIES

The Schitsu'umsh were divided into three generally recognized groupings, or "bands," each of which was associated with particular winter village regions. The first division, the Coeur d'Alene Lake band, consisted of some sixteen villages of families located at sites on Hayden Lake, near the current cities of Coeur d'Alene and Post Falls, along the Spokane River near Green Acres, and on the shores of Liberty Lake. The second band, the Coeur d'Alene River families, consisted of some eleven villages located along the Coeur d'Alene River, including sites near what would become the city of Harrison and the Cataldo Mission. The St. Joe River families made up the third band and were located in six villages along the lower St. Joe River, at the future site of St. Maries, with a single village located at the upper reaches of Hangman Creek. There might have been an additional Schitsu'-umsh band, with those families living around Liberty Lake and along the Spokane River, separate from those living at the north end of Lake Coeur d'Alene. The larger of the winter villages often numbered up to some three hundred individuals. Each of the three bands was made up of interrelated families who would typically winter in their band's established area, though individual families might not winter in the same village from year to year.

Within the seasonal transhumance pattern, individual families congregated and cooperated together during certain times of the year, as in communal deer hunts; at other times of the year, they dispersed throughout the land into smaller groupings of related families, as when they were berrying in the mountains. Thus it was necessary for Schitsu'umsh social structure to remain flexible enough to provide for situational cooperation and leadership. Reflective of these needs, traditional Schitsu'umsh society was fundamentally egalitarian, without hereditary, unilineal descent clans, or class structures. Although slaves acquired through capture or purchase were known, they were few in number, and the Schitsu'umsh did not systematically practice slavery.

Given this flexibility and the situational realigning of family groupings throughout the year, it is little wonder that the Schitsu'umsh had a bilateral kinship system. One's own family was made up of members from both his father's and his mother's families. This emphasis on both the paternal and maternal sides is expressed in the classificatory merging of siblings and cousins. Distinguished only by gender, the equivalent terms of "brother" and "sister" were used to address cousins from either side of the family. At the same time, such merging did not take place in the parental generation (Palmer: 1998: 321). It was an individual's closely aligned kinsmen—his brothers and sisters, as well as his father and mother and grandparents—that he would most rely upon for hunting, fishing, and gathering endeavors, as well as for the entire series of life-cycle rituals and activities. From vision questing and marriage to child birthing and raising, culminating in one's own funeral and burial, the life-cycle support provided by an individual's family allowed him or her to mature successfully and become integrated into Schitsu'umsh life.[6]

There were no prescribed marriage patterns between designated families and kin groups among the Schitsu'umsh. Marriage selection was largely by the mutual consent of the two individuals involved, though parents would sometimes attempt to "meddle." Despite this relatively open system, the phrase "You are like a dog" was applied to anyone who married a "close relative," i.e., someone to whom paternal or maternal ties could be traced directly.

Upon marriage, the bride typically moved in and traveled with the groom's family. A strict taboo against speaking with one's mother-in-law existed for the groom and, in some families, the bride was prohibited from speaking with her father-in-law. Polygyny was allowed, but was practiced by only a few. Marriages could be dissolved easily, though without severing affectionate and supportive ties with children, and between ex-spouses and their once-aligned families.[7] Should a wife's husband die, it was the responsibility of the deceased husband's brother to look after his brother's wife and her children. The result of such nonprescriptive marriage and relative ease of divorce and remarry was a wide dispersal of affiliations and alliances between and among varied families, further integrating Schitsu'umsh society.

THE CHIEFS

Reflecting the egalitarian and flexible qualities of the Schi̱tsu'umsh band and family structures, leadership positions were typically achieved, not ascribed or inherited. Each of the three bands had its own elected head chief, with subchiefs living in each of the other associated band villages. Any man was eligible to become a chief, though sons of former chiefs were often elected. While no woman could become a chief, women were allowed to speak at social gatherings; and many women became well respected for their wisdom and "chieflike qualities," exerting considerable influence over public opinion. It was often true that the chief residing at "Head Waters" (or "Surface on the Head of the Water"), the large village located at the mouth of the Spokane River (at the future site of the city of Coeur d'Alene), was the "head chief" of all three bands. The leadership position of chiefs at all levels was signified by public possession of a "stone pipe." The role of all chiefs was advisory; they led by example and ruled by consensus. Chiefs, whether village or band, had no coercive or punitive powers. Thus there was no need for a "police society" to carry out and enforce decisions of the chiefs.

The influence of the chiefs was often first articulated and then expressed through the actions of the village and band council meetings. Made up of the village elders, the council meetings were facilitated by the chiefs. But all decisions were arrived at by a consensus of the elders, based upon their consideration of the entire village or band's welfare. When the pipe was finally smoked at these councils, the decisions agreed to were binding by all families represented by the elders in attendance.

The influence of the chiefs was also expressed at the talks and storytelling sessions held during the winter ceremonies and social gatherings. The chiefs encouraged the people to conduct themselves properly and morally, and to be industrious. They would emphasize the importance of cooperation and generosity: "Don't put yourself above others." Lawrence Aripa recalled, with a big laugh, his father saying, "If you look down your noise at someone else, all you'll see are your moccasins." The chiefs would also publicly admonish those who were acting selfishly, cowardly, or who were quarrelsome, calling them "coyote." In fact, the most important social control of deviant behavior was in public joking and ridicule, and, if necessary, in the threat of ostracism. A thief or vain person would be laughed at and socially isolated from his or her family. Lawrence Aripa and his uncle, Felix Aripa, both told of a man, Cosechin, who was "mean and no good" (Frey

1995:177–79). The only way to control his "cruel ways" was to banish him to the mountains. While the mountains were part of a hospitable landscape for Schi̲tsu'umsh families, attempting to live there alone was sure to be fatal.

Additional responsibilities of the chiefs included helping in the regulation and distribution of food stores. The chiefs' ultimate responsibility was always to attend to the welfare of all members of their villages or bands, seeing to it that no individuals or families went without proper provisions throughout the year. A chief would continue to provide leadership so long as his decisions were sound and his actions moral. He ruled by the consensus of those he represented.

In addition to the village or band chiefs, specific ad hoc leaders, or "headmen," were selected for particular tasks. In communal hunts, fishing camps, and warfare, separate hunting and fishing headmen, and war chiefs, would be elected, but they served in that capacity only for the duration of the activity at hand. Men so elected had distinguished themselves as great hunters, fishermen, or warriors, possessing expert knowledge and perhaps *suumẹsh* relating to their particular skills. And like the role of village chiefs, the hunting and fishing headmen supervised the redistribution of the game meat and fish, assuring that those in need were cared for.

The social and political organization of the Schi̲tsu'umsh was thus marked by its flexibility and transitory qualities, lacking the rigidity found in hereditary, unilineal, descent-based groups and in ascribed, inherited leadership positions. Given the situational leadership structure, when individual extended families undertook an activity that isolated them from their village or band leadership for a short time, the eldest male within the group could easily assume decision-making responsibilities. Thus each family could effectively function both alone and as part of a larger whole. In order to pursue more communal-oriented tasks, individual families could, with relative ease, align themselves with other paternally or maternally related families. At all levels of social alignment, whether a single family, a hunting or gathering group of several extended families, or an entire winter village, leadership roles were clearly delineated and their responsibilities carried out.

THE SHAMANS

While the chiefs and headmen helped coordinate social and economic activities, the shamans facilitated spiritual affairs among the people. In turn, when spiritual endeavors were properly conducted, all aspects of Schi̲tsu'umsh life potentially benefited. While the power base for a chief lay in his ability to lead by consensus, the position of shaman was based upon his seeking and his successful acquisition of medicine, or *suumęsh* power, from an animal guardian spirit. His power was ultimately derived by the consent of his *suumęsh*.[8]

As virtually all adults, men and women, sought a vision and received a guardian spirit, shamans were distinguished from others by the degree of their power and the number of guardian spirits they possessed. Both men and women could become shamans, though there were more male than female shamans.

The roles of the shamans, in consort with the headmen or themselves acting in that capacity, included conducting hunting rituals prior to a hunt and helping in the coordination of hunting and gathering activities. In songs and prayers, the shaman sought to apply his *suumęsh* to assure a successful outcome in the hunting and fishing endeavors. As he sang his *suumęsh* song, a shaman would attempt to locate and draw in the game toward the hunters. In the following vignettes, "Somesh" and "A Medicine Lodge Ceremony prior to the Hunt," we have eyewitness descriptions of the application of *suumęsh* for hunting purposes, albeit from a less-than-sympathetic Jesuit perspective. Through the shaman's coordination of the ritual activities following a hunt or berry gathering, he would also see to an equitable distribution of the venison or berries among all the families.

In addition to specific hunting and fishing applications of their *suumęsh*, shamans prayed throughout the year for abundant rains and bountiful growth of camas and huckleberries. Besides addressing *Amǫtqn* and his spirit guardians, shamans might also beseech the aid of Thunder Man, "who lives on the high mountains" and announced when the rains would fall, or Sky Chief, who brought the snowfall and summer rains needed to nurture the roots and berries, and to sustain fish and deer.

Somesh

Yes the savages believe in an invisible power superior to his: they call that power Somesh [*suumęsh*]: but where it is . . . nobody could say: they would invoke: the bear, the deer, the wolf, every thing but God: I asked once a good old man whether and how he prayed before he knew almighty: "I was always a poor man, never had any Somesh medicine: going hunting I would embrace a tree and tell him: have pity on me, let me find a deer or bear. Another time I questioned one of our ~~most intelligent~~ Coeur d'Alene: whence did you get your Somesh. [In the original handwritten journal, "most intelligent" was crossed out.] He told me: when I was about 12 one of our dogs died, my father told me, take that dog . . . and go look for Somesh. I went to the mountains, the evening of the 2nd day I came to an old sweat house: it spoke and said you will take fire in your mouth without burning yourself: the dead dog spoke . . . and said you will be a great deer killer. But it was a dream? [asked Joset]. By no means, I was well awake! [answered the man]. The man was serious. (From the letters of Father Joset 1838–77, JP 69: "A Quarter of a Century among the Savages.")

The *suumҽsh* songs of the shaman were also sung in the Sweat House and during the Winter Medicine Dances (Jump Dances), or at anytime during the year inside a family's tule-mat lodge, in applying medicine powers to those who might be ill.[9] It was understood that when an individual family member was ill, the cooperative role he or she provided to the other members of the family would not be fulfilled, and consequently the entire family was ill and would suffer. The shaman thus played a vital healing role in Schitsu'umsh society. Incorporated into the shaman's healing procedures were the singing of his *suumҽsh* songs, the ritual painting of the patient as prescribed by the shaman's dream, and the application of a vast botanical pharmacology, administered as salves, drinks, or incense. Among the devices used by the shaman was a "sucking tube." An illness might be diagnosed as coming from an "object" shot into a person from a malevolent spirit, jealous rival, or because of the breaking of a taboo, and the treatment required that the shaman suck the object out of the patient with a hand-held sucking tube. Once removed and publicly shown to the family gathered around the patient, the object, such as a small bone or tuft of hair, would then be "thrown away" and the patient allowed to recover. If "soul loss" was detected, however, it was typically fatal, and could not be treated by the shaman.

It would also be the shaman's responsibility to help facilitate the transformation of and ultimately control the "Blue Jays" that would come out during the Medicine Dances. With blackened faces and bodies, individuals with Blue Jay power would "become" their patron spirit, "flying" to the rafters of a lodge and then out into the night, only to be "captured" eventually and brought back by the shaman.

It was sometimes one of the shamans who, in the winter communal house, told the stories of the First Peoples, of the adventures and misadventures of Coyote. The stories taught and helped vitalize the meaning of the landscape. And it was the shaman, "with his knowledge of the dead," who presided over the rituals of burial. Placed in a flexed position on a side or as if sitting, the dead were wrapped in robes, skins, or tule mats and buried in the earth or under rocks. The body was placed in a westerly orientation, as "the west is the end of the day and the end of life." Such items as blankets, a canoe, and other personal property, as well as small quantities of roots and berries, were included in the grave. The "ghost" of the deceased often remained near the grave and occasionally attempted to "visit" its living relatives for a while after the burial. These visits could bring illness if not repelled through the prayers and songs of a shaman.

If the role of the chiefs was ultimately to help regulate the social and economic relations between the people and the landscape (by influencing the proper behavior of people), the paramount role of the shaman was to help regulate the spiritual relations between the people and the landscape. If properly traveled, the landscape provided for the material needs of a people, through food, shelter, and transportation, as well as the spiritual needs, through *suumesh* songs. Camas and venison could nourish a body, but the *suumesh* could heal the body, as well as help assure the health of the roots and deer, and bring about a successful gathering and hunting season.

A Medicine Lodge Ceremony Prior to the Hunt

To give credit to their sacrilegious practices, until recently supported by hard-felt want, all the medicine men, recalling the time of their supposed efficacy, were pleased to repeat, "One day, after having invoked our manitous [*suumesh*], we bagged one hundred eighty deer."

"And we," replied the true believers, "by the power of Him Who created and redeemed the world, have, almost without the aid of our bows or guns, in less than six hours bagged as many as three hundred."

The last medicine lodge kept by the Coeur d'Alenes may give some idea of what one is like. The grand officiating priest was the youngest of medicine men, but, since he was the richest and the most generous, the others were willing to cede him the honors. In order to live up to the exalted idea of his merit, he began by decorating, as well as he could, a lodge capable of holding all the believers of the tribe. At about the height of a man, there is a sort of grille on which he arranges the objects relating to his medicine. Then he asks the eight people having the most striking appearance to seat themselves at either extremity of the lodge, four men on one side and four women on the other. Their duty is to assist the grand priest in his functions. The simple attendants are placed in two lines running the length of the lodge. These arrangements having been made, the grand master, his head decorated with elegant feathers and his body streaked with various colors, opens the session with a mysterious chant. After this, at a signal from the master, several cry out, "Kill the fire! Kill the fire!" At these cries, an indescribable confusion ensues, which does not end until the master pronounces the sacramental words, "My medicine is hidden." Then the fire is rekindled and the search for the medicine begins. In the midst of the milling about, begin the fainting spells, delirium, visions, revelations. What has the great manitou revealed? It is very cold, but, regardless of this, it is necessary to swim across the river and return with a certain kind of wood. Or stones of a certain kind are to be heated to red heat in the fire, extracted with the bare hands, and held between the teeth while one walks around the lodge. All these things are done. Then a voice cries, "The hunt has opened." Everyone leaves the lodge and makes a common invocation. The voice cries again, "Before taking the first shot, turn the rifle toward the sun. If the first animal killed is a male, it should be brought into the lodge head first; if it is a female, the rump should be first." Thus prepared, it is said, the results of the hunt were abundant. (From Father Nicolas Point's winter 1842–43 observations [1967:67–70].)

❧

Winds of Change: Contact History

Winds of change swept over the landscape of the Schi̱tsu'umsh with the coming of Euro-Americans and their imposition of the name "Coeur d'Alene" onto its people.[1] Many of these winds would bring a harsh chill over the Schi̱tsu'umsh landscape, threatening its integrity and incorporating much of it into a Euro-American landscape. While these winds severely threatened, they did not obliterate the trails over which Crane and Coyote and the other First Peoples continued to travel. And, more recently, warmer winds have contributed to a rekindling of a sovereign Schi̱tsu'umsh landscape.

THE HORSE

The first winds of Euro-American change actually occurred long before any Euro-American and Schi̱tsu'umsh set eyes upon each other. The initial Euro-American impact was set in motion by the arrival of a new animal—the horse—in the Schi̱tsu'umsh landscape. Horses were reintroduced to the New World during the Spanish Conquest, but it is not entirely certain when the Schi̱tsu'umsh first acquired horses and under what circumstances. James Teit offers the following account.

The First Horse

The first horse came to the Coeur d'Alene country at a place about 3 ¹/₂ miles northwest of DeSmet. A large number of people were gathered there, digging camas. They saw a man approaching on horseback, and became greatly excited. The rider was a Kalispel Indian, who remained several days with the Coeur d'Alene. The people examined the horse closely, and wondered much at the strange animal. As the horse was gentle, many people tried to ride him; but when he trotted, they fell off, excepting one man. (Teit 1930:109.)

By the 1760s the horse had likely become a fully integrated member of the Schı̣tsu'umsh landscape and society. With that integration also came changes. The horse provided a means to travel farther from the home territories. Access to the important Columbia River salmon fishing and trading sites, such as Kettle Falls and even as far away as The Dalles and Celilo Falls, was made much easier. The distances now traveled could, in fact, be quite significant. Gone for up to nine months of the year, individual Schı̣tsu'umsh families, often joining with Spokane families, traveled over the Bitterroot Range, meeting up with Flathead families, and hunted buffalo in the valleys east of the Bitterroots and farther onto the Plains east of the Rocky Mountains. Leaving in August, "after the harvesting of the principal root and berry crops, and after the salmon had been put up," the Schı̣tsu'umsh traveled "by a short trail over the Bitterroots, by Old Mission [and likely along the St. Regis and Clark Fork rivers], returning in April by Kalispel River [likely the segment of the Clark Fork River running from the St. Regis River to Lake Pend Oreille], where the snow goes off early in the spring, and grass for horses is abundant" (Teit 1930:97).

Buffalo hunting soon became a regular part of a changing transhumance pattern. Entire families went on the hunt: "Women and children went along with their husbands and other relatives. Only the oldest and a few others remained behind" (Teit 1930:96). Thus, while many families traveled to the winter villages along the lake's shore, some began their trek over the mountains into buffalo country. The following year, some of those who had wintered along the lake's shore were among those buffalo hunting in the valleys east of the Bitterroots; those who had hunted buffalo the year before now hunted deer in the Coeur d'Alene Mountains.

Buffalo Hunt

Buffalo were hunted by parties of mounted men advancing on them in a line, usually not far apart, and often quite close together. At a signal by the hunting chief, the hunters dashed at full speed at the herd of buffalo, stampeding them. They shot and speared the animals in the rear and sides of the herd. The pursuit and slaughter continued until the party considered that they had sufficient meat and skins. (Teit 1930:103.)

In search of a more mobile form of lodging, the Schı̣tsu'umsh soon complemented their use of tule-mat lodges with the skin-covered tipis of the Plains peoples; they also adopted the horse-travois. After a successful

Susan Michel with her pitse' and horse, 1920s (photograph by Dick Lewis; courtesy Northwest Museum of Arts and Culture and Eastern Washington State Historical Society, acc. no. L91–167.218)

The Dalles near Celilo Falls on the Columbia River (from John Mix Stanley's lithographs in Stevens 1855, pl. XLIII)

hunt, much of the buffalo meat would be smoked and brought back home. In addition to the sustenance acquired, travel across the Rockies provided opportunity to educate the young. As Lawrence Aripa emphasized: "They didn't go to the buffalo country just to hunt. They had plenty [of deer and elk to hunt] right here. They'd learn about different things, pick up things along the way. And they'd say, 'The children would leave as children, and they'd come back as grown-ups.'" The nine-month journey acted as a kind of "rite of passage" for the young and inexperienced of the family.

The adoption of the horse also meant that families, throughout the year, had to find good grazing lands for their herds close to their home territories. There were incentives to spend less time in the heavily forested mountainous country to the east and north of Lake Coeur d'Alene and more time in the grass-covered prairie country north of the Spokane River, along Hangman Creek, and south into the Palouse River region. Berries continued to be gathered, deer hunted, and fish caught, but buffalo meat and a new rite of passage were now added to the diet and well-being of the Schitsu'umsh. In this sense, the range of travel through the Schitsu'umsh landscape was expanded.

While in buffalo country, hunters searched the horizon not only for game but for Blackfeet and Crow warriors as well. After the arrival of the horse, intertribal warfare escalated for the Schitsu'umsh, as did the importance and power of the "war chiefs." While traveling in the valleys and on the open plains, much was vested in the sound judgments made by these leaders. Unlike travel within the boundaries of their traditional landscape, virtually all trips by Schitsu'umsh families into buffalo country and the territory of the Blackfeet and Crow were preceded by "war dances and war ceremonies." The warriors sang their *suumesh* songs and imitated the deeds they might have to accomplish in battle. These dances were also held at intertribal gatherings and at fur-trade rendezvous. While not preparations for battle per se, these "intertribal war dances" were held to celebrate past war exploits, to reaffirm resistence to any and all adversaries, and to reestablish kinship relations with families and friends. They typically lasted for several days, with intervals of feasting and games held throughout the dance. In the songs and dance, protection from the increased and inevitable danger was sought. With the coming of the horse, even travel within the boundaries of the traditional landscape became less safe.

Buffalo Country on the Northern Plains
(from John Mix Stanley's lithographs in Stevens 1855, pl. x)

Crow War Party

A large Crow war party traveled into Coeur d'Alene country and was poised to attack the Coeur d'Alene village located near Cataldo. The Crow chief came to the Old Mission because he was mad the Coeur d'Alenes no longer went through their territory, and thus the Crows could no longer raid them and make their children and women slaves. They were looking to count coups and make war on the Coeur d'Alenes. The Coeur d'Alene headman asked to first parlay with the Crow war leader and challenged him to a contest. Who were the better marksmen with the bow and arrow, the Crow or the Coeur d'Alene? Now the Crows, a tall and physically strong people, are well known as great warriors. A huge fellow came forward, with a long and powerful bow. So the Crow hung a large bag full of straw from a rope and behind it a smaller bag and a wood plank with a target on it.

He had the two bags swung in opposite directions. He took aim and shot his arrow through both bags and hit the target The Crows cheered and felt real confident. Now the Coeur d'Alene bowman came forward, a rather short fellow, with a small bow. You wouldn't think he could do much against that Crow. As he took aim, he signaled to some women who were hidden on the other side of the hill below the Mission to chase the horse up and over, and into range. "Oh, no! No!" the Crow chief shouted. It was his stallion. With his little bow, the Coeur d'Alene shot the white stallion as it came over the hill. The arrow went straight through the horse and into the wood plank, the target.

Oh, that Crow chief was mad. It was his prized horse. He was very angry, and about to have his warriors come down and take care of the Coeur d'Alenes. But the Coeur d'Alene headman came forward and reminded the Crow chief of his word. And he honored it. Indeed, that short Coeur d'Alene bowman had triumphed over the best Crow archer. And the Crows left the Coeur d'Alene country never to return. (Abbreviated, as told by Lawrence Aripa, April 15, 1995.)

Teit suggests that there were occasions when "nearly the entire tribe" hunted buffalo, sometimes for up to eight or nine months, leaving in the fall and returning during the spring months (1930:97). Most likely, more individuals participated in the hunt each year until nearly the entire tribe went. This was probably sometime "before 1800, when the Coeur d'Alene were well equipped with horses, and the Blackfeet were often attacking the Flathead, [and] the latter extended invitations to the Coeur d'Alene and other western tribes, and welcomed them to hunt buffalo in their territory" (Teit 1930:97).

The number of such tribal hunts is not clear. They were likely initiated as ad hoc responses to provide military assistance to the Flathead against a common foe, rather than a reflection of a permanently changed transhumance pattern based upon subsistence considerations. Given the winter dispersal of the buffalo, the cold and heavy snows in western Montana that inhibited travel during winter, and the prevalent method of buffalo hunting, most buffalo hunting probably took place during the fall and spring seasons. The winter saw individual Schitsu'umsh families scattered among their Flathead relatives, sharing their hospitality and food, and living with them throughout the season in their longhouses. Having abandoned their own long communal houses along the shores of Lake Coeur d'Alene, the Schitsu'umsh Jump Dances, one of the most important of all ceremonials,

Blackfeet Indians on a buffalo hunt
(from John Mix Stanley's lithographs in Stevens 1855, pl. xxvii)

were held among the Flathead, who shared the same religious tradition. The last Schitsu'umsh buffalo hunt occurred in 1876, after which the virtual extinction of the herds on the Montana plains made these trips impractical.

The Schitsu'umsh, while known as good warriors, may have found themselves at a distinct military disadvantage against the numerically stronger Blackfeet and Crow within their own landscape, expanded by introduction of the horse. These tribes had much more developed traditions of coup counting and more organized warrior societies than did the Schitsu'umsh. The expanded Schitsu'umsh landscape was thus now also a less hospitable landscape.

SMALLPOX

As with the horse, a second wind of Euro-American influence was felt before the eyes of any two strangers met. A new, unseen, and deadly presence roamed the Schitsu'umsh landscape: smallpox. The Schitsu'umsh suffered from smallpox epidemics perhaps as early as the mid-1770s, with the virus likely carried inland along the Columbia River in the wake of Euro-Americans exploring the west coast of the Pacific for fur-trade opportunities. Smallpox may also have spread from epidemics occurring on the Plains, transplanted via Schitsu'umsh buffalo hunters. The Schitsu'umsh certainly suffered the ravages of smallpox in 1801, and again in 1830 or 1831, and in the 1850s. While smallpox was the most destructive of the infectious diseases for which there were no natural immunities, chickenpox, measles, scarlet fever, and whooping cough also likely took their toll, especially among children. Healthy bodies, the advice of chiefs, and the *suumęsh* of shamans were inadequate protection.

Disease decimated the population of the Schitsu'umsh. Entire families and camps were wiped out. From an estimated 5,000 before the epidemics, by the 1850s the Schitsu'umsh numbered only some 500 individuals (Joset 1838–77, JP 69; Stevens 1854).[2] If a person lived through these epidemics, dying of old age in the 1850s, he would have survived episodes during which nearly every Schitsu'umsh he knew died a horrible death.[3] One cannot imagine the terror and sorrow such a person must have felt. The U.S. Indian Department reported that the Schitsu'umsh population remained fairly steady at 494 individuals in 1905, all of whom lived on the Coeur d'Alene Reservation.

Smallpox and the Five People

It was about the 1870s and the people were preparing to go to the reservation. Some of the Coeur d'Alene people were living on both sides of the Spokane River, at the mouth of the river, near Fort Sherman. It was during the winter and it was very cold. There were probably 200 people there. The lake itself froze over with ice. And at the time there was a smallpox outbreak in the fort; but because everybody was quarantined, it stayed in the fort.

There was a young lieutenant, from back East. He felt sorry for the Indians. So he ordered his men to gather the blankets and clothes from the dead soldiers, and give them to the Indians so they could warm themselves. And soon after, the epidemic hit the Indian camp. The people were just dying, and they were very sick, and it took a lot of our people.

At the same time, there was a young boy and his grandfather out on the lake, fishing through the ice. They had with them a young girl and two women, who were trying to gather some food from the shores of the lake. A pretty bad storm came up. They had been gone from the camp for five days after the smallpox came.

So when they came back to the camp all their own people, their own families, were dying. Only five people were still alive. The boy and the old man helped bury them, and helped to comfort the ones that were dying. And it was very, very sad and very bad.

All the rest of the people were over in the Harrison area, and up at Hayden Lake, and so they weren't here at that time of the outbreak. But they came back and heard the news that the people were dying. When they arrived these five people, the little boy and his grandfather and the three women, were busy burying the dead and doing all they could to help. But one of the medicine men said, "These five people must be the cause of the dying, because they are not sick. They have a bad spirit—the devil in them! And we must get rid of them!" And so without consulting the Black Robe like they usually do, the subchief gave the order, "Those people are to be banished, because they have bad spirits within them." So they are banished from the tribe. And they were told to get away.

And so they leave and go up to the Cusick area [in Washington]. The old man knew some people up there who would feed them—the Kalispel. But somehow word already got there. And when they arrived the people there told them to leave. So they went to the Spokane Tribe. But as they got close they were met again, and told to leave. They next went to the Nez Perce, but they were kicked away.

It was a very hard winter, but those five people stayed away. They lived in a little tipi they made. They never had enough to eat and were always near starvation. But for five years they wandered, these five people. People would pass by, traveling to the reservation or going to trade over in Spokane. They'd see these five pitiful people out there all by themselves, but nobody would talk to them, nobody would even look at them. Their clothes became ragged. They were in very, very bad shape. Their camp was down towards Tekoa, and they were out there.

The people had embraced the Catholic religion. The priests at Cataldo Mission told the people that what they were doing was wrong and that they should not be banished. So some Coeur d'Alene went out to bring the five people back. They wouldn't come at first, but finally did. For five years they were gone. They were accepted by the people again. And they became very strong Catholics. The young woman had a large family. And the young boy grew up to become a well-known man on both the Coeur d'Alene and Kalispel reservations. (Abbreviated, as told by Lawrence Aripa in April 1991.)[4]

The smallpox epidemics not only took their toll in Schitsu'umsh lives lost, which was disastrous in itself, but for those who lived through the devastation life became far more challenging. While traditional transhumance patterns had spawned a degree of social and economic autonomy among families, the loss of life from epidemics threatened the integrity of the society at large. Much of the expertise and collective wisdom necessary for leadership, subsistence, and religious expression was removed within a relatively short time. In addition, with the sheer loss of able-bodied men came a loss in warriors, and thus an increase in the threat posed by the ever-menacing Blackfeet and Crow. Much of the Schitsu'umsh landscape became even more inhospitable.

THE FUR TRADE

Under the leadership of President Thomas Jefferson, the United States purchased the Louisiana Territory from France in May 1803. Soon after, President Jefferson authorized Meriwether Lewis and William Clark to undertake a transcontinental expedition to map and report on what had been acquired, and to discover a water route to the Pacific. On their return trip from the Pacific coast, near the confluence of the Clearwater and Potlatch rivers, the men of the Corps of Discovery and three Schitsu'umsh first set eyes upon one another. It was May 6, 1806. A competing set of eyes, accustomed to another landscape, would now also view the landscape of the Schitsu'umsh. We have the words of Clark recorded from his journal entry.

The Skeet-so-mish

At this place we met with three men of a nation called Skeets-so-mish [Schitsu'umsh] who reside at the falls of a large river dis[c]harging itself into the Columbia on its East side to the North of the entrance of Clark's [Fork] River. this river they informed us headed in a large lake [Coeur d'Alene] in the mountains and that the falls below which they reside was at no great distance from the lake. these people are the same in their dress and appearance with the Chopunnish [Nez Perce], tho' their language is

intirely different, a circumstance which I did not learn untill we were about
to set out and it was then too late to take a Vocabulary. (Thwaites 1904–
05 [4]:363.)

The journals of Lewis and Clark record, in total, 120 "Skeet-so-mish"
lodges with "Probable No. of Souls" of 2,000 (Thwaites 1904–05 [6]:119).
Also referred to was "Waytom Lake" (Lake Coeur d'Alene), which is "10
days around it, has 2 Islands and is 7 days from the Chopunnish" (Thwaites
1904–05 [5]:94). The landscape of the Schitsu'umsh would soon be frequented and inhabited by many more Euro-Americans.

Three years later, in 1809, David Thompson of the Northwest Fur
Company built the Kullyspell House near the modern town of Hope,
Idaho. This was the first fur-trading post in the Pacific Northwest. The
Schitsu'umsh were also noted by Thompson in his journal writings. On
September 9 of that year a group of twenty-three "Pointed Hearts" "made
a handsome present of dried Salmon and other Fish with Berries and a
Chevruil [deer]" (Elliott 1920:52). While the Kullyspell post existed only
briefly, it succeeded in opening a door for fur trade with the Schitsu'umsh.
It was at this time that the first guns were introduced to the Salish peoples,
along with other trade objects.

The following year, Spokane House was established by Jaco Finlay, at
the confluence of the Spokane and Little Spokane rivers, a short distance
downriver from Spokane Falls. The Northwest Fur Company and the
Hudson's Bay Company were merged in 1821, thereby establishing a virtual monopoly over the fur trade throughout the Northwest. Fort Van-
couver, founded in 1825, became the center of this new empire. Spokane
House was abandoned after a few years in favor of its close neighbor, Fort
Spokane. But by 1826 Fort Spokane was also closed, and the regional center of the fur trade had moved to Fort Colville at Kettle Falls. However, the
distance to this post seems to have inhibited the Schitsu'umsh from continuing their active participation in the fur trade. By the early 1840s the short-
lived fur trade had all but ended throughout the region.

In addition to trade goods, the Schitsu'umsh acquired something else
from the fur traders. While the precise origin of the name is unknown,
"Coeur d'Alene" was likely used by French-speaking fur traders of European
or Iroquois descent in their initial dealings with the Schitsu'umsh.[5] The term
"coeur d'alene," which means "heart of [like] an awl" but is often loosely
translated as "pointed hearts," refers to the tough bargaining conducted
by the Schitsu'umsh with the fur traders.

The fur trade was a period of mixed blessings for the Schitsu'umsh. From the Euro-Americans came such trade goods as glass beads, wool blankets, cotton shirts, and an assortment of utilitarian metal products, such as knives and axes, cooking pots, arrow points, and eventually rifles. The great trade gatherings, or "rendezvous," were also an exciting time of games and family renewal. While there was no overt attempt by fur traders to alter the institutions or way of life of the Indians, changes did occur. With those few white traders and trappers who spent extended time among the Schitsu'umsh came the first exposure to Euro-American attitudes and values.

The fur traders were, at best, an interesting lot of emissaries. The reliance on the landscape for certain bone, wood, and stone materials was now also augmented by inclusion of new technology that generally made life physically easier. But continual access to metal axes, rifles, and the like meant dependency on these entrepreneurial and not-always-honest traders, reliance on distant Euro-American manufacturers, and attachment to a capitalistic-based, market economy. The Schitsu'umsh became linked to the oscillations of continental and global markets, economic processes over which they had little control. When beaver-felt hats were no longer in fashion, beaver belts lost their value, and acquisition of new axes as well as gunpowder and lead for muskets became far more difficult.

The Schitsu'umsh were also introduced to a new way of viewing the phenomena of the landscape itself. Furs and other items, once used only for subsistence needs, were now collected in ever greater quantities and began to assume new meanings. The "fairly abundant" beaver (Teit 1930:97) came to be valued relative to what its pelt might command in exchange for trade goods; the beaver thus became valued as a commodity. Any spiritual or social significance the animal once had was now supplemented by its market significance.

It was also during the fur trade era that alcoholic drink was introduced. The long-term effects of excessive liquor consumption were devastating both to individual lives and family structures.

With the Louisiana Purchase and the ensuing fur trade, the Schitsu'umsh landscape obtained new "gifts," but also an increased dependence on distant forces beyond the control of the Schitsu'umsh. With the relatively sudden collapse of the fur trade also came societal disruptions caused by lack of access to certain commodities and trade goods recently integrated into Schitsu'umsh society. And it was now a landscape increasingly inhabited by Euro-Americans, who were redefining it and making it a part of their own landscape.

THE JESUITS

Even before the Jesuit priests arrived, their coming was foretold. Living "a couple of hundred years before the coming of the White man," Circling Raven was given "a great vision." Joseph Seltice noted that Circling Raven was head chief of the Schi̱tsu'umsh "for a hundred years," from 1660 to 1760 (Kowrach and Connolly 1990:13). His *suumẹsh*, Raven, would circle above his head and tell him the location of game animals or an enemy. On one occasion, Raven told of the coming of men wearing "long black robes with crossed-sticks under their belts" who would teach the Schi̱tsu'umsh a "new way to the heaven trails."

Among the Flathead there was also such a visionary. As a small boy, Shining Shirt was out with his parents on a hunt when they were killed, leaving him orphaned (Peterson 1993:14). When he returned to his people, he went to the mountains to pray. He spent many days there, and finally a vision came. In his vision he was taught the ceremony of the Winter Jump Dance, and learned that he would be able to help others when he did this dance. He was told that he would become a powerful shaman, and that "when he died, lightning, thunder and hail would shake the earth" (ibid.). In his vision the future was also seen. Teaching a new way to pray, "fair-skinned men wearing black robes" would come. These "Black Robes," as the Jesuit priests were called, would not only bring a "new way to the heaven trails," but, in so doing, they would indelibly alter the Indian way of life.

During the fur-trade era, before the Black Robes actually arrived, Christianity began to make an impression on the Plateau peoples. By the 1820s, several French-speaking Iroquois families had settled among the Flathead to trap and trade fur. They began sharing their version of Catholicism, which included elements of their own Indian ritual and belief. Spokane Garry had spent two years at the Anglican mission's Red River School (near present-day Winnipeg, Manitoba), and by the early 1830s he was teaching the tenets of the Protestant faith and the King James Bible to the Spokane, and was very likely influencing the Schi̱tsu'umsh as well.

Beginning in 1831, the Flathead and Nez Perce sent three successive delegations to St. Louis to request the Black Robes. It was a dangerous journey: The 1837 delegation, the third to set out, was "attacked and wiped out by Sioux warriors." In 1836 Presbyterian missions were established by Henry Spalding on Lapwai Creek in Nez Perce country and by Marcus Whitman at Waiilatpu in Cayuse country, near Fort Nez Perces (Fort Walla Walla). A fourth delegation of Flathead and two Iroquois who had settled among the Flathead, Pierre Gaucher and Young Ignace, left in 1839. At Council Bluffs, Iowa, their requests were heard by the Black Robe, Father Pierre-Jean DeSmet, a thirty-eight-year-old Jesuit priest from Belgium. For DeSmet "the appeal came as a voice crying from the wilderness" (Peterson 1993:23), and his was the vision of establishing a "wilderness kingdom for God."

DeSmet first traveled to the Bitterroot Valley in 1840, and then he returned the following year with Jesuit Fathers Nicholas Point and Gregory Mengarini, and three lay brothers. They established the St. Mary's mission among the Flathead in the Bitterroot Valley, in what would become western Montana. The prophecies of Circling Raven and Shining Shirt were being fulfilled.

Finding the Lost

The Black Robes were found wandering around on the prairie out there by Hayden Lake area. They were lost and trying to find the Coeur d'Alenes, but they were lost. The Flatheads that were with them were trying to find them, but they were just wandering around. They were found out there wandering around looking for the Coeur d'Alenes, by Stellam, which was Thunder, was his name. (From an interview conducted on June 7, 1996.)

In the spring of 1842, while on his way to Fort Colville, Father DeSmet first met with Stellam, the head chief of the Schitsu'umsh, at a location just west of Hayden Lake.[6] It was noted by one elder that the encounter with Father DeSmet was seen by some Schitsu'umsh less as an opportunity "to learn from the priests [than] to teach the priests about the Coeur d'Alene ways and traditions!" DeSmet, in turn, instructed Father Nicolas Point to work directly among the Schitsu'umsh and to begin a modest mission among them. Built the following spring near the north bank of the St. Joe River, the Mission of the Sacred Heart of Jesus was established.

Father Point discovered a landscape abundant with life. He noted with interest that fishing and hunting were done year-round and, where the Spokane River meets the lake, that "the catch is usually so abundant that canoes are filled and emptied within a space of a few hours" (Point 1967: 175). He also observed that in one day 180 deer were killed by a single group of hunters, and another group killed 300 in the space of six hours (Point 1967: 67).

*Mission of the Sacred Heart, overlooking the Coeur d'Alene River
(from John Mix Stanley's lithographs in Stevens 1855, pl. xxxv)*

*DeSmet, Idaho, c. 1909; on the ridge overlooking the community is the Convent
of Mary Immaculate and the Mission of the Sacred Heart (courtesy Northwest
Museum of Arts and Culture and Eastern Washington State Historical Society,
acc. no. L95–109.206)*

As the mission was initially located on a floodplain and thus not well suited for long-term habitation, in 1845 Father Joseph Joset, who had replaced Point, surveyed the lake and river region and moved the mission to a hill overlooking the Coeur d'Alene River. Here the mission was built near a traditional village and burial site. Father Joset served the Schįtsu'umsh until his death in 1900, at the age of ninety. He learned the language of the people and was extremely influential in their lives, as well as with the growing Euro-American community. By the 1850s, under the architectural guidance of Father Antony Ravalli, the Mission of the Sacred Heart of Jesus or what is known today as the Old Mission or the Cataldo Mission had been constructed with the labor of the Schįtsu'umsh "without the use of a single nail." In the years following, as many as forty to fifty Schįtsu'umsh became closely associated with the mission's activities and likely settled at the site in a semisedentary fashion. The children of these families were, in turn, instructed by the Jesuits in Catholicism, as well as in farming techniques and animal husbandry.

Beginning in 1876, under the direction of Father Alexander Diomedi, who arrived that year, and assisted by Father Joset, the Jesuits began moving the Mission of the Sacred Heart to a new site near Hangman Creek and Moses Mountain. This new "DeSmet Mission" was fashioned after the Cataldo Mission. Flanking the mission, a girls' and boys' dormitory was built and a boarding school established by the Sisters of Charity in 1878. To the north of the mission, and under its watch, a small community of Schįtsu'umsh living in wooden houses flourished. The settlement was named DeSmet, in memory of "the beloved" priest who had died in 1873. After fire consumed the church building in 1939, the mission was soon rebuilt. To this day, the Sacred Heart Mission continues to serve the Schįtsu'umsh actively.

The Jesuits' desire to move the mission to Hangman Creek was the culmination of several concerns.[7] Among the considerations was the completion of Mullan Road in 1862, which passed right by the Cataldo Mission. Literally thousands of settlers, on their way to a new start on the Pacific, traveled through the Schįtsu'umsh landscape each year. In 1866 alone, an estimated 20,000 people, 5,000 head of cattle, and 6,000 mules traveled the Mullan Road between Montana and Walla Walla, Washington (Winther 1945). And many stayed. By 1870, hundreds of gold seekers were in the mountains along the north forks of both the Clearwater and Coeur d'Alene rivers. Thus continued the growing encroachment and influence of the white settlers, especially miners, in the Coeur d'Alene River basin. The Jesuits feared the moral influences of these whites on the Schitsu'umsh. Mean-while, the Sisters of Charity needed additional land to support a school they sought to establish among the Schitsu'umsh. Larger tracts of good farm-land were also needed if more Schitsu'umsh families were to settle around the mission. The Cataldo site had only limited land for such expansion. With only a small percentage of the entire tribe living permanently at the mission, the Jesuits exercised only marginal control over the movements and lives of the Schitsu'umsh (Palmer 1981b: 1). Most of the Schitsu'umsh families lived in their traditional villages and camps, and they continued their traditional transhumance pattern on the landscape. Removal of the entire tribe to a "remote location" with good farmland would, it was hoped, address these concerns.

Do You Wish To Be a Great People?

I have many times spoken to you before, to kindly ask you to leave these rough mountains where there is not enough land to raise feed sufficient for animals, where there is not enough vegetables for all your people.

Therefore, go to the vast prairie lands where you can raise all the wheat and all the vegetables you need for both your stock and yourselves, and also for your children's children, and children to come for always.

The White people will come in great numbers. As they are so many, you cannot count them. Across the big waters where they come from are thousands upon thousands of them. You would not know how many they are. They will come across and settle upon all the buffalo plains in the land of the Rising Sun and upon these, our camas plains of the Setting Sun. They will settle upon the shores of all our lakes and rivers, they will settle in the forests, in the hills and even on the very summits of our high-est mountains.

There will be no more vacant or open land. They will kill off all the buf-falo, the elk, all the big game, the birds of game. They will destroy all the salmon, trout and all fish in our lakes and streams. They will plow up the prairie lands where the camas and all eatable roots grow, and there shall be no more camas.

They are now many in our country and have their laws, and they shall still come a thousand fold more times than what they are now.

No doubt this is a serious matter. Now I want the Sisters to come and teach your children. Suppose the Sisters come; they must have a house and a mile square of good tillable land, and very well you, yourselves, know that cannot be had here, and therefore we ought to leave this place, and go to the region where such land is available.

Moreover, let me tell you that this moving of the Mission is for the greater good of all of you, old and young. Do you wish to die? Then remain here; live by hunting and fishing, spend your time, the Church will be in mourning. She will mourn for her children and have no comfort because they are gone.

Do you wish to be a great people? Go to the beautiful land; break the sod and grow grain, plants, vegetables, and your children will live, your wives will be safe and well dressed and you will have plenty. (Reported by Basil Peone of Father Diomedi's 1876 speech to the Coeur d'Alene people, attempting to convince them to move to Hangman Creek. *Coeur d'Alene Teepee* 1938 March 1 [5]: 14; 1981:85.)[8]

By November 1877, the move of the Schi̱tsu'umsh to the traditional camas region along Hangman Creek had been completed, with construction of the church finished in 1882. By 1880, Cataldo was no longer used as a permanent Schi̱tsu'umsh village site, though it continued to produce hay for the horses at nearby Fort Sherman, located at the mouth of the Spokane River.[9] At Hangman Creek, Schi̱tsu'umsh settled in permanent homes near the new mission and began supplementing their camas digging, berry gathering, deer hunting, and trout fishing with agricultural pursuits. After the move, the annual trip over the Bitterroot Range to hunt buffalo with their Flathead relatives all but ended.

While the move to Hangman Creek was desired by the Jesuits, the resettlement was not supported by all Schi̱tsu'umsh. Besides Agusta (see "Must We Leave?" below), many others spoke out against the move. Among those dissenting were "Isadore Bernah (Bernard), Joseph (Old Agath's husband), Aripa [Rufinus Shi'itsi̱n] of the St. Mary's clan, Francis Regis, the Rocky Mountain Steer (Zu-lemi-gu-zo) and his brother Basil (Kui-kui-sto-lem) Blue Steer" (*Coeur d' Alene Teepee* 1938 April 1 [6]:17; 1981:110). Upon arriving in the Hangman Creek area, Stanislaw Aripa recounted to his son, Felix: "We look around, we're lost. All we seen was tall grass and prairie chickens. We look around, we felt lost." Even after the resettlement to Hangman Creek, many families, albeit in modified form, continued their transhumance travels over the traditional landscape. For example, "From 1883 to 1900 Coeur d'Alene were seen hunting mule deer and berrying along the Little North Fork of the Coeur d'Alene and on Grizzly Mountain," despite the move to DeSmet (Palmer, Nicodemus, and Felsman 1987:59).

Must We Leave?

Must we leave this land where the bones of our fathers mingle with those of our children? Must we leave these woods which supplied us with fuel and game? This prairie which has fed our horses? This river which has given us trout and beaver? We are good and healthy. Our children are fat. Our wives are comfortable in our lodges and log houses. We are not like you. You need bread. We have camas. You require good clothing; we are satisfied with deer skins and buffalo robes. We can live comfortably on what you would think poor and wretched. I know not what my fellowmen may decide but as for myself, I will stay to live and die in my native land and there will my bones be buried with those of my fathers, and children's bones. There ends my talk from heart. (Reported by Basil Peone of the response given by Agusta to Father Diomedi's speech urging a move to Hangman Creek. *Coeur d'Alene Teepee* 1938 March 1 [5]: 14; 1981:85. Peone described Agusta as "a good man, but overfond of his native land.")

The appeal of Christianity to the Schitsu'umsh was unmistakable. The vision of Circling Raven had established an indigenous legitimization for the Jesuits. The years immediately preceding their arrival had been exceedingly chaotic, disruptive, and dangerous. Smallpox, Blackfeet raiders, and the collapse of the fur trade meant population decimation, economic hardship, and social strain. The skills and *suumesh* powers of the shamans, warriors, and hunters could not completely abate these challenges. But the power of the Black Robes promised to do so. A sharing of certain values and ritual behaviors contributed to the appeal and eased the transition. For example both the Jesuits and the Schitsu'umsh valued generosity and respect for family and community. Catholic rituals, such as the use of chants and prayer, the application of sacred objects, the uses of water and incense for purification, holding processions and feasting days, and accessing the sacred through spiritual intermediaries, had general parallels in Indian rituals. The importance of religious practitioners—shamans and priests—was also well established in both traditions.

Burn Their *Suumesh*

But the Coeur d'Alenes was ruined by the priests coming in. They took everything away from them. They made them give it up. They made them burn their *suumesh*, their bundle. A lot of them died because of that. And some, I guess, hid theirs, and some got away with some. (From an interview conducted on February 11, 1998.)

Unlike the fur traders, the Jesuits sought to transform the way of life of the Schitsu'umsh. Using varied techniques, the Jesuits tried to undermine and suppress all forms of traditional culture that they felt would prevent the Indians from becoming "civilized." The priests became well versed in the language and customs of the Schitsu'umsh people. One of their first actions was to replace traditional Indian names with "Christian names." Upon baptism, a name from the Bible, such as Andrew or Debra, would be assigned. The Christian name helped displace the Indian identity from its family ancestry and perhaps animal *suumesh* power, from which the traditional name was derived, and to associate it instead with the Scriptures. The priests targeted the established native leadership for conversion. To convert the chiefs would win important allies and provide Christian role models for the others. The Jesuits brought many families together under those chiefs who became Catholic.

The Sisters of Charity of Providence of Montreal founded the Convent of Mary Immaculate and opened a boarding school at DeSmet in 1878. The children of the Schitsu'umsh were "forced to attend." Upon arrival, children had their long hair cut and, throughout their stay, were prevented from speaking their native language. This haircutting must have been particularly traumatic, as the act was so closely associated with mourning the death of a relative. Upon the death of a parent, for example, immediate family members would cut their hair to shoulder length. Hence these policies had the effect, figuratively and literally, of severing ties with parents and grandparents, and thus with the traditional culture of the Schitsu'umsh. By removing such "negative influences," and in assuming many of the parental responsibilities over Schitsu'umsh youth, the Sisters could more easily teach a new moral code, as well as the economic skills and technical expertise integral to a Christian and "industrious" life-style. The intensive education of the Schitsu'umsh youth was an essential prerequisite to successful transformation of the society.

With the loss of the Schitsu'umsh language came an eroding of social cohesiveness and a singular cultural identity rooted in a language distinct from one's neighbors. With the loss of language came a loss of the unique linguistic markers that help connect a people with their landscape. For example, *Q'emiln* would become Post Falls, "celebrating the settling" of that area by Frederick Post in 1871. Thus no longer anchored to the landscape's significance is the story of a boy whose canoe capsized on *Hnt'ąq'n* (Hayden Lake) and after a three-day journey emerged from an underground passage near the falls on the Spokane River. The opening became known as *Q'emiln*, or "Throat" (Palmer, Nicodemus, and Felsman 1987:85–86). Lost also were such descriptive names as *'L'lkhwi'lus*, "Little Hole in the Head," for the site of DeSmet, named after a small spring near DeSmet Hill; *Hnch'mqinkwe'*, "Surface on the Head of the Water," for the large village site at the mouth of the Spokane River (later to become the city of Coeur d'Alene); *Stseqhwłkwe'*, "Splashing Water," for Spokane Falls; *Hnch'emtsn*, "Inner Mouth," for the site of one of the largest villages (the future St. Maries) along the St. Joe River, at the confluence of the St. Joe and St. Maries rivers; and *Ałkwari't*, "Source of Gold," for the village site at what would become Harrison (Palmer, Nicodemus, and Felsman 1987: 24, 43, 64, 79–80, 119). As Felix Aripa recalled, the "gold" of Harrison refers to the golden appearance of the lake's surface as one looks out toward the sunset from the Harrison area. Today only a handful of Schitsu'umsh speak their native language with fluency.

The Jesuits made every effort to discourage certain social and religious practices. The priests attacked traditional marital habits, ceremonials, dances, and gambling, such as the stick game. For the Jesuits, the war dances were "evil." Indian dance regalia was burned and participants fined for dancing. Medicine bundles, the tangible representation of one's *suumesh*, were also collected and publicly burned. *Suumesh* songs were not to be sought in the mountains, and the stories of Coyote and Crane were held to be of little importance other than as fairy tales. With the assistance of the Soldiers of the Sacred Heart, the Jesuits sought to curtail the Jump Dances and use of the Sweat Houses, as both were considered evil. The Soldiers of the Sacred Heart were a "type of police force" made up of Schitsu'umsh who helped enforce the policies of the Jesuits and their allied chiefs. Members of the Soldiers of the Sacred Heart exemplified the values of the church—"industriousness, honesty, respectful for authority, good ways." If the Soldiers of the Sacred Heart heard of a Jump Dance, for example, they attempted to "put a stop to it." The use of "whipping," a form of corporal punishment previously unheard of, was instituted for continued offenders. The priests also imposed fines, incarcerated "troublemakers," and threatened to withhold communion from those deemed lazy and evil. As one elder explained, referring to the priests, "Not only did they bring the word of God, but they acted like they were God." Those who followed them "were sort of fanatics."

None Take Part

To Superintendents:
  1. That the Indian form of gambling and lottery know as the "giveaway" be prohibited.
  2. That the Indian dances be limited to one in each month in the day-light hours of the midweek, and at one center in each district; the months of March and April, June, July and August are excepted.
  3. That none take part in the dances or be present who are under fifty years of age.
  4. That a careful propaganda be undertaken to educate public opinion against the dance and to provide a healthy substitute.
  5. That a determined effort be made by the Government employees to cooperate with the missionaries to persuade the management of fairs and "round-ups" in the town adjoining the reservations not to commercialize the Indian by soliciting his attendance in large numbers for show purposes.
  6. That there be close cooperation between the Government employees and the missionaries in those matters which affect the moral welfare of the Indians. (From the Department of Interior, Office of Indian Affairs, on Indian Dancing, dated February 14, 1923.)

Many of the efforts of the Jesuits coincided with those of the U.S. government. Policies aimed at "assimilating" Indians into American society predominated in federal relations with the tribes throughout the late-nineteenth and early-twentieth centuries. In 1884 the U.S. government formally prohibited most forms of traditional ritual practice, such as Sun Dances and dream societies, on all Indian reservations. The so-called war dances did continue on the Coeur d'Alene Reservation as "exhibition and for exercise until about 1900," when they were finally discontinued at the behest of the priests.

Everything We Do a Sin

We the undersigned wish to call your attention to some conditions existing on the Coeur d'Alene reservation which are greatly annoying us and causing a great deal of dissatisfaction among the Indians and particularly among the younger members of the tribe, Joseph Caruana the priest has with the assistant of one of the Indians Bonamancha who he calls an Indian police, made a rule and is endeavoring to enforce it to the effect that all Indian clothing and Indian ware which we wish to wear on the 4th of July and on other occasions, shall be burned up and destroyed and that if any of the Indians refuse to deliver this property to them then and in that event they will not let us attend church and to go to confession and communion, now the priest has such control over the Indian police and even with Peter Wildshoe one of the chiefs that he makes rules without calling in the head chief Peter Moctilma, and after he has made the rules then some of the Indians over whom he has control will endeavor to enforce the orders delivered by the priest. . . .

The priest has also issued orders that no Indian shall go from one reservation to another especially on the 4th of July, and if they do they will be arrested.

They have done this three or four times in the past, and will not let them go to church but will lock them up.

The priest will not allow us to have any races on the reservation and no war dancing as a past time in our idle hours, as he claims it is a violation of the laws of the Catholic church and the worst sin on earth.

It is not only the young fellows who are complaining against these rules but one half of the old ones are complaining but are afraid of the priest and therefore submit to these conditions and say nothing.

Now if any of the young fellows drink anything while away from the reservation and should get arrested as soon as they come home they will be arrested and fined and possibly be confined in jail for a couple of weeks.

Now we would like for the department to investigate these matters at its earliest convenience as we believe that we can show what we say is absolutely true and is not at all satisfactory to a majority of the Indians on the reservation.

The young fellows who like to enjoy themselves in racing and all kinds of sports are continually being called down and the priest calls everything we do a sin. (From an undated letter addressed to the Commissioner of Indian Affairs. It was signed by Morris Antelope, principal writer, and ten other Schi̱tsu'umsh, around 1907).[10]

If the Jesuit vision of establishing a "wilderness kingdom for God" was ultimately to succeed, the priests would need absolute control over the lives of the people. A "wandering, nomadic people," whose subsistence and identity were so interwoven with an expansive territory, would not conform to such plans. But a sedentary, self-sufficient agricultural community fit perfectly. The Jesuits applied a management style known as the "reduction system." Having been successfully applied in Paraguay among the Guarani Indians, Father Point drew up plans for its implementation among the Schitsu'umsh. Point sketched actual architectural plans for the reduction site, which included row houses and fields radiating out from a centrally located cathedral. The priests tried to convince individuals of important families from the dispersed areas to relocate into an all-Indian town, called a "reduction." Over time the town would become self-sufficient, supported by its own agricultural harvests and livestock raising. The relocation of the Schitsu'umsh families from the Cataldo area, and from the Spokane and St. Joe River regions, to Hangman Creek was a direct reflection of this policy. The Hangman Creek area, with its good camas prairie, was ideal for farming and ranching, and was isolated from white settlements and other influences felt harmful to the Indians.

The eventual success of the reduction policy thus hinged on the adoption of farming by the Schitsu'umsh and their settlement in a permanent community.[11] The practice of horticulture may actually have been adopted by the Schitsu'umsh prior to Jesuit instruction. As noted by the anthropologist Gary Palmer (1981b), German botanist Charles Geyer observed the Schitsu'umsh growing potatoes successfully along the Coeur d'Alene River in 1843. Geyer believed the Schitsu'umsh had obtained the English white potato from Hudson's Bay Company fur traders, likely at Fort Spokane, "about ten to fifteen years ago," which would date potato cultivation among the Schitsu'umsh to as early as 1828 (Geyer 1846). In any case, it is not difficult to understand an easy transition to tuber cultivation by a people who relied so extensively on a root-digging tradition.

Under the supervision of the Jesuits, the scale of plant cultivation intensified significantly. No longer were the Indians *gathering* a "camaslike" tuber, but now potatoes, wheat, and hay were *harvested* and cattle *raised*. Agriculture had been fully introduced, and with it came new ways of viewing the landscape. The land became "sod to break" and to fence with barbed wire. New technologies, such as plows and threshers, were to be applied to the land in the expectation that a cash crop would be harvested.

By 1845 Father DeSmet had reported that the Schitsu'umsh families associated with the mission harvested "upward of 1,200 bags of potatoes; some families had each upward of 100 bags" (Chittenden and Richardson 1905: 997). Palmer has noted, however, that given the amount of land under cultivation, ranging from 100 to 200 acres, and the number cows and pigs raised, most of the harvest was probably consumed by the priests and visitors to

Sch̲i̲tsu'umsh farmer, 1920s (courtesy Northwest Museum of Arts and Culture and Eastern Washington State Historical Society, acc. no. L95–109.131)

the mission, and used "to supplement the subsistence of a larger number of families who still derived their primary subsistence from the prairies, woods and streams" (1981b:81). Besides farming around the mission, Sch̲i̲tsu'umsh families were also observed cultivating on the prairie adjacent to the Spokane River and along the St. Joe River, providing evidence that members of all three bands had begun farming to complement their transhumance subsistence (Palmer 1981b:83).

Sch̲i̲tsu'umsh agricultural "success" was most noticeable after the resettlement to Hangman Creek, and particularly following "the 1892 payment." That year the tribe received a half million dollars from the United States in compensation for ceding their northern territory as part of the Indian Commission's Agreement of 1889. The money was divided equally among the families, each member receiving a payment of approximately $1,000. Most funds were, in turn, invested in state-of-the-art farm implements, wire fencing, and workhorses. According to the reports of the Indian agents, wheat production alone rose from 8,000 bushels in 1892 to 27,600 in 1893, then from 45,000 in 1894 to 100,000 bushels in 1896 (Commissioner of Indian Affairs Reports 1892–1896).

Besides wheat and potatoes, Schitsu'umsh families successfully grew oats, peas, and hay for cash income. This level of production suggests that Indian agriculture was moving beyond the subsistence needs of individual families.[12] Some families had fenced farms and ranches ranging in size from several hundred to 2,000 acres. This was the era when many families kept two homes, one on their farmland and another as a "weekend home" in DeSmet. On the weekends, the families would congregate at and around the mission for religious services and social gatherings. As Felix Aripa remembered, this was a time when "we even hired whites to help in the farming." He referred to this period as "a time of good feeling."

Despite initial success, resistance to the teachings of the Jesuits was evident. Many families secretly held on to their medicine bundles. Jump Dancing continued at remote and hidden sites. "You knew which families not to tell," as "our religion sort of went underground." "You couldn't even get the older ones to talk to you about it." As ethnohistorian Jacqueline Peterson has put it: The Indians never understood "why a loving God would send his children to hell. Nor did they at first understand the appeal of heaven, since there were no relatives or buffalo there" (1993: 98).

Indeed, the Schitsu'umsh had looked to the teachings of the Animal Peoples, such as Badger and Coyote, for their guidance. In contrast, the Jesuits asked the Schitsu'umsh to look to the example set forth by a wandering Hebrew tribe and a man from Galilee. The Schitsu'umsh were now being taught not to look to the landscape for guidance and life's lessons. The Indians objected to, and refused to conform to, "Catholic authoritarianism, the concepts of sin and hell, and the imposition of European social, political and economic structures" (Peterson 1993:24). Since the Schitsu'umsh had themselves sought out Jesuits, the priests' decision to establish a mission among the Blackfeet was viewed as a betrayal. Now their most feared enemies would also acquire from the Black Robes what was protecting them.

While both traditions relied upon religious practitioners and intermediaries—priest and shaman, saints and guardian spirits—there were also fundamental differences. The *suumesh* power of the shaman was ultimately derived from his personal relationship with the landscape, with an animal guardian spirit. In the Schitsu'umsh tradition, spirit was inherent throughout the landscape. In the tradition of the Jesuits, with its focus on the redemption of human souls and saints coming from human communities, the natural world was, in essence and by contrast, rendered temporal, secular, and "wild." The Jesuit emphasis was on a spiritual domain residing only within the human portion of the landscape. Believers sought personal and exclusive relationship with the "human son of God."

While agriculture established them "as the most successful of all the tribes in the northwest region of the United States," the reduction did not prevent Schítsu'umsh families from continuing their seasonal round of digging roots, gathering berries, catching fish, and hunting deer (Palmer 1981b:66; undated manuscript). As noted by Palmer, some families did not even move to DeSmet until after 1900, but continued to rely on hunting and gathering (undated manuscript). The Vincent family, before moving to DeSmet, lived at the southern end of the lake, hunting waterfowl, digging water potato, and fishing the lake. Even after their migration to DeSmet (sometime after 1914), when they took up subsistence farming, the Vincent family continued to depend upon winter deer hunting and trout fishing. Hunting along the Little North Fork of the Clearwater River, the "meat from over 30 deer shot on a hunt would go into jerky. They also caught a lot of trout which they smoked and dried" (Palmer, undated manuscript). The anthropologist Roderick Sprague has suggested that "political pressure" influenced the Indian Agents to emphasize Schítsu'umsh farming successes and to inflate their reports on the grain and produce harvest (1996:59). While the Indian Agent reported in 1902 that, acknowledging family variation, "75% is gained from 'civilized pursuits' and 25% through hunting and gathering, . . . the true figure thus was easily 50%" (Sprague 1996:59).

Not only did the Jesuit priests and the Sisters of Charity bring a "new way to the heaven trails," but they imposed a new form of leadership and a new view of the land itself.[13] With the power of the priests unquestioned and the Catholic chiefs becoming more absolute, the *suumesh* power of the shaman was further undermined. There was a shift toward the use of punitive measures, enforced by the Soldiers of the Sacred Heart. A competing view of the landscape took root. Under the stewardship of the Jesuit priests, the landscape would no longer be viewed as a source of guidance, conveyed in *suumesh* song, an Indian name or a Crane and Coyote story. With an accompanying loss of language, the uniquely Schítsu'umsh identification with the landscape was diminished, and the oral traditions themselves were further detached from the landscape. The landscape came to be viewed as "sod to break" for the cash crops it would produce. It became a commodity to be fenced and "owned." Ironically, in seeking to establish a "wilderness king-dom for God," the new spiritual leaders ushered in a far more secular view of the landscape. Along with the "reduction," the spiritual and subsistence connections and transhumance patterns linking the people with their land-scape were thus compromised, though not discontinued. The Jump Dances and stories of Coyote continued, though "in secret." For most Schitsu'umsh families, the new agricultural pursuits more typically supplemented rather than replaced the gathering of camas and the hunting of deer, as well as the singing of the *suumesh* prayers that accompanied such activities.

It should be pointed out that the restrictive efforts of the Jesuit priests were most pronounced during the first third of the twentieth century. But as federal policy toward Indians took new directions in the 1930s, under John Collier's administration of the Bureau of Indian Affairs, and solidified under the Indian Reorganization Act of 1934, so too did the Jesuit policy on the Coeur d'Alene Reservation.

The changed policy was exemplified in the work of Father Cornelius Byrne, who helped initiate the newsletter *Coeur d'Alene Teepee*, which was published from 1937 through 1940. Father Byrne wrote in the newsletter's first "Editorial" that "the Coeur d'Alene Teepee is dedicated to the preser-vation of Indian culture and advancement." He continued: "We maintain that there is no conflict between the Indians' ancestral heritage of a pecu-liar art and his Christian Faith. . . . The Indian's culture and art, unlike his pagan beliefs, are eminently true, beautiful and good. These we accept, to preserve for posterity. The latter we reject" (1937:2). Today, Father Thomas Connolly of the Sacred Heart Mission is a "strong supporter of the Indian way," able to speak much of the Schitsu'umsh language, eminently knowl-edgeable in the native traditions, history, and culture, and a regular and "well-respected" participant (often asked to give the opening prayer) and dancer at the Schitsu'umsh Powwows. The changed attitude is reflected in the comment by some Schitsu'umsh that a Jump Dance would "not be com-plete" without a priest present!

While my focus has been on Jesuit influences on the Schitsu'umsh con-nection to their landscape, the legacy of the Jesuit experience must be appre-ciated in the full context of "good deeds" brought by the Black Robes. Motivated by a sincere desire to "help the Coeur d'Alene people," the Jesuit priests and the Sisters of Charity implemented a Euro-American educa-tional system, encouraged agricultural and other "industrial pursuits," challenged alcohol abuse, improved health-care delivery, opposed various

The Cataldo Mission, August 1997

outside economic and political interests who sought to control the Schitsu'umsh, and brought celebration to birth and marriage, comfort in death, and a "new way to the heaven trails." Among many devout Catholic Indian families today, the teachings of Jesus Christ are central to their lives, fully integrating Catholicism into a Schitsu'umsh way of life. For them the Fathers and Sisters are indeed "beloved."

WAR

As Felix Aripa related: Late one night, while looking for some water to refresh himself, a Schitsu'umsh saw something "shining in the hillside." He had found a large gold nugget, and it was immediately hid. He knew of "the white man's greed. 'Gold becomes their God' was a common expression." Should they learn of the gold, "the whites would take our lands." With the opening up of Schitsu'umsh territory in the 1850s and the influx of Euro-American settlers came additional competing perspectives on the landscape, leading inevitably to conflict, war, and displacement.

Beginning in the early 1850s, various Indian tribes grew steadily more concerned over the ever-increasing numbers of white immigrants. Enticed under the federal government's 1850 Donation Land Law, in which half-section grants of land (320 acres) were offered to U.S. citizens in return for a promise to till the soil for four years, white farmers rapidly settled the rich agricultural lands of both Oregon and Washington territories. Their initial route of entry was primarily the Oregon Trail. In addition, white encroachment onto Indian lands escalated with the discovery of gold. Prospectors eventually invaded virtually every corner of the new territory. The newcomers held little regard for Indian claims to the land.

In 1853 Washington Territory was established by the U.S. Congress, placing the Schitsu'umsh within it. The territory's first governor was thirty-five-year-old Isaac Stevens, a West Point graduate. The ambitious Stevens also assumed responsibility as ex-officio Superintendent of Indian Affairs for the region, and in 1853 he led the search for a suitable northerly railroad route through the new Washington Territory.[14] His roles as governor and Indian superintendent had interlinking goals. Stevens envisioned a grand design in which all the Indian tribes of the territory would be placed on a single reservation, thus extinguishing Indian title to vast tracts of land and opening the land up for the railroads and homesteading by whites. For the loss of title, annuities and other assistance would be provided by the government. Stevens had also promised the Indians that they would be paid for any lands taken by white settlers. In 1855 the Schitsu'umsh witnessed Governor Stevens, in what has been characterized as a rather "heavy-handed" and "intimidating" manner, complete the Walla Walla Treaty with the Cayuse, Umatilla, Walla Walla, Nez Perce, and the Yakama, and the Hellgate Treaty with the Flathead, Pend Oreille, and one band of the Kootenai.

For the Schitsu'umsh, in particular, tensions further escalated over the surveying of the Mullan Road, which ran through the heart of Schitsu'umsh country. In 1854 the U.S. Congress had authorized funding for a 600-mile, transcontinental road linking Fort Benton on the Missouri River with Fort Walla Walla near the Columbia. Under the direction of Capt. John Mullan, who had assisted Governor Stevens in his 1853 railroad survey and who would serve under Col. George Wright in the 1858 war, actual construction of the road began in 1859, with completion in 1862.[15] For some Schitsu'umsh, the effort to build this road was proof that the U.S. government intended to take Indian lands.

1885

Fort Coeur d'Alene at the Mouth of the Spokane River, 1885;
note tipis in the foreground and the steamboat in the background on Lake Coeur
d'Alene (courtesy Museum of North Idaho, Coeur d'Alene, acc. no. FHS-3–10)

Despite the peacemaking efforts of Father Joset and, initially, Head Chief Vincent, open revolt against the whites began in 1858, and the Schitsu'umsh became involved in armed conflict with the U.S. Army. As Felix Aripa put it, "We didn't want to go to war, but what would you do when someone breaks into your home?"

During the first part of May, Lieut. Col. Edward Steptoe, with 152 enlisted men and 5 officers, two mounted howitzers, and insufficient ammunition, left Fort Walla Walla on an assignment in Colville country. After he crossed the Snake River, he proceeded northeast through territory used by the Schitsu'umsh, Palouse, and Spokane. This was not a direct route north but a rather undiplomatic detour through the heart of Indian country. Women digging camas fled at his advance, fearing an attack. Adding to the tension, Steptoe had some 50 Nez Perce scouts with him who taunted the tribes, claiming "they were going to help the soldiers take your lands."

After being shadowed on their northerly march, fighting broke out on May 17 near *Hngwsumn* Creek (meaning "Rope Place," in reference to an area where ropes were made, and called Pine Creek by whites). The creek runs by the present town of Rosalia, Washington. Under the command of Vincent, in addition to the Schitsu'umsh and Spokane, the fight was joined by the Kalispel, Palouse, and Yakamas, a force numbering around 500 warriors in all. Outnumbered, Steptoe's troops fought a running retreat south. Steptoe was in a hopeless situation and defeat was immanent. Recognizing Steptoe's dilemma, and after conferring with leaders such as Andrew Seltice and Peter Wildshoe (who would themselves later become head chiefs), as well as with Father Joset, Vincent sent a message to Steptoe. The Schitsu'umsh would allow his troops safe passage through their lines that night, provided that they leave their weapons behind. Under the cover of dark, Steptoe and his detachment of soldiers and Nez Perce scouts withdrew to Fort Walla Walla. As the troops passed through their lines, the Schitsu'umsh "drummed loud to cover their retreat." Under Steptoe's command, 2 officers, 5 troopers, and 3 Indian scouts were killed. For the Schitsu'umsh and their allies, at least 9 were killed, with some 40–50 wounded. Among the Schitsu'umsh killed were Jacques, Victor, and Zachary. The conflict is referred to by many Schitsu'umsh as the *Hngwsumn* Battle.

Many of the "spoils of war" went to the Schitsu'umsh. At a Veterans Powwow I attended in 1993, I saw a saber from the Steptoe Battle held in honor by a Vietnam War veteran during his induction into the Schitsu'umsh veterans honor guard. The lives lost at the Steptoe Battle, both Indian and soldier, are commemorated during the annual Memorial Warriors Horse Ride, or also known as the *Hngwsumn* Memorial Ride. The ride begins at the Agency grounds near Plummer and finishes in the hills near the actual battle site, close to the modern town of Rosalia. At the end of the ride, families share stories, song, meals, and sweat prayers at a tipi encampment.

At the 1996 Memorial Ride, I again saw the saber I had seen displayed at the 1993 Veterans Powwow. Held in a beaded case, it was passed around and closely inspected by everyone seated around a family drum. It had been taken in "hand-to-hand combat," when a Schitsu'umsh warrior struck down its owner. The family of the warrior has kept it as "a symbol of bravery." When worn in a special dance or brought out at a family gathering, such as the *Hngwsumn* Memorial Ride, "you are honoring the soldier who had given his life for it and the Indian men who took it from the soldiers, who

Cliff SiJohn with the flag at the Hngwsumn Memorial Ride, May 1996

met the soldiers with only a bow and arrow and maybe a musket and met the encroachers."

Steptoe Warrior

When the hostilities were going on and just before the Steptoe Battle, an old man, once a great warrior, from the Cataldo area, wanted to go and fight. He encouraged others to join him, but none would. The priests at the Mission told him not to go, that it was wrong, and if he went, they would not allow him to go to mass or even to work on the construction of the church building. Everyone turned their back on him, including his wife. She said that she would cook and clean for him, but in every other way, she would not be a wife to him. But he just couldn't resist the fight. This was the only way he knew how to get honors, for his bravery.

So he got on his horse and went to the Tekoa area, the Steptoe area. But it took him quite a while, for it was many miles from the Mission. When he arrived, the battle was already over. And everywhere, there were pots, blankets, horses, a big mess. But no battle to fight. So he loaded up a horse with all kinds of war booty and went back to his village near the Mission.

When he arrived, he expected everyone would cheer him, but they all turned their backs to him. None would give him any honor. In fact, the priests said that he must return these things at once. "But these things are won by me, my honors; if I try to return them, the soldiers would kill me!" The priests insisted, as did everyone else.

So he loaded his things onto his horse and headed to the nearest fort, Fort Walla Walla, many miles away. It took him a long time to travel there, and he knew he'd be shot as soon as the soldiers saw him. But he went anyway. Finally he arrived close to the fort.

He hung his head down. His horse knew something too. It hung its head down and slowly they approached the gate. All the soldiers were at the wall looking down. He knew he'd be shot soon. But he continued. His horse knew as well. Slowly they entered the fort, with all the soldiers' rifles pointed at them. He got off his horse and laid out a blanket. On it he laid all the things he had taken from the battle site. After he had done this, and without a word, he got back on his horse and headed out slowly. He knew he'd get shot. Slowly he rode out of the fort. All the rifles were still pointed at him. After he had gotten out of the firing range of the rifles, he held his head high, and as if his horse knew they were out of danger as well, they galloped over the hill and back to the Mission.

But this time, when he arrived, expecting the same cold shoulder, everyone cheered him. And the priests welcomed him back to the Church. This was indeed a brave deed! (Abbreviated, as told by Lawrence Aripa in April 1991.)

In August of 1858, a punitive reprisal for the Steptoe "disaster" was led by Col. George Wright, a veteran of the Seminole (1835–42) and Yakama (1855) wars. Wright's command included well-equipped infantry and calvary, with the new, long-range .58-caliber Springfield muskets and accurate howitzers. His forces engaged several hundred warriors from the area's

The Steptoe saber

tribes, first near Medical Lake in the Battle of Four Lakes, and then several miles west of the city of Spokane in the Battle of Spokane Prairie. As the Indians approached, they and their horses were easily shot, and as they retreated the howitzers scattered their ranks. The two battles were decisive encounters. For the tribes, there would no longer be any hope for a military challenge to the white encroachment onto their lands.

Following these initial defeats, the tribes sought peace. However, the campaign was not over, as Colonel Wright pursued a "scorched-earth policy." In the days following the two battles, literally hundreds of horses were shot. Food stores of grain for the coming winter were burned. Upon reaching the Cataldo Mission, Wright wrote: "For the last eighty miles our route has been marked by slaughter and devastation; 900 horses and large number of cattle have been killed or appropriated to our own use; many houses, with large quantities of wheat and oats, also many caches of vegetables, kamas, and dried berries, have been destroyed. A blow has been struck which they will never forget" (Wright 1859). Though many Schitsu'umsh, out of respect for Father Joset, had remained neutral and did not participate in the Steptoe Battle, Colonel Wright's troops nonetheless killed their horses and cattle, destroyed their wheat and hay, and burned their barns.

Heroism

There were always one or two gentle ponies kept in the log barns, and these too were burned by the troops. These belonged to the innocent children of the Coeur d'Alenes whose parents had been willing to remain neutral, out of respect for Father Joset. The cattle that were killed for only their hind quarters also belonged to these neutral Coeur d'Alenes. So Wright's troops displayed their heroism by seeing who could destroy the most property of the innocent. All the other cattle and horses became very wild, as the troops stampeded everything in sight. (From an account of Joseph Seltice, based upon the memories of his father, Andrew Seltice, in Kowrach and Connolly 1990:131.)

On his return to Fort Walla Walla, Colonel Wright "lured" several Palouse and Yakama leaders, along with members of other tribes, into his camp. Without benefit of a formal trial, Wright selected "at least twelve men" and had them hanged. Some of the men were put onto a wagon and had ropes tied around their necks to a tree. From atop the wagon they told their families "not to be afraid of these soldiers." Then they deliberately jumped off the side of the wagon, denying any pleasure to the soldiers. "They hung themselves to show how brave they were." The hangings took place along a creek in the general region of Steptoe's defeat, and where the Schitsu'umsh traditionally gathered to make ropes. The creek was subsequently named Hangman Creek by local residents, and the Schitsu'umsh learned of a new application for ropes.

The Hangman Creek tragedy had a personal and lasting effect on at least one Schitsu'umsh family, as they are descendants of one of the men hanged that day. At the hanging this warrior gave his family "some words and a song," which are vividly remembered and still sung today. While sitting on the horse with the rope around his neck, the warrior asked to speak with his relatives, who were gathered on a nearby hillside. After he spoke (see the following vignette), he sang the song. "It is somewhere between a death song and a medicine song for our young people." When he finished, "a man with marks on his arm" (a sergeant) whipped the horse, and he swung there "until his tongue came out."

Don't Be Sad

If things are going bad and your people are suffering and your children are crying, this song will heal you. So don't be sad because of the death around us, because these men who are being hung were fighters and they faced the soldiers. Don't be sad that the young girls who followed the battle and some of them even getting involved with killing soldiers. When they get old and they are feeling bad for what they had to do, sing this song. When your children and grandchildren are hurting or having hard times, then sing this song. (From an interview conducted on October 3, 1997.)

On September 17, 1858, conditions for peace were established by Colonel Wright. Treaty articles called for immediate cessation of hostilities, return of all property belonging to the United States and its citizens, assurance that whites would be "unmolested" while traveling through Schitsu'umsh country, and the holding as hostages "at least one chief and four men" responsible for "initiating hostilities," and their families for one year (Wright 1859). Payments for destroyed property belonging to neutrals were supposed to be made, including payments to the Schitsu'umsh who had stayed out of the fighting. But such payments were never made. Among those who signed the Peace Treaty of 1858 were Head Chief Vincent, Andrew Seltice, Peter Wildshoe, and Tecomtee, a son of Stellam.

The landscape of the Schitsu'umsh could no longer be protected with bow and arrow and the deeds of its warriors. It was a landscape in turmoil. Colonels would ultimately triumph over war chiefs. And never before had humans so deliberately and woefully destroyed those things on the landscape that had nurtured life. It must have been a sight incomprehensible for the Schitsu'umsh to behold.

One of the Old-Time Indians

There was one time, my uncle and my dad, I went with them, they took me along. . . . My dad always called Spokane, Spokane City. He said we'll have to camp in Spokane City. Something went wrong with the Model-T truck. My dad went and told my uncle, and we had Grandmother with us, too. . . . "Well, we'll camp here in Spokane. We'll get a hotel." They got rooms and Grandma got her a best room. My uncle said, "Let's go to a movie." My uncle couldn't speak English or read or write, but he could understand English. He enjoyed watching them, silent movies then.

Troop G of the 4ᵗʰ Cavalry, Fort Sherman, c. 1890
(courtesy Museum of North Idaho, Coeur d'Alene, acc. no. FSH-6-8)

After the movie, we went back to the hotel. My dad went to check on Grandma. Got no Grandma. My dad went back to our room and looked around and Grandma not here. He went down to the desk and asked the clerk, "Has the old lady gone by?" He said, "No, I haven't seen her." We walked around and walked around looking for her. So my dad saw a policeman. He told the policeman to look. Can't find the old lady. They were all going to help. We all went to Grandma's room. All of her stuff was there. My dad happened to look. The beds were higher. There her moccasin was sticking out from under. . . . She crawled underneath the bed. She never used the bed. She always had to lay on the ground or on the floor. That's what she did [laugh]. You couldn't see she was underneath there. But my dad saw her moccasin sticking out [laugh]. My dad went back down and told the police he found her.

She was one of the participants in the Steptoe Battle. She was one of the old-time Indians who never believed in sleeping on the bed. (From an interview conducted on May 20, 1996.)

EXECUTIVE ORDER AND ALLOTMENT

In June of 1855, while briefly stopping at the Sacred Heart Mission on his way to Blackfeet and Flathead country, Territorial Governor Isaac Stevens spoke of negotiating a treaty with the Schi̱tsu'umsh. In the agreement the Schi̱tsu'umsh would sell a portion of their lands in exchange for life on a reservation. This may have been the first time the Schi̱tsu'umsh heard from a representative of the U.S. government that they were to be confined to "a reservation."

In the Hoodoo area on the North Fork of the Palouse River, a traditional hunting and camas-digging region of the Schi̱tsu'umsh, gold was found in 1860. Because northern Idaho was so rich in minerals, with an ever-increasing population of "squatters seeking their fortune," on June 14, 1867, President Andrew Johnson sought to establish a quarter-million-acre reservation for the Schi̱tsu'umsh. In confining the Schi̱tsu'umsh to a reservation, large tracts of land could thus be opened up for settlement. But Congress never ratified the "agreement." In fact, no attempt was made to inform the Schi̱tsu'umsh of their new territory until 1871. Upon hearing of the arrangement, the Schi̱tsu'umsh refused to accept it, claiming the area was much too small.

During this period of negotiations between the various Indian tribes and the U.S. government, certain legal principles were established that would set the tone for subsequent agreements. The legal status of the tribal entities was conferred and acknowledged to be that of "sovereign nations." Treaties were nation-to-nation agreements, intended to be legally binding for all time and recognized as "the supreme law of the land" under Article VI of the U.S. Constitution. Property would not be taken without consent of the Indian. Ownership of the land and resources was to be held by the tribes, unless explicitly relinquished in the language of an agreement. For example, the ownership of a lake or river, if not explicitly granted to the United States, would remain with the tribe. As such, and as upheld in *U.S. v. Winans* (1905), the agreements entered into were not grants of rights to Indians but rather grants of rights *from* Indians *to* the United States, the "reserved rights doctrine." In exchange for the cession of vast tracts of land and resources, the tribes would receive educational and health benefits. Such contracted services are thus "purchased" services rather than social entitlements. Especially during the nineteenth and early twentieth century, the federal government's record of adhering to these principles was poor. One

Logging white pine on the North Fork of the Coeur d'Alene River, 1918 (courtesy Museum of North Idaho, Coeur d'Alene, acc. no. LOG-2-17*)*

party's failure to honor the accords of the agreement did not negate the legal status and continued integrity of the agreement, however.

In 1871 the Indian Appropriation Act put an end to the making of treaties between Indian tribes and the federal government. All future nation-to-nation agreements would be carried out by executive order, with full congressional approval. In June of 1871, Frederick Post, a German immigrant, purchased land around the falls near the mouth of the Spokane River from Andrew Seltice. Post had been attempting to secure the land since as early as 1867, offering $500 to Moses Seltice, the father of Andrew. Post would soon build a mill at the site in hopes that a town would flourish there. It did, and the community quickly grew into the city of Post Falls.

In 1873, at a site along Hangman Creek, a three-member Indian Commission, sent by the Commissioner of Indian Affairs and led by Indiana Rep. John Shanks, reached an "agreement" with Head Chief Andrew Seltice, former Head Chief Vincent, and other subchiefs. A reservation would be established "for the exclusive use of the Coeur d'Alene Indians." It would include land extending south and west from the site of the Sacred Heart Mission (see the map on page 8), and from Cataldo the border would proceed west to the mouth of the Spokane River and then along the center channel of that river to the Washington territorial line. The boundary would then run south, paralleling the Washington-Idaho territorial line, to the mountain ridges just south of Hangman Creek. Moving east along that ridge, the boundary would then run directly northeast back to the area just west of Cataldo. This reservation, of some 598,000 acres, would include Lake Coeur d'Alene. In return, the Schitsu'umsh would give up claim to the rest of their aboriginal lands, over 3 million acres, and would allow the government the right to build roads through the reservation. In exchange for these lands and right-of-way, the Schitsu'umsh would also receive a mill, blacksmith shop, school with supporting personnel, farm implements, and $170,000.

While the necessary congressional approval was not forthcoming, President Ulysses S. Grant, in an executive order and as a temporary measure, established the "Coeur d'Alene Reservation" on November 8, 1873. Hence the Schitsu'umsh became known as an "Executive Order Tribe." However, without congressional approval, the order could not provide remuneration for the lands ceded; nor did it confer "title" to the tribe. And it did not include the lands of the Sacred Heart Mission, leaving the church facility outside the confines of the reservation. In addition, the precise boundaries of this 1873 reservation were not immediately surveyed and publicly disseminated. With the influx of settlers and miners, particularly in the northern sections of the region, this lack of clearly delineated borders would fuel increasing white-Indian tensions.

In 1875 the Schitsu'umsh endeared themselves to the local white community by not taking part in the Sioux uprising. There was fear among white settlers, at the time, that hostilities would spread from the Dakotas into the western territories. In addition to staying out of the uprising, the Schitsu'umsh sent a representative to the Sioux requesting that they stay out of Schitsu'umsh territory. Then in 1877 the Nez Perce War broke out. Again the Schitsu'umsh chose not to get involved in the conflict and, in fact, assisted many local whites. In the area of the Palouse River, Schitsu'-umsh actually looked after the livestock of whites who vacated their farms in fear of Chief Joseph.

Soon after the relocation of the Catholic mission to Hangman Creek in 1878, the U.S. Army established Fort Coeur d'Alene to help "resolve" the increasing tension between settlers and Indians. The post was renamed Fort Sherman after Gen. William T. Sherman, who helped establish the post. With the start of the Spanish-American War, Fort Sherman was essentially abandoned in 1889 and was entirely vacated by 1901.

Indian Uprising on the St. Joe

My family lived up on the St Joe. And before the place was settled, before it was completely taken over, they met just a very few white men, mostly trappers. I don't know, maybe some of you here are familiar with Rochat? [the French pronunciation of "Rocher"]. My great-grandfather [Rufinus Shi'itsin-Aripa] had a beaver line with him; they trapped together. And so they had this special place where they would go together and they would set out their traps.

And that was when Fort Sherman was still going in Coeur d'Alene, . . . and everything was at a point where it was very uneasy; there was still a lot of trouble between the soldiers and the Indians. And so it was very, very shaky.

And so a group of soldiers, about seven of them, got leave and they didn't have any place to go, so they decided to ride over here and go up the St. Joe and just camp. When they come up, without realize it, they run into my great-grandfather and Rochat's trap lines. And so they saw these beaver ponds, and it was beautiful; the water was just clear, and cool, and so they decided to swim. And then when they got into the water then they saw the traps. So they start snapping them. They'd say, "Here's one," and they'd take it out and snap it and then they'd pick up another one.

And about that time the two came back to the point and then they saw what was going on. So Rochat told my great-grandfather, he says, "You go over this side. I will go over here." It was a big area where there was a lot of beaver dams. So he says, "When I give you the signal"; he says, "you fire your rifle and yell"; he says, "and we'll chase them away. So they won't bother our traps anymore." So they did that. And when they fired and they yelled, the soldiers got scared and they ran out and jumped on their horses and they took off. And they went back to Coeur d'Alene.

And about three or four days later, there was a whole company of soldiers coming up the river. The paper—I don't know if it was Wallace or Kellogg—the paper had, "Indian Uprising on the St. Joe" [tremendous laughter from the audience]. And here they were just protecting their traps.

Rochat went up there and he talked to the commanding officer, and he straightened everything out. And he says, "There was no uprising"; he says, "All the Indians are peaceful up there, and they were just protecting their traps." (Transcribed from an audiotape recording of Lawrence Aripa telling this account to an audience in April 1991.)

In another attempt to establish a permanent Coeur d'Alene Reservation, the Northwest Indian Commission met with the Schitsu'umsh in council, and an agreement was reached on March 26, 1887. This agreement included retention of the area specified in the original Executive Order of 1873, but it also allowed members of some thirty-two Spokane families, approximately a hundred individuals, to relocate on the Coeur d'Alene Reservation, settling in the Worley area and becoming enrolled tribal members. The agreement stipulated that no part of the reservation could be sold, occupied, or opened to whites without consent of the Schitu'umsh. It ceded all nonreservation, and thus aboriginal, lands to the U.S. government. But again the agreement failed to receive congressional ratification.

Another three-man Indian Commission was sent in August of 1889. Under pressure to secure federal recognition and title to their lands, and thus protection against further white encroachment, the Schitsu'umsh reached an agreement with the Commissioners on September 9. Among the numerous leaders who marked X's by their names were Head Chief Andrew Seltice, former Head Chief Selepsto Vincent (Vincent), subchiefs Pierre Wheyiishoo (Peter Wildshoe) and Pierre Bartholomew (Peter Moctelme), and such family headmen as Louis Arripa (Louis Aripa), and Nicodemus (Croutous Nicodemus).[16] The agreement called for the tribe to cede the northern portion of their 1873 reservation in exchange for a $500,000 per-capita payment (divided among some five hundred Schitsu'umsh) and annual payments over the next fifteen years totaling $150,000 for the construction of a "saw and grist mill" and other purchases, "under the direction of the Secretary of the Interior," that would "promote the progress, comfort, improvement, education, and civilization of said Coeur d'Alene Indians."

Starting at the northwestern corner, the northern boundary of the "new" reservation was moved twelve miles south, and then south along the shoreline. It then ran east across the lake to the mouth of the Coeur d'Alene River and continued east to the border of the reservation (see the map on page 8). The 184,960 acres of ceded land returned to the public domain. The village of *Hnch'mqinkwe'* ("Surface on the Head of the Water") was supplanted by the rapidly growing "Coeur d'Alene City." Cession of the rest of the Schitsu'umsh aboriginal territory was thus made to the United States, some of which would soon become extraordinarily valuable once mining began. The agreement also assured the Schitsu'umsh that no part of their reservation lands would be sold or occupied by whites without their consent.

Unlike the previous agreements, by March 3, 1891, the Agreement of 1889 (inclusive of the Agreement of 1887) had been ratified by the U. S. Senate and House. The year before, on July 3, 1890, Idaho had been granted statehood. Added as defining properties of the traditional Schitsu'umsh landscape were thus "tribal," "state," and "federal" jurisdiction status.

The exterior boundaries of the Coeur d'Alene Reservation were given their final definition with the "Harrison cession" of 1894. Soon after the establishment of the reservation, settlers began occupying the area at the mouth of the Coeur d'Alene River. They named their community Harrison after the current president, Benjamin Harrison. But the community was clearly within the boundaries of the reservation. Instead of removing the squatters the federal government obtained an agreement from the tribe to sell the northern strip of the reservation, one mile wide, from the mouth of the Coeur d'Alene River east to the border of the reservation. The tribe was paid $15,000 for the land cession. Harrison, and this traditional village of *Ałkwari't*, thenceforth fell outside the reservation boundaries.

In 1887 the federal government passed the General Allotment Act (more formally known as the Dawes Severalty Act for its sponsor, Sen. Henry Dawes of Massachusetts). But it was not until 1906 that the allotment process was authorized and in 1909 completed on the Coeur d'Alene Reservation. The act decreed that each tribal member—man, woman, and child—be assigned 160 acres and relinquish all other land claims. Its intent was to "civilize and make farmers" of the Indian. What better way for the Indian to learn American values then by owning and learning the value of "private property"? Such ownership would, at the same time, undermine the main impediment to that goal: the "unproductive," "communal" nature of Indian land tenure. The Indian would finally become self-supporting. In turn, the "surplus" lands not allotted to Indians would be brought into public dominion. The reservations would thus be opened up further to expansion of a white population hungry for inexpensive land. No compensation would be given to the Indian for the loss of these lands once designated by treaty. The act was unilaterally imposed by the federal government, ignoring all previous treaty and agreement negotiations, obligations, and rights.

Broken Promises

It has not been so very long ago that the President of the United States and his Lawmakers promised, after they had bought the district of Coeur d'Alene mines, that this present reservation was to be ours for all time to come. And when our late Chief Seltice made his treaty the Government, the White Man, promised that no White Man would ever set a foot on our land, that we were to have and control our own laws, that the Reservation was never to be surveyed, or sold without our consent. They broke their promises and bought the northern part of our reservation when valuable and rich gold mines were discovered there, and this against our will. The Indian did not want to sell. They were almost forced to sell, and now at the present time, today, the Whites have decided to allot our Reservation. They already have started surveying it without consulting us, without even asking our consent, without any offer of compensation. What are we to do about this? My dear people, I want you to speak up and say what you think is best to be done. (Speech given by Head Chief Peter Moctelme in 1907 at a General Council meeting of the tribe. Peone 1938 May I [7]:17; 1981:134.)

What actually ensued for the Schitsu'umsh under the General Allotment Act was very different from the act's stated purpose. By July 1909 some 638 allotments had been assigned for a total of 104,077 acres set aside for the Schitsu'umsh. Of the 638 allotments, 97 went to Spokanes and 66 to whites who had been "adopted" by the tribe and who were living on the reservation. Schitsu'umsh allotments were typically too small to be economically viable. While each adult received 160 acres, the holdings of a single family were often not contiguous, resulting in fragmentation of the family's holdings. While many of the allotments were located on good farmland near and along Hangman Creek, other allotments were in forested and mountainous regions, not on the once agriculturally productive camas prairies. Productive thousand-acre family farms were reduced to a few hundred acres.

Since the act's original stipulation that land would be held in trust for twenty-five years was removed in 1906, individuals were henceforth allowed to lease or sell their landholdings to whites. Further escalating the loss of Schitsu'umsh sovereignty over their land was the manner in which land was inherited. Upon the death of a parent, for example, each child received an equal, albeit fractional, share of his or her parent's landholdings. Over time, this splintering of land inheritance resulted in a "checkerboard" pattern of landownership. Any given acre of land could be owned by numerous, potentially unrelated individuals. Consequently, rather than attempting to farm their fragmented parcels of land, many Schitsu'umsh found the only economic option available to them was in leasing their scattered landholdings to white farmers. This lease pattern continues into the present. In the decades to follow, more than a third of the original allotments were sold to whites. By 1921 only four Schitsu'umsh families were able to continue farming their own allotments productively.

Loss of lands resulting from individual sales of allotments to whites paled in comparison to the loss of vast tracts of "surplus" lands not allotted to the Schitsu'umsh in the first place. At the time of allotment, the Schitsu'-umsh immediately lost claim to an estimated 310,000 acres of land. These lands—all within the boundaries of the Coeur d'Alene Reservation and all confiscated without compensation to the Schitsu'umsh—were, in turn, opened up for settlement to whites.

Besides loss of major portions of their reservation, the General Allotment Act also resulted in the removal of many families from their traditional homelands around Benewah Creek, near Lake Coeur d'Alene, and at the mouth of the St. Joe River. For these Schitsu'umsh, their cultural and subsistence links with the lake were thus severed. And finally, with the allotment process and its emphasis on individual ownership of land and property also came the further erosion of the traditional collective orientation of family and kinship obligations, and the landscape's further redefinition as an economic commodity. The allotments were intended to be owned and operated in the manner of a Euro-American nuclear family.

When asked how he remembered the effects of allotment on his family, and on the Schitsu'umsh generally, Felix Aripa replied simply: "It broke every one of them." Once successfully integrating hunting and gathering with agriculture, Schitsu'umsh families would now face a severe period of dislocation and poverty. The federal law that sought economic self-sufficiency for the Indian accomplished just the opposite.

While not part of the Allotment Act, the few remaining Schitsu'umsh families living along the shores of Lake Coeur d'Alene were removed with the installation of a dam and the establishment of a park. Frederick Post had begun work on a mill and dam as early as 1871. But it was not until Washington Water Power of Spokane (now the Avista Corporation) completed their dam and hydroelectric power plant at Post Falls in 1906 that the lake's water was fully harnessed, providing electricity, irrigation water, and seasonal flood control. Soon after the damming of the river, the character of Lake Coeur d'Alene's shoreline was significantly altered. While estimates vary, the lake rose at least six to seven feet above its former yearly average level (personal communication, Robert Singletary, October 1997). With the increased volume of the lake came permanent flooding of thousands of acres of land, as well as destruction of many traditional sites associated with residence, fishing, and water-potato gathering. In raising the lake's level, a series of small lakes were also fully etched out along the lower section of the Coeur d'Alene River: Rose, Bull Run, Killary, Medicine, Cave, Swan, Black, Blue, Thompson, and Anderson lakes; and at the southern end of the lake, Benewah, Round, and Chatcolet lakes. The waters of Lake Coeur d'Alene no longer ebbed and flowed with the changing seasons but were monitored and controlled for the electrical power that the water produced.

In 1911 Heyburn State Park was established at the southern end of the lake to provide recreational opportunities for local residents. Though the land had been deeded by the federal government to the state of Idaho, for the several Schitsu'umsh families who had traditionally resided in cabins along the lake's shores, the park meant eviction without compensation. The money received from the state for the purchase of the trust lands (some $11,000) did not go to the tribe but was allocated to cover the costs of developing the state park.

The processes of executive order and allotment, in combination with a subsequent wind of change, resulted in a landscape that could no longer provide economic self-sufficiency for the Schitsu'umsh, in any combination of a transhumance or "reduction" mode. Not unlike the consequences of the buffalo's demise on the Plains for the tribes of that region, with their loss of land came a loss of access to fishing, root gathering, and game hunting, and the Schitsu'umsh entered an era of devastating poverty and dependency on the U.S. government.

The Schitsu'umsh families were now legally defined and limited to some 100,000 acres within a reservation one-twelfth the size of their once 4-million-acre aboriginal landscape. With the growing white desire for and incursion onto Schitsu'umsh lands, the federal government's solution was to remove the Schitsu'umsh rather than the white squatters. Traditional village sites at the mouths and along the Spokane and Coeur d'Alene rivers were replaced by commercial centers, all of which were part of a new and burgeoning economy that essentially excluded the Schitsu'umsh. As the warriors had failed to meet the military challenge of the colonels, the chiefs could not successfully bargain against the commissioners. The executive order process saw the power and prestige of the chiefs further undermined. The landscape was increasingly dominated by Euro-Americans who sought ownership of the land to fulfill their own desires for independence and economic security. It became a landscape legally redefined as a "reservation"; it become an "economic commodity" over which "federal," "state," and "tribal" authority was asserted and contested.

MINING

The 1880s saw a rush of miners to the Coeur d'Alene River basin, staking out claims and cutting timber.[17] Discoveries included placer gold in the Coeur d'Alene Mountains in 1880 and near Murray on the North Fork of the Coeur d'Alene River in 1883. During the following year, lead and silver veins were discovered on the South Fork of the Coeur d'Alene River, and in 1885 major silver strikes resulted in the opening of the Hecla, Bunker Hill, and Sullivan mines. In 1880 the first of several steamboats, the *Amelia Wheaton*, was launched, providing easier transportation of people and supplies up and down the rivers. The power plant at Post Falls began delivering electrical power to the mines by 1906. Chief Seltice had earlier requested that the U.S. government send representatives to negotiate with these new arrivals and see to their removal. His requests went unheeded and the newcomers stayed.

The Coeur d'Alene Mining District, located primarily along the South Fork of the Coeur d'Alene River, is the world's largest source of silver production. Since 1884, it had "produced over 1 billion ounces of silver, 8.5 million tons of lead, 3 million tons of zinc, and substantial quantities of antimony, cadmium, cooper, and gold. The total value of this production

*Hecla mine near Burke, Idaho (photograph by T. N. Barnard, 1923; courtesy
Northwest Museum of Arts and Culture and Eastern Washington State Historical
Society, acc. no. L88-154.12)*

is over $4.8 billion" (Bennett, Siems, and Constantopoulos 1989: 137). The
Bunker Hill mine contains more than 150 miles of underground workings.
At 7,900 feet deep, the Star-Morning mine is the deepest in the United States.
And the Sunshine is the richest U.S. silver mine, having produced more
than 350 million ounces of silver. The mines continue to be very productive, yielding more than 3 million ounces of silver annually, representing
approximately 10 percent of U.S production.

From the mines also came industrial by-products and waste. Heavy-metal pollution began accumulating in impoundment ponds. The contaminants included lead, cadmium, zinc, mercury, and arsenic. But spring runoffs and floods, which eroded the containment dikes, spread the contaminants throughout the Coeur d'Alene River basin, down to Harrison and into Lake Coeur d'Alene. The floods of 1913 forced complete abandonment of the once-fertile hay fields around Cataldo. The following vignette presents the account of a young white girl traveling by steamboat on Coeur d'Alene Lake just before 1911.

Liquid Lead

At Harrison the Coeur d'Alene river, flowing with liquid lead, empties into the lake, bringing as tribute a fortune in solution every year, the loss from the flumes at the mines. These lead-laden waters are death to animals and vegetable life; a dog or cat drinking from it dies. (Mock 1980:2)

Relocation to Hangman Creek, the intensification of agriculture, and the establishment of reservation boundaries had inhibited, but not curtailed, access to or reliance upon the northern reaches of the Schitsu'umsh landscape. As discussed previously, families continued to hunt, berry, and fish that region, as reflected in the sightings of Schitsu'umsh hunting mule deer and berrying along the Little North Fork of the Coeur d'Alene and on Grizzly Mountain up to 1900. But just as smallpox had decimated the human population, pollution from mining in the Coeur d'Alene River basin brought illness and death to the other populations of the landscape—the fish, animal, and plant inhabitants. As a result, Schitsu'umsh activity in this region of their landscape all but ceased after 1900. It is ironic that this economically redefined land would so enrich one population at the expense of another.

Dishwater

Back when I was, from what I recall, age five to age ten [approximately 1950], my dad used to go fishing in Chatcolet area, Harrison area, and he just didn't go anymore. A lot of the older people that he was fishing with would say that the fish were sick. "They are sleeping." Those are the words that he came back with. "The fish are sleeping all the time." We never got the advantage or the opportunity of eating a lot of fish anymore. I remember distinctly the fact that in order to get any fish, we would have to go to Spokane. Or we would go up on the Spokane Reservation to fish. For whatever reason, what I remember him mentioning was that the fish were "sleeping." What he told was, "They were soft. They didn't taste good anymore." So we never got any more fish. . . .

I used to get water potatoes and things like that that my grandma and them used to go around Cataldo and there; even before there was the pilgrimage, they used to go there because one of our family is buried there. . . . They would dig for cub ears and water potatoes and for what they used to call the wild carrot. Then they quit and moved the whole area from digging around there and they began to have to dig with the Spokane, down to Davenport and Wilbur and Creston area [Wilbur is some sixty miles directly west of Spokane]. That is where they would go digging after that. . . . They would travel around, but they didn't go to Harrison anymore. They didn't go to Cataldo anymore. They didn't go that way at all anymore. They just quit going.

I remember asking him, my Hoppy, why we didn't go to the Coeur d'Alene River anymore and he mentioned that it was gray. His exact words were something like, "The water looked like dishwater. It looked like dishwater." So he just didn't go there anymore. There was an area where they used to go around Harrison and something about a cave. It must be Cave Bay or somewhere over in there [Cave Lake or Bay is on the Coeur d'Alene River, just a few miles east of Harrison]. They used to go over in there and pick water potatoes, and then they just didn't anymore. (From an interview conducted on June 7, 1996.)

SELF-DETERMINATION

The 1920s and 1930s signaled the blowing of a new, warmer wind across the landscape of the Schitsu'umsh. Congress bestowed U.S. citizenship on all Indians in 1924. Citizenship was in part granted in gratitude for so many Indians having served the country during World War I, but the new law was also enacted to help curb the authority of the Interior Department by "getting them out of the Indian business." However, the granting of citizenship did not remove the treaty and executive-order obligations entered into by sovereign nations, the tribes, and the U.S. government. Dual citizenship was thus established. A Schitsu'umsh individual is both citizen of the United States and of the Coeur d'Alene Nation.

In 1934 the federal government enacted the Indian Reorganization (Wheeler-Howard) Act, and the thawing of the landscape thereby deepened. The goal of the act was to rehabilitate tribal economies, promote self-determination via local rule, and provide religious and cultural freedom to Indians. It also formally ended the allotment process. Funding was provided for education. Each tribe had the right to accept or reject the act.

In 1947 the Coeur d'Alene Tribe formed its first tribal government independent of the traditional head chiefs' control. This set the stage for a form of government that would provide the Schitsu'umsh people with most of their executive, judicial, and legislative needs. The Tribe established an elected council of a chairman and six board members, each serving three-year terms. All enrolled members, with at least "one-fourth Coeur d'Alene blood" or by adoption, were entitled to a vote and voice in the governance of the tribe. Leaders would be chosen by consensus of those represented.

The Indian Reorganization Act of 1934 also lifted the governmental ban on ceremonies and dances. The repressive policies of the Jesuits ceased, and, as we observed in the example of Father Byrne, the priests even began encouraging many forms of traditional culture. With improved roads and the automobile, contact between various reservations, nearby and distant, increased tremendously. As a consequence, the 1930s witnessed the syncretism of at least two dance traditions—the traditional war dance and the Lakota Omaha dance—to form a new expression: the Powwow. The term "powwow" likely derives from the Algonquian word "*pauau*," or "*pau wau.*" Powwow originally referred to a gathering of spiritual leaders; but, as with so many Indian words, it was frequently mispronounced and misapplied by early Euro-American observers of the dances, who believed it referred simply to a large gathering of Indians. In turn, the usage spread and has become adopted as a pan-Indian term. Arrival of the Lakota Omaha dance brought certain associated dance regalia—for example, the eagle-feather bustle and the porcupine hair roach. Like the term powwow, the Lakota Omaha dance became widely shared throughout Indian country. In the songs, dances, and regalia of the Powwow, the Schitsu'umsh could continue to express the prayerful and celebratory desires that were so central to their war and harvest ceremonies of old, as well as develop a new forum in which to reaffirm to a hostile world their identity as Schitsu'umsh. The nature and significance of the Schitsu'umsh Powwow will be considered more fully in a subsequent chapter, "Sharing the Gifts."

Leadership

I admire Joe Garry; I grew up when he was a leader, and I heard him speak. I thought Ozzie George could mesmerize the whole audience. And I saw the humility and the humbleness in him. And they looked at Happy LaSarte and the compassion he had for the people. And probably those three men had a great impact on my values. . . .

And we're a matriarch tribe, where our grandmothers, our *T'upye's*, are really the important women in our families. I got to spend a lot of time with my grandmother; saw how strong willed she was and I admired her for that. And I learned how to maybe make decisions for the rest of her family, at that time. They taught me that decisions have to be made. . . . You couldn't put them aside. They had to be made. And if you didn't make those decisions, then things wouldn't be right. Procrastinating. You couldn't procrastinate. So I thought those people influenced me quite a bit. . . .

The leaders I talked about, I felt had a commitment more than anyone I knew, to the whole tribe, where the tribe was most important. And if they took care of their tribe, then the families would be taken care of. And they sensed that. That they really, really cared. That they weren't in those positions for money; they weren't in those positions for esteem. But there was a sense that they had to protect the tribe, they had to lead the tribe, they had to really take care of them. (From an interview conducted on February 19, 1997.)

It was under the leadership of such Council Chairmen as Joseph (Joe) Garry, Oswald "Ozzie" George, and Bernard "Happy" LaSarte, beginning in the 1950s, and in conjunction with the Indian Self-Determination Act of 1975, that the Tribe further extended its autonomy and its influence on the lives of its own people and the landscape.[18] Marceline Kevis, granddaughter of Andrew Seltice and herself a member of the Tribal Council "for thirty-two years intermittently," vividly remembers the leadership of Joe Garry and others. During the 1950s, these leaders not only thwarted the efforts of the federal government's "termination policy" on the Coeur d'Alene Reservation but championed resistance to the federal government's abrogation of its responsibilities to many of the tribes throughout the region.

The Self-Determination Act provided the Coeur d'Alene Tribe with the authority to control and operate many services previously provided by the federal government. Final transfer of the remaining functions of the Bureau of Indian Affairs was assumed by the Tribe. It is important to note that the qualities that helped guide the chiefs of the Schitsu'umsh families through the seasonal rounds of bygone days are similarly expressed in the recent past and still today among the elected members of the Tribal Council. The thawing winds brought by the Indian Reorganization Act and the Indian Self Determination Act encouraged from within the Schitsu'umsh landscape a reflowering of what had long been suppressed and lay dormant.

Today the Tribe has its own court and police system, along with Departments of Environment and Natural Resources, Education, Health Services, Housing, Planning, and Social Services. As a function of the Law and Order Department, the Tribe has civil jurisdiction over all inhabitants living within the reservation boundaries; the federal government retains judicial responsibility over felony issues. As in former times, the Tribe also has the power of "banishment." If an individual's behavior is judged continually "harmful to his neighbors and to the children," he can be expelled from the reservation. In addition, health services were transferred from the Indian Health Service to the Tribe's own contracted providers when the Benewah Medical Center was established.

In 1989 the Tribe entered into an agreement with the state of Idaho allowing the Schitsu'umsh to hunt, fish, trap, gather, and camp in the territory ceded by the 1887 and 1889 agreements with the U. S. government. The Schitsu'umsh are thus allowed limited access to much of their aboriginal territory. This agreement excludes privately owned lands and any portions of the states of Washington and Montana. The Natural Resources Department has expanded its scope of services to include management of fisheries, wildlife, water resources, air quality, pesticide use, and environmental planning on the reservation. Today the Coeur d'Alene Reservation boundaries include 345,000 acres, of which about 70,000 acres are actually owned by the Schitsu'umsh themselves. The enrollment of the tribe numbers some 1,725 individuals.

The Schitsu'umsh people continue to strive for even greater economic and political sovereignty. Successes include the Benewah Medical Center (in Plummer), the Tribal School (in DeSmet), and the Wellness Center (near the Medical Center)—each opening state-of-the-art facilities in 1990, 1997, and 1998, respectively—the Schitsu'umsh language programs in the tribal and public schools and local college, the Benewah Market, and the Coeur d'Alene Casino. In seeking to develop its economic self-sufficiency, the Tribe has formed an Economic Development Corporation, which, among other enterprises, oversees operation of the 6,000-acre Tribal Farm. The Tribal Farm received its initial impetus in 1958, when the tribe was awarded approximately $4 million dollars from the Indian Claims Commission for lands ceded in 1889. Of that award, $1.5 million went to the purchase of agricultural lands for the Tribal Farm.

We're on an Expedition

We try to hire our people [for the Coeur d'Alene Casino]. We try to believe in them. We try to give them a chance. We try to train them well and right. We included in our training program things about who they represent and taking pride in it. Wearing the uniform, so to speak, with a great deal of pride. Before we opened up, there were a lot of people who came to me and said, "you're doing this wrong. It isn't going to work. It's going to fail like the pig farm and the construction enterprise. You're hiring the wrong people. You're training them wrong. If they've never had these kind of jobs before, why don't you get people out of Spokane who already worked in bingo halls and let them do it." Some of our own people were telling me that, too. I just figured, I don't think that can be true. It's not brain surgery. It's not rocket science. If we believe in them, they know we believe in them. They're not feeling like I can't do it because people are treating me like I'm stupid, but we treat them like they're intelligent, like they have a reason to have pride and try hard and encourage them. Where we see they're weak in an area, we train them in that area and it worked. We're known around here as being the operation with the greatest level of customer service in gaming, bingo, or maybe just about anything. It's because our people who work here are primarily tribal members or other tribes married in. They've done an excellent job.

After that, after this is all done and set and we're moving and going, the way I run it here, there are no titles. Nobody has got to come in and call me, "Mr. . . . ," or anything. We're all first name. I try to tell them we're a team, we're a family. We're like a band or a war party or a hunting party. We've been sent out to do something. This is what we're doing. If we succeed, then our people are going to be protected. Elders are going to have care. The children are going to have a future. That's the way we have to look at it. We're on an expedition. We have to do something here. We have to be careful. We have to be alert. We have to be on time. Put it in those kinds of context. The Indian mind, our employees here, can see that.

They can understand that's what's at stake. That's what it's all about. (From an interview conducted on May 24, 1996.)

The Coeur d'Alene Tribal Bingo and Casino was established in 1993 at a initial cost of $2.7 million. Deliberately electing to forgo an outside financial partner, after three years of profitable operations, its ten-year mortgage was paid off. A $14-million expansion soon followed, and by 1998 the additions were paid for completely and net profits from the gaming operation totaled $9.2 million. In keeping with a tribal decision, profits from the revenues of the casino have gone back into such endeavors as education—both for the Plummer-Worley School District (publicly funded and administered elementary and senior high schools) and the Coeur d'Alene Tribal School (a tribally operated K–8-grade elementary school)—into Schitsu'umsh language programs, and, most important, into the purchase of land, especially forest and farmlands, to help enhance and eventually sustain future tribal economic independence. Funding would also be directed toward neighboring school districts off the reservation. In 1999, for example, $794,000 was given to various educational endeavors: $255,000 to the Plummer-Worley School District; $394,000 to the Coeur d'Alene Tribal School and Department of Education; $40,000 to the American Indian Art Institute in Santa Fe, New Mexico; $30,000 for North Idaho College; and to white communities just off the reservation, $20,000 for the St. Maries School District and $10,000 each for the Coeur d'Alene, Kootenai, and Post Falls school districts. Additional funding was also distributed to area libraries. The funding was designated for use entirely at the discretion of each school's administration.

Since its inception, the casino has thus generated more than $3.5 million for educational endeavors. According to Tribal Chairman Ernie Stensgar, "This is not a donation; rather it is an investment in our Indian and non-Indian children." In 1999 the Coeur d'Alene Casino, as it is now called, embarked on an ambitious $32-million expansion, which includes a 5,000-seat arena for boxing, concert, and rodeo events, a twenty-seven-hole golf course (including a nine-hole "executive course"), an RV park, and a 104-room motel and conference center.

Leadership for the various tribal initiatives has come from such individuals as Ernie Stensgar, a descendant of Circling Raven, who has been Tribal Chairman since 1986, and David Matheson, who served as Tribal Chairman from 1982 through 1984. Matheson also served at the national level as the Deputy Commissioner of Indian Affairs in President George

Bush Sr.'s administration, and he has been the Chief Executive Officer for Gaming at the Coeur d'Alene Tribal Casino since its inception. As of 1999, the Coeur d'Alene Tribe, in all its operations, had become one of the largest employers in the region, with more than 700 employees.

With the Schitsu'umsh language now being taught in elementary, high school, and college-level classrooms, the uniquely Schitsu'umsh names for their landscape are now once again spoken aloud: *Q'emiln, Hnt'aq'n, 'L'lkhwi'lus, Aƚkwari't, Hnch'mqinkwe', Stseqhwƚkwe',* and *Hnch'emtsn.* These efforts are being greatly assisted by such linguists and teachers as Raymond Brinkman, who is teaching and developing a college-level language curriculum; Ivy Doak, who is updating and expanding the Schitsu'umsh dictionary; and Reva Hess and Jill Wagner, who are teaching and developing a high-school-level language curriculum. A strong advocate for such endeavors has been Dianne Allen, the Coeur d'Alene Tribe's Director of Education. At all levels of instruction, the ninety-year-old Lawrence Nicodemus continues to guide and inspire the Schitsu'umsh language revitalization.

In coordination with various state and federal agencies, and led by the efforts of such individuals as Henry SiJohn and Alfred Nomee, the Coeur d'Alene Tribe is in the forefront of mining-pollution cleanup efforts throughout the Coeur d'Alene River basin.[19] "We want a clean and pristine and healthy lake for our children and their children's children, for all the peoples of this region." In July of 1998, U.S. District Court Judge Edward Lodge ruled that the tribe was "entitled to exclusive use, occupancy and right" to the bed and banks of the southern third of Lake Coeur d'Alene. His ruling was, in part, based upon the Executive Order of 1873. On June 18, 2001, the U.S. Supreme Court upheld the Lodge decision. Thus the Schitsu'umsh added to their claim as legitimate stakeholders in the Coeur d'Alene River basin cleanup efforts, and reaffirmed their desire to nurture and restore to health all the members of the Schitsu'umsh family—human, animal, and plant.

Despite the strong winds that have blown a freezing chill over the landscape—disease, conversion, war, executive orders, allotment, pollution, as well as the secularization and economic and legal commodification of the land—the teachings of the Schitsu'umsh continue to flower, helping to contour and animate a landscape. Many of the holes in the Schitsu'umsh flag are, in fact, being mended. And as testament to a people's perseverance against overwhelming odds, their Indian flag flies with the stars and stripes of the United States and the crucifix of the Jesuits patched

Coeur d'Alene Casino, January 2000

alongside the stories of Crane and Coyote. While retaining their core values, their teachings, the Schitsu'umsh have flourished not by attempting to exclude but by embracing aspects of educational, health-care, economic, political, and religious institutions once alien to their own society. In turn, these institutions are given a uniquely Schitsu'umsh orientation as they are integrated into their society. Thus, for example, a tribal chairman, who governs by consent of the people, embraces the same values that would have elected a traditional chief, and a multimillion dollar gaming operation is run in the spirit of a hunting expedition.

"From where we stand [whether in Plummer or DeSmet] we once could see the dust rising from the feet of our grandmothers as they walked the trails over the hills and into the distant mountains." Much of the Schi̱tsu'-umsh landscape is no longer accessible, incorporated into another people's landscape or now diseased and inhospitable. While the dust no longer rises, trails through the Schi̱tsu'umsh landscape are still traveled. The Coeur d'Alene Tribe, as its highest priority, is attempting to regain tribal and economic sovereignty within their landscape. Leadership is again by consent of the people, and is spearheaded by astute and visionary Schi̱tsu'umsh. New gifts have been discovered and are brought forth from the landscape, providing expanded economic opportunities. At the same time, when the story of Crane or Coyote is told, or a Memorial Giveaway is held, the landscape is also reinvigorated.

✻

Preparing the World

The *Amotqn*

I was taught a long time ago that the Father of everything, the *Amotqn*, lived in the sun. And he was the Father, and that's where he lived, and that . . . his brightness was there for a purpose, other than to warm your face on a cold morning. When it would come up in the morning, you would pray to the *Amotqn* and we still do, thanking him for this day, and that from the Father and the sun, where he lived, and he warmed the earth, and that's where the Mother lived. From the earth the Father would touch the Mother and things would come, new things, new growth, the Animals would get busy and they would take the things that would grow out of the ground and nourishment, and they would eat it so they could be strong, so they could continue that same thing. So the Father was responsible for everything, the *Amotqn*. He brought about life and the Mother was the earth who nurtured all of us, and that's where we all came from this. So when the Animals had a chance to eat all the berries and all the roots and all the plants and all the grasses, and they, in turn, giving thanks to the *Amotqn*, they would create things among themselves through this blessing and that's where they would have their babies. And because of that and us, as Human Beings, began to do the same thing as a tribute or a thank you, to be able to have others to come about, to be able to look at the *Amotqn* and thank you, Father, for this life. Thank you for my child's life. Thank you for my grandchild's life. And because of that virtual and that feeling of *Amotqn* and how he came to be the sun and where he lives, and how he would smile on the Mother, and they would create things, and out of that creation would create, in turn. . . . And we could go to the Mother and say I can't create, I need strength, and she would give us things to eat, to consume, so we could be good people. And that we would be able to bring about grand-children and children and so on and so forth. (From an interview conducted on June 4, 1996.)

THE CREATOR

It is the Creator who is responsible for the world of the Schitsu'umsh. He is said to have sent the First Peoples, such as Crane and Coyote, to "prepare the world for the coming of the Human Peoples." Once the world was prepared, all that followed—the deer hunted, the camas dug, the huckleberries gathered, and the *suumesh* song acquired—also derived from the Creator. It is the Creator who is the ultimate benefactor of all these gifts. While it may be one of the Animal People, such as Eagle or Elk, who offers a *suumesh* song to a young man who is fasting for a vision on a nearby mountaintop, that medicine song is ultimately granted by and, when sung, heard by the Creator.

Among the Schitsu'umsh two primary terms are used for the Creator: *Amotqn* and *K'u'lnsutn*. One of the earliest references to the term *Amotqn* comes from Father Diomedi. While traveling in Schitsu'umsh country in 1876, he was told of *"Amotkan"* by his Indian guide, Felician (1978: 75–76). As reported in Father Diomedi's "Sketches," which he wrote in 1879, *Amotkan* was said to be "a monstrous being, like a man, stationed at the head of the river and ruling over the waters." Given the prevailing nineteenth-century Jesuit perspective, we can infer from Diomedi's characterization that he was not equating *Amotkan* with the idea of a supreme being.[1]

On the other hand, James Teit, an ethnographer working under the direction of eminent anthropologist Franz Boas, continually referred, in his 1904 descriptions of Schitsu'umsh life, to *"Amo'tqEn,"* "who lives on the highest mountains," as the chief deity, "the deity prayed to most" (1930: 184–85). "He could see all lands, and understand what was required for the benefit of the Indians." This notion of a central deity and use of this specific term are shared among other Salish peoples. For the Thompson Indians, *Amo'tqEn* is a central deity located on one of the highest mountains in the area (Teit 1900:345). For the Flathead, *Amo'tqEn* "sits on top of the tree," "makes food plentiful and tries to benefit people," and "is the deity who sent Coyote into the world to make life easier for the people" (1930:383).

The term *Amotqn* (pronounced ah-môt-kin) has continued in use by the Schitsu'umsh. Gary Palmer, a linguistic anthropologist, translates *Amotqn* as "one who sits (presides) at the head (peak)" (Palmer, Nicodemus, and Felsman 1987:115). While the *Amotqn* "sits at the head" and is considered the "father," life itself could not be maintained without the "mother," the earth. In prayer to the *Amotqn*, the Human Peoples are "his children" (Teit 1930:185).

In addition to current use of the term *Amǫtqn*, reference is also made to *K'u'lntsutn* (meaning, literally, "the means of making oneself" or "he who creates himself," and loosely translated as "the maker"), as well as to the "Creator," the "Grandfather," and the "Father." Some Schitsu'umsh distinguish between *Amǫtqn* and *K'u'lntsutn*, the first referring to the non-Christian Creator and the latter referring to the Catholic notion of God or Jesus Christ. One current elder understands *Amǫtqn* to be a "modern term" that can mean "headwater." *Amǫtqn* can also be interpreted as "president" (Nicodemus 1975[1]:25), or can refer to the Tribal Chairman, the "head of the family." Still others use only the term *K'u'lntsutn*, even as active Jump Dancers. Several elders see the two terms as fundamentally synonymous, i.e., both mean Creator. And two individuals I interviewed suggested that the Indian term for Creator is "too difficult to translate into English." Nevertheless, all my consultants seem to agree that the Schitsu'umsh held to the belief in a single supreme being prior to the coming of the Jesuits, and that they continue to do so today. Unless another term is specifically cited in quotes, Creator will be used to refer to the Schitsu'umsh understanding of a supreme being.

THE FIRST PEOPLES

As established by the Creator, the world was initially inhabited by the powerful First Peoples, such as Chief Child of the Yellow Root, Crane, Rabbit and Jackrabbit, the "famous and, at times, infamous" Coyote and his wife, Mrs. Mole, along with a host of other beings.[2] Each of the First Peoples embodies the qualities of animal, human, and *suumesh*, simultaneously. As with the other tribes of the Plateau, the oral literature of the Schitsu'umsh and the tellers of those narratives do not attempt to describe the physical appearance of Crane, Chief Child of the Yellow Root, or even Coyote. In the instance of *Skwarchn*, or Crane, we learn from his story accounts that he lives in a lodge with his grandmother, wears a belt, hunts deer with bow and arrow, boils and smokes venison, and eats from plates. He exhibits the proper etiquette when guests arrive, hunts only two deer at a time, and provides for a hungry village. But Crane also demonstrates his *suumesh* when he causes a tree to burn, and he carries enough deer under his belt to feed an entire village. And Crane is also understood as one of the Animal Peoples. That which defines Crane, as well as the other First Peoples, is not delimited but inclusive. By extension, the landscape traveled by Crane is thus endowed with animal as well as human and transformative qualities.

Rabbit and Jackrabbit[3]

Rabbit and Jackrabbit are cousins and friends at the same time. Rabbit lives in the mountains around DeSmet, near Moses Mountain here. Jackrabbit lives on the prairie of the Big Bend country, from Rosalia out toward the Davenport area there.

The winter is hard. When it clears after a big snow Jackrabbit looks toward the mountains here. The trees are heavy with snow; the branches interlock. Jackrabbit says, "I wonder what he eats? I think Rabbit must be dead." Then Jackrabbit says, "I think I'll take my cousin some bitterroot, camas, dried salmon eggs." He puts them in a bundle and packs it on his back. Then he starts off to Rabbit's home.

Rabbit looks toward the prairie there. Then he says, "Poor Jackrabbit! I wonder if he has a fire in this cold weather. I'll go see." He gathers pitch shavings, makes as large a pack as he can carry. Then he starts off with it toward Jackrabbit's home.

Rabbit comes up the north side of Tekoa Mountain. Then he sits down at the edge of the woods. He says, "I wonder where Jackrabbit lives? I don't know exactly."

Jackrabbit comes over the prairie, up the south side of the mountain. Then he sees Rabbit sitting. He says, "Why, here he is!" Rabbit stands up. He sees Jackrabbit. Then they walk toward each other, shake hands.

"You're still alive, my cousin!" says Rabbit. "And you're still alive, my cousin," says Jackrabbit. "I was just coming to look for you. I was worried about you," says Rabbit. "Why, I was coming to look for you too. I was worried about you. I thought you might be hungry," says Jackrabbit.

"No, I'm not hungry. I found green grass under that tree. I ate it. It's you I worry about. I thought you might get cold so I brought these pitch shavings for you to start a fire," says Rabbit. "No, I'm not cold. You worry for no reason. When it snows and drifts, I find a dry spot under this sagebrush. That's where I stay. I thought you might need some food so I brought you some camas and bitterroot," says Jackrabbit. Then they both laughed.

"I'll throw away the pitch." Then Rabbit unties his pack, dumps it out. "I'll dump what I brought to feed you." Then Jackrabbit unties his pack, dumps it out. Then Rabbit and Jackrabbit go their separate ways.

The next spring the pitch grows into pitchy trees and the bitterroot and camas into rock roses. When you go to Tekoa Mountain, you will find pitch pine trees. You will find patches of bitterroot and camas.

Then, the end of the trail.

The ultimate role of the First Peoples was to "prepare the world for the coming of Human Peoples." In addition to the First Peoples, the world was originally inhabited by a host of Monsters and "man-eaters." There was Rock Monster who rolled about the country, destroying the camps of the First Peoples, and there was the giant Gobbler Monster, who "swallowed up" all the First Peoples. Even Awls, Combs, Pestles, Bladders, and Lassos were man-eaters, until Chief Child of the Yellow Root subdued their "chiefs" and commanded them to serve "the people who are coming." It was the First Peoples who rid the world of these Monsters, rendering it hospitable to Human Peoples.

Hawk and Turtle

All the People were gathered there [near Little Falls Flat, north of Spokane Falls in Spokane country]—the First People, the Animals, the Bear, the Deer, the Elk, the Eagle, even the Turtle. The earth shook. They were looking at the situation. The earth was moving and settling. [An earthquake was occurring, and those who walked upon the earth were having a difficult time.] It was the Hawk who began to dance and laugh at all the ones who were walking on the earth. He said, "I don't know how to do that. I'm much better than you. I can just fly and let the earth rumble all it wants. It would never scare me."

It was the Eagle that came over and told him, in so many words, to shut his mouth, because he didn't know what he was talking about. The Hawk wouldn't do it. He kept prancing and moving his head. [The storyteller moved his head to-and-fro as if dancing.] He'd walk in front of the People. The Fish were sitting along the bank, like that, watching. The Turtle and the Rabbit, all those People were there. The Hawk would walk around and move his head like this, like he was dancing and he would sing a song about how powerful he was. His head would move like this when he walked.

And so it was the Turtle who came up and told him, "You shouldn't do this to the People, just because you are more skillful than us, you think you have more skills than us. We're all equal, we're all the same." The Hawk told him, he says, "No we're not, we're more powerful because we fly. Look at the Eagle, he's close to the *Amotqn*." The Turtle said, "But yet the Eagle doesn't come and hold it over us. He comes and sits at our camp. Sometimes he'll bring us something to eat. He's a good person." Hawk just walked around, his head would come up, his feathers would come up like that—really proud, walk around, strut around. So he says, "I can fly

St. Joe Baldy overlooking the St. Joe River, c. 1925
(courtesy Museum of North Idaho, Coeur d'Alene, acc. no. SJR-1-16)

faster. I can do anything better and faster than anybody." The Turtle said, "No you can't." He says, "What do you want to do, race? You think you're fast?" The Turtle said, "I can outrace you."

All the People stood up then. They knew something was going to happen. All the Chipmunks quieted down. They all gathered around him, listened to these two guys talk. Hawk says, "How are we going to race?" He says, "He's too slow." The Turtle says, "Take me way up there, just as high as you go, you pick me up and take me way up there. Eagle can go with us. He'll say go. And you just drop me and we'll see who comes down." So they did. All the People were hollering and war whooping as they went around through the camp. The Turtle would barely move like that, and he would wave once in a while at his best friends. They would say, "All right, Turtle, go, go, go. We know you can do it." Hawk would walk around and he would dance and he would sing and move his head like that [storyteller continues to move his head as if dancing], and he would sing a special song [storyteller sings the song], just showing off.

So finally Eagle says, "All right, let's go." So he [Hawk] picked Turtle up and they took off. They went way up high, high, high. "Is this high enough?" The Eagle says, "You can go higher than that, Hawk." "I don't want to hurt this guy." "No, you won't hurt him. Keep going." He went as high as he could and his wings couldn't go any higher with this guy he was trying to carry. The Eagle says, "Okay." He looked down. All the First People are looking up. The Elk and all of them are standing there. Little Birds took the best seats, it was said, on the antlers of the Elk. His head was just full of little Birds, like that, because they all wanted to see. They had the highest seat.

Finally they said, "All right, go." Hawk let him go. Here comes Turtle, just straight down. Hawk turned, let out a big war whoop, screeched and came straight down. Just came right after Turtle. Caught up with Turtle and they were just neck and neck. The Turtle looked at him, like that. He was going so fast, the Turtle's eyes began to get narrow. There were tears coming out the side of his eyes he was going so fast. They got closer and closer to the ground. The Hawk pulled ahead a little bit, like that. He'd look back and he'd laugh. Pretty soon here comes Turtle catching up with him. The closer they got to the ground, the faster the Turtle seemed to go. Finally they get close to the ground. Just moments before they hit the ground the Turtle pulled his head in, pulled his arms in. Boom. [Storyteller slaps hands at each boom.] Hit the ground. Boom. Hawk hit the ground. Nothing but feathers all over the place.

The People ran over there. Badger, his family starts digging. They finally found Turtle's shell and they started pulling him out. Bear went over, great big chunks of dirt. He started digging. Finally found Hawk's feet, the first thing he saw and he kept going. Pulled him out like that. Hawk was still, still all messed up. Dirt in his eyes and in his little nose, his little beak. Turtle came out and shook his head, stretched. The People all cheered and hollered. All looked over at Hawk and he's dead, just dead—feathers missing, body all broken up.

So they called the Mole, Coyote's old lady, to come over and fix that Hawk up. She came over and stood there for a long time and then she turned and she told the People. "Now you look at this. How pitiful this guy looks. He thinks he was so smart and he strutted around because he had a powerful body, and he thought he could do things more than this poor slow person over here. This old person, this Turtle, was old. And now the Turtle is going to go over and get a drink of water. He's going over to the river now and get a drink of water. The People are going to fix him supper and he'll have a good rest. He won the race." She said, "Look at this guy [referring to Hawk]. Pretty soon the ants will be over here trying to tear him apart. The other scavengers will be here, scatter his bones all over here. And for what? He thought his pride was so strong and he thought he was better than anybody else. We can't be like that. We can't be like that. Someday we're going to have to teach somebody [the Human Peoples] how to do these things, how not to do these things. How to do and how not to do. I'll bring this one back to life, but only we have to mark him forever, because of that."

So she jumped back and forth over him and she would sing her song. Pretty soon Hawk's leg, his foot, started going like this. [Storyteller moves and kicks his leg.] His talons started moving a little bit. Finally he woke up. She looked over and Coyote was sitting over there, his legs crossed like that and he'd laugh and he'd point at that Hawk and he'd laugh. And Mole told him, "You better be quiet. You're going to do stupid things, too. You're going to be in the same situation." He said, "Yes, yes, right, right" [in a sarcastic voice]. She jumped back and forth over him and pretty soon Hawk finally sat up, looked a little dazed. Before, when the Creator first made Hawk, he had a real nice pretty beak. Gee it was pretty. Very beautiful. He'd sit there with his foot sometimes and rub it. It was so straight. He could really pick up little things, like that. Finally he come to, dazed, like that. His nose was turned, his beak was turned down when he hit the ground. At the back of his head there's little rings because he used to have kind of little long neck. When he hit the ground so hard, he just pushed his neck right up into his body. So Mole marked him, little rings on his neck and turned his beak.

She says, "Every time you see Hawk now, you remember. Nobody should be dancing around other people, parading themselves that they're better. Everyone is equal here on this earth. Everybody. We all live together. We don't talk smart, we don't act smart." Hawk got up and he kind of shook his head like that.

The Eagle came walking over there. "Hawk, you want to race some more? You want to race anybody else here?" Hawk says, "No." He says, "You going to dance? Move your head around when you walk now?" He says,

"No." He [Eagle] says, "Okay. To remind everybody, you look at him." And he says, "Dove, you're the one who gets to walk around and move your head like that from now on. But when you do that it's a pretty thing. To remind all the People about the prettiness of our lives. Not to show off, but as pretty." So they said, "Okay." Eagle told everybody, "Okay. Let's go have supper." They all left the ground.

Later that afternoon, the only one that was still out there was the Coyote. He's looking in the hole, he would look up at the sky and he'd look in the hole and he would look up in the sky. They told the Mole, "Your husband is out there. He can't figure it out yet. He can't figure it out." She says, "He'll never figure it out" [followed by a big laugh]. (From an interview conducted on July 3, 1996.)

Also through the actions of the First Peoples the landscape was inundated with gifts that would nourish and heal the bodies of the Human Peoples. It was Blue Jay, Hawk, and Badger, for example, who came to the Human Peoples during a time of suffering. There was "a great sickness," and the "medicine people" could do nothing for those who suffered. Blue Jay, Hawk, and Badger appeared before the people one night and took them to a particular tree to pray. It was the Cedar Tree. They showed them how to use the "whole tree, the roots, bark, and leaves." The roots would heal the sick, the bark would be made into baskets, and the tips of the needles would purify. The landscape was rendered hospitable and prepared with gifts for the Human Peoples.

COYOTE

One of the most important of all the First Peoples is *Smiyiw,* or as Lawrence Aripa would say, "the Coyote."[4] As reflected in the text "Coyote and the Salmon," Coyote releases the salmon that had been captured by the man-eaters or, as in another version of this account, by the Swallow Sisters, who live on the Columbia River (see below and Reichard 1947:101–5; Teit 1917:121). Coyote turns the sisters into swallows, and thus provides salmon as food for "the people who are coming." The swallows are to signal the coming of the salmon upriver each year. The cycle continues with Coyote making his way up the Columbia River, encountering other monsters. Using his skills of deception, Coyote often attempts to take advantage of his foes, but just as often he gets duped by his own trickery. The outcome is generally to "prepare the world for the coming of Human Peoples."

Post Falls, c. 1910 (photograph by Frank Palmer; courtesy Northwest Museum of Arts and Culture and Eastern Washington State Historical Society, acc. no. L84-327.979

In one of these encounters, Rock Monster is crushing all the villages, destroying everything in its wake (see below). The First Peoples seek the help of Coyote, who responds by asking, "What's in it for me?" And they respond, "You want mice, you want snakes, we'll give them to you." After being taunted and teased, the Rock Monster finally gives chase to Coyote. Through the country the Rock pursues Coyote and, in so doing, brings out many landforms, mountains, and prairies. All the trees on the Palouse prairie were cut down and the top of Plummer Butte made treeless, for example. After a long chase and becoming very exhausted, Coyote dares the Rock to follow him through a patch of huckleberries and then off a cliff into the lake, as Coyote hangs on the cliff's edge. Thus the Peoples are saved, and the "blue of Coeur d'Alene Lake" is created (Frey 1995:71–75). Coeur d'Alene Lake, now complete, is ready for use by "the people who are coming."

It is also Coyote who encounters the Gobbler Monster who has swallowed up all the First Peoples (see below). Yelling and waving at him, Coyote entices the monster to swallow him. Once inside, Coyote "cuts out the heart," killing the monster and allowing all the First Peoples to escape. Cutting up the parts of the monster, Coyote throws the head, arms, legs, and belly in all directions, the parts becoming the various tribes of Human Peoples (e.g., Diomedi 1978:76; Reichard 1947:70–71; Teit 1917:122). From the hair the Nez Perce are made, as they have "long, shiny, beautiful hair." From the stomach come the Gros Ventre, as they have "large bellies." From the legs, the Blackfeet and Crow are made, as "they are tall, have long legs." As Lawrence Aripa related at the conclusion of this story, "And so he [Coyote] takes the heart and he throws the heart, and of course, naturally, here is where the Coeur d'Alenes come from. And so the Coeur d'Alenes have real good hearts" (Frey 1994:7–11). But one more tribe was left to be made. As there are no more parts of the monster left, Coyote wipes the blood from his knife on a clump of grass and throws the clump away. "That's where the Spokanes came from. They are poor," Aripa explained, a remark that was followed by a big laugh.

Salmon up Hangman Creek

But salmon, they used to come up Hangman Creek. I heard my dad refer to it. It's red salmon or the chinook. They call it *chillwidst*, "salmon when it's red," when it comes up. But according to the Coyote stories, he's the one that stopped the Coeur d'Alene getting salmon because Coyote fell

Beauty Bay on Lake Coeur d'Alene, c. 1910
(courtesy Museum of North Idaho, Coeur d'Alene, acc. no. LCDA-2-11)

for a young, good-looking Coeur d'Alene, the chief's daughter. My God the chief wouldn't allow it. He says, "You're Coyote. You can't have my daughter." He went back a couple of times. . . . He's going to plug off the river. That's the Spokane River now where the falls [are]. When he plugged that up, the Coeur d'Alene never could get any more salmon. (From an interview conducted on May 20, 1996.)

And finally, as told by Lawrence Aripa, Coyote travels around Lake Coeur d'Alene, whereupon he encounters a "beautiful girl," whom, of course, he desires and wants to marry (Frey 1995:188–94; also see "Coyote and the Salmon" below). The Schitsu'umsh people, who are fishing salmon at the time, refuse his wishes. After several requests, denied each time, a vengeful Coyote moves great boulders and creates the falls on the Spokane River at Post Falls and Spokane Falls, thus preventing the salmon from entering Lake Coeur d'Alene. The Schitsu'umsh are thus deprived of this important food source. Coyote is later found "dead" or, as in the account to follow, made into a "rock"

Coyote and the Salmon[5]

Coyote is thirsty. Then he comes to some water there and drinks. Then he thinks that he would take a bath. So he undresses and swims. As he is bathing he sees a waterfall. He thinks that he'd like to go over the falls. As he lets himself float over it, he says, "My, is that pleasant!" He wishes there was a larger falls like it. Then he sees a larger falls. He floats over it and comes to where a wide pool spreads into a river [perhaps the Columbia or Snake River].

Then he follows that river and sees some people. They are talking about not having any salmon to eat. There are four little girls, the man-eaters, who have dammed them all up. The Coyote laughs, saying, "How could little girls be man-eaters! I'll go and break it up." But the people warn him that he'll be killed. Coyote says, "Who is afraid of four little girls? I'll go and break up the dam. What are their names?" "They are called Snipe, Waterbird, *xwi'u xwi'u*, and Killdeer." Then the Coyote goes off.

Then Coyote arrives at the house of the man-eaters. Here is the cliff over which water falls. This cliff made the dam and stopped the salmon. Then Coyote calls his powers. They tell this Coyote that the people are hungry for salmon. Then the first power becomes a digging stick. The second power becomes his armor, a hard thing to protect his hands and the back of his head. The third power becomes the Coyote in the form of a baby. Then the fourth power becomes a log. Then they tell the Coyote that he will be a baby in a box on the log.

Then the log is rolled into the water. Right here, Coyote becomes a baby in a box on the log. As the man-eaters are sitting in their house they hear the cry of the small baby, "*wr wra.*" They think it sounds like a person. They look toward the water here and see the log with the box on it. They say, "Surely some people must have tipped over. Doubtless the parents are drowned and only the child is left. Let's go get it. The one who gets there first can have the child."

Then they jump into the water and swim toward the log there. They catch hold of it and push it ashore. The baby is crying. Then one of them puts her finger in its mouth and it sucks in the whole finger. She jerks it out.

Spokane Falls (from John Mix Stanley's lithographs in Stevens 1855, pl. xxxvi)

Then one makes a kind of mush of salmon and the baby stops crying at
once. He is satisfied and goes to sleep. Then he wakes up and cries. Nothing
but salmon will satisfy him. He grows up very fast. He is learning to crawl.

Whenever the girls go to dig camas roots in Nez Perce country they
take the baby with them. Then they make a little shade for him and feed
him salmon. Soon he is able to eat by himself. They dig and dig. Then the
baby tells Waterbird, "I am thirsty." She says, "I am too busy now; go get
a drink by yourself." He crawls off as a baby. But as soon as he gets out of
sight, he becomes Coyote and runs to the dam. He digs at it for a short
time, then runs back. When he comes within sight again, he creeps.

One of the girls says to the other, "Go look after the baby. He might fall
into the water." One goes and sees him creeping back. Then she picks him
up. He is crying. She quiets him with some salmon gruel. About an hour
later he wants a drink again. He is told that he knows how to get it, and
to go on there.

This time the Coyote digs a larger hole in the dam. He keeps doing this
for many days. One day Coyote puts on his armor and takes his digging
stick. Then he stays so long one of the girls says, "He may have fallen in."

One of the girls goes to look and sees it is Coyote. She calls to the others, and they all run with their digging sticks. Then they came up and club Coyote over the head and all over his body. His armor protects him. As they beat him the dam breaks. Then the Coyote sings, "Come! Salmon come!" Then the salmon are released and go one after another upstream there. Then the man-eating girls wept bitterly.

Then the Coyote goes along the stream there and becomes hungry. He calls in the salmon and clubs one. Then he makes a fire and roasts it. He is tired and will eat it after a little nap. Then four Wolves and Fox, Coyote's friend, come and take the salmon. They took grease and rub it on his hands and mouth. They take a burned stick and burn around his nose and eyes. They go up to a hill there. Then they eat his salmon and watch the Coyote.

The Coyote wakes up. He thinks he must have eaten the salmon. There is grease on his hands and mouth. But he is still hungry! He hears laughter and looks up there to see the four Wolves laughing. Then he knows what has happened and runs after the Wolves.

Then the Coyote tires and turns back. He is thirsty. He bends over to take a drink from the stream there. But he sees a very frightful thing and runs off. Then he consults his powers, he says, "When I am thirsty I see a frightful thing in the stream there. Get it out." They say, "It is your own face. The Wolves have done this. You can find the Wolves there."

The Wolves are at the lake swimming for eggs. Then they roast and eat them. The Coyote finds them asleep. Their eggs are baking. Then he breaks one egg over the face, hands, and body of Fox here. Then he defecates and replaces the eggs with his excrement. The Coyote takes the other eggs up to a hill. Then he eats them and watches below there.

Then the Wolves wake up. They find only the excrement baking and know Coyote must have done this. They run after the Coyote. Because the Fox is the fastest, he catches up with him. Coyote asks his friend, Fox, "Instead of smearing the eggs all over yourself, why didn't you eat the eggs? Why were you baking your own dung as food? Why did you turn against me?" Fox says, "I was just going along with the Wolves." Then the Coyote and the Fox go on together. Then Fox leaves.

Then Coyote goes to the salmon. Then he takes the salmon to the rivers in Nez Perce and Colville country there. Drops them off. When he goes to the Schitsu'umsh, he says, "I want a wife." Coyote is refused. Then he goes to Lake Coeur d'Alene there, and St. Joe River and Liberty Lake there. Again the Coyote asks the Schitsu'umsh for a wife. Each time he is refused.

Then the Coyote shouts to the salmon, "Don't come up river here where the Schitsu'umsh live, but swim there" [to the Nez Perce and Colville].

Then Coyote goes to the Nez Perce. There he gets his wife. Then the people hear a great sound. Where there had been a very large, smooth rock, the Coyote becomes the rock.

Then, the end of the trail.

It is interesting to note that when Coyote seeks to benefit others who are in need, such as by releasing the salmon to feed the people, he generally succeeds. When his actions are directed toward "preparing the world for the coming of the Human Peoples," his deceptions and trickery result in the demise of the Rock Monster or the Gobbler Monster, for instance. But when Coyote is self-serving, as when he desires "a good-looking woman" or "wife," and threatens to withhold salmon from the people if his wishes are not met, his actions typically fail and result in his being duped by his own scheme and made "foolish" (Frey 1995:65–66). His reward is to be "found dead" (Frey 1995:194) or as a "rock." When Coyote chooses not to follow the proper hunting rules and attempts to "take too much," or when he is rude and discourteous to his host (as, for example, with Woodtick), he will likely find himself going without that which he seeks.

Coyote and Woodtick[6]

There is Coyote at his lodge there. He is starving. Then he is lying on his back by the fire. "I wonder what I will have to eat." For many days he has not eaten. Suddenly he smells something. "It must be my blanket burning." He feels around and finds a half a deer foot lying by the fire there. He wonders why it is only a half a foot, why not the whole thing. Then he chews on it and eats it all. Coyote lies down again.

Then the next morning the same thing happens, but this time it is the whole foot there. "Thank you," Coyote says. He chews it all up, even the bones.

Then the next day a whole shoulder lies there. He gets water and cooks it, serves it, and eats it all. He even drinks the broth. Nothing is left. "Thank you, I've had plenty," he says.

Then the next morning he hears something fall. Half of a deer cut from the neck to the tail lies there. This time he cooks half of the piece, thinking to save the other half for tomorrow.

Then the next day he decides to find out where the meat came from.

He pulls a corner of the blanket over his eyes. The other half of the deer falls down there. He looks and sees Woodtick. She says, "Don't look at me." Coyote says, "Oh, it's you who haven't even a neck."

Then she goes away. Coyote uses up the deer. In a few days he is hungry again. Then he lies down like before and listens for Woodtick. He gets up and looks around. There is no sign of her. He remembers where he had seen her before and goes to her house there.

At Woodtick's house a woman sits there. She looks up. Then she puts her head down again. Coyote sits down here. He sees that she is making sacks with grass. After a while she puts her work away. Then she gets meat, cooks it, and serves it. She sets the table for two. Coyote sits there watching. She eats, but does not invite him to eat. When she finishes she takes up her work again. He stays all night.

Then the next morning she again sets the table for two, but eats alone. Then Coyote gets up, takes meat, cooks it, and eats alone. "You are not a real person, you don't share your food," Coyote says. He eats alone. "I set the table for two, but you didn't come and eat with me," Woodtick says. "Did you say, 'Come eat?' No, you said nothing," Coyote says. "Did I not take pity on you a few days ago? I fed you, but you didn't leave me alone, so I left. I wanted you for my husband, but you called me names, so I left," Woodtick says. "Well, I came here looking for you," says Coyote. "All right. You may stay," says Woodtick.

Then Woodtick says, "We'll have some fresh meat to eat. You go into that corner and sit still." She called, "Deer come!" Soon they heard, "*xumuumumu*" [the sound of deer running on the snow]. They galloped into the house. Then Woodtick takes the tongs and pierces a hole in the ear of one and then another. [Note that she takes just two deer.] The rest run out. She says, "Skin and butcher it." They have fresh meat to eat.

Then the same thing happens again.

Then Coyote thinks, "I'll kill Woodtick. Then I'll be the one who calls in the deer." He takes this stick and clubs her over the head. He lies in a corner and covers her with a blanket.

After a time he thinks he would like some fresh meat. Then he calls the deer. Then they come in. He chooses the largest. As he pulls on its ear to try to pierce it with the tongs, he pierces his own ear. "*Anininin*, I punched myself." Then the deer goes out, but there is meat. When Coyote goes out to get water, Woodtick's spirit says, "Run away, deer! Coyote has smoked eyes. Run away!" [speaking in Spokane to the deer meat]. It keeps repeating this in a voice which becomes weaker and weaker.

Then the dried meat hanging on a rock above the fire falls down here. Coyote hangs it up again. Then it keeps falling. Then Coyote hangs it up. It becomes deer and runs out, saying, "*xwau xwau.*"

Coyote stuffs some of the meat in his quiver. Then the deer busts it and runs out. Soon it is all gone. Woodtick told the deer to run away.

Only that which Coyote is cooking is left. Then when it comes to a boil it turns into a deer and runs out.

Then there is nothing but bones tied up in a sack. Coyote thinks, "I'll cook them and make some soup. I can drink that." Then as soon as it boils the bones becomes deer and runs out. Then Coyote throws Woodtick out. "It's your fault the meat is gone."

Then, the end of the trail.

In the words of Lawrence Aripa, let us now "listen" to three of his favorite Coyote stories. In the first two, Coyote, "being Coyote, being happy," uses his particular skills— "teasing" and "calling names"—to overcome the Rock Monster and then the Gobbler Monster, thus helping to prepare the world for the coming of Human Peoples. In the second of these first two stories, we have an account of Coyote creating the Human Peoples. In the third story we glimpse Coyote's less noble side, the "mischievous, crazy" Coyote.

As each text is based upon a verbatim transcription of either an audio- or videotaped recording, and on my own participation in the telling, as part of the audience, I have thus been able to convey some of the oral nuances in the act of storytelling. To better emphasize the dramatic rhythm and pacing in Lawrence's storytelling, I have formatted each text in a poetic style, with verse demarcations. Lawrence's patterns of intonation and stress (voiced inflection of morphemes), evident in the oscillations of his voice, are marked by italicizing the appropriate words. Pauses are marked by commas and periods, and, within verses, by a series of dot ellipses. Commas indicate brief pauses, periods mark longer pauses, and dot ellipses note pauses from a half-second to up to two seconds. Lawrence uses these patterns of intonation and pauses very deliberately to add dramatic effect. Some of Lawrence's hand and facial gesturings, and, in the second story, some audience responses, are also noted in accompanying brackets. The second story, "Coyote and the Gobbler Monster," was told before a live, primarily white audience of some fifty individuals. The audience for the other two stories consisted of four Indians and three whites.

While these renderings are certainly only approximations of Lawrence Aripa's storytelling, in formatting the texts in this fashion it is hoped that

his voice will continue to be heard and his story listeners made participants
with Coyote and the First Peoples in the unfolding landscape. This formatting style is based upon a form I had previously developed in collaboration with Lawrence and incorporated in our book, *Stories That Make the
World: Oral Literature of the Indian Peoples of the Inland Northwest As Told
by Lawrence Aripa, Tom Yellowtail and Other Elders* (Frey 1995). Additional
comments on the oral dimensions and techniques of the storytelling will
be addressed in the chapter "Sharing the Gifts."

Coyote and the Rock Monster[7]

One time . . . there was a *Rock* . . . that was a great . . . big. . . round Rock
that . . . all of a sudden went *crazy*,
   went *wild* [slow, deliberate pace].
He decided he was going to . . . *smash everything* in his . . . path . . .So he
started to *roll* [pace picks up]
   and as he rolled [motioning with his hands],
     he's wrecked everything in front of him.
       He knocked down trees.
         He made new . . . creek beds.
          He just went *wild*.
           He was just going in *all* directions.
And so . . . he started out in the country . . . towards Yakama, [pointing to
the west],
   in that direction,
     and that's why a lot of those lands out there don't have any trees,
       because . . . the Rock Monster had knocked them all down.
He would roll,
   roll [motioning with his hands]
     and he would take everything with him,
       knock everything over.
And he was ruining the habitat for the . . . Animals.
But they couldn't stop him,
   and he was just getting *worse*.
And so they all . . . all got together and they said,
   "We have to *do* something.
     That Rock is just going to *ruin us*.
       So we have to do *something* to *stop* him."
So they thought for a while and they said,

"*Well*, . . . the Coyote has *powers*.

 Maybe he can stop him.

  He's *crazy*.

   He's *mischievous*.

    But, . . . still at times he can do *good things*.

   Let's call the Coyote."

So they went out to the Coyote and there they found him . . . as usual,

 playing around,

  having fun,

   jumping,

    yelling,

     being Coyote,

      being *happy*.

And they told him what happened and they said,

 "Now we want you to stop that *Rock*."

And the Coyote says,

 "*How* am I going to *do that?*"

And they said,

 "*Well*, . . . you have the *power*,

  you can do it."

And so the Coyote goes over to where the Rock is.

 The Rock is going around in circles flattening the whole country [motions with hands].

 He's just going crazy.

And so the Coyote looks at him and gets in front of him,

 and he *yells*,

  and *shakes his hands* [motions with both hands],

   and he gets the attention of the Rock.

    He calls him all kinds of dirty names and gets the Rock mad.

    And the Rock goes after him.

And he knows that he can run faster than the Rock can roll.

He takes off and . . . the Rock is right behind him.

 And he knocks over all kinds of . . . trees and *everything* [motions with left hand].

And the Coyote is just running as fast as he can right in front of him.

And then finally the Coyote stopped and he says,

 "I have to do something,

  I have to . . . get rid of him somehow.

How can you *kill* a *Rock?*
A Rock is *hard.*"
And so . . . he says,
"Well, I just have to keep going."
So he'd *run*
and *jump*
and he'd make *fun of the Rock,*
and gets him *mad*
and he'd chase him
and they went *all* over the country.
And that's why you see these bare spots . . . all along the countryside.
And that's where the Coyote *ran*
and that's where the Rock *knocked down* all the trees
and all the vegetation
and *everything* [motions with his left hand].
And so . . . he came back to this part of the country [motions with his left hand],
and he would *jump* from mountain to mountain,
and that's why a lot of these mountains you see here like Plummer Butte . . . have
no trees on the top [points toward butte].
That's where the Coyote *jumped* [motions with left hand]
and the Rock was right behind him
and he *took down* the trees.
The Coyote *jumped* to another mountain [motions with hands]
and he just went in circles
and he just went all over
and the Rock was right behind him.
He says,
"*I've got to do something,*
I have to *do something* to stop that Rock,
to *kill him.*"
And he says,
"O-o-o-h, I know what to do."
He says,
"I'll . . . take him to the lake
and drown him,
he'll go into the lake

and he can't get out."
So he starts looking,
    looking,
        "How can I get him to the lake?"
So he starts through the woods.
And at that time of the year the *berries* and
    all of the vegetation is ripe.
So as the Rock *rolls* [motions with his hands]
    he is running over *huckleberries*
        and the Rock *turns blue*.
And he just keeps on a going
    and the Coyote keeps going.
        They just *go*
           and *go*
           and *go*.
And finally the Coyote says,
    "I know where there is a ledge . . . over by the lake."
He says,
    "I'll run over to this ledge [points with his left hand]
        and jump down
           and I'll hide,
                and the Rock will keep right on a going [motions with hands]
                  and he will hit the lake
                      and he will drown.
                          He will be down there where he can't get out."
So he goes around and he again teases the Rock
    and *calls* him names
        gets him *mad*.
And the Rock doesn't even pay attention to where he's a going.
    He just wants to run over the Coyote.
So the Coyote runs
    and he gets over to the lake,
        and then he gets close
           and then he remembers that particular place.
He runs and he jumps over the cliff [motions with hands]
    and he stops right below [motions with left hand].
And the Rock is coming . . . just as fast
    and he has picked up *huckleberries*,

serviceberries,
    all kinds of *bushes* that he had run over.
He rolled right over Coyote and he rolled right into the lake.
    He fell off the bank [motions with hands]
        and *splash!*
            He made a big splash into the lake,
                and then he settled down to the bottom.
And all the juices from the huckleberries
    and the serviceberries,
        they *all came* off the Rock,
            and that's why . . . Benewah Lake and Coeur d'Alene Lake are *blue*
            [big smile on his face].

(Transcribed from a videotaped recording made in April 1993.)

Coyote and the Gobbler Monster[8]

And . . . so . . . one day Coyote . . . is enjoying himself [slow, deliberate pace].
He is going along the prairie . . . having a lot of fun,
    enjoying life,
        enjoying the Sun,
            enjoying the warmth,
                and just being a good, good Coyote.
And as he ran along . . . singing,
    "*Hey he yaa, hey he yaa!*"
        He is *happy.*
        He is sitting on top of the world.
And all of a sudden he comes to a village.
    And the village is . . . *all* empty.
        There are empty tipis,
            only poles around there.
            All the fires are gone,
                there are no people.
And so he starts to worry.
So he looks around and then he sees Mr. Fox . . .
And he says,
    "Mr. Fox, what . . . is going on?
        Why aren't there any people?

Why can't we see people?
They are all gone."
Mr. Fox says,
"Well, . . . it is because . . . they have been . . . eaten up!"
And the Coyote says,
"*Who would* do such a thing . . . ?"
And Mr. Fox says,
"It is . . . the Gobbler Monster!"
"*Gobbler Monster?*
Now who is the Gobbler Monster?"
And Mr. Fox says,
"He is something that is bad.
And he *eats* everything in his way.
He *gobbles* up everything.
So he's a Gobbler Monster.
And he never stops.
He never fills up.
He just keeps eating and eating."
And the Coyote says,
"Alright, I will get him.
I will take care of him" [in a slow, confident voice].
And so he looks around,
and it doesn't take long
and he runs across the Gobbler Monster.
And so he *intimidates* him.
He goes over
and calls him names,
and *yells* at him
and *waves*
and gets the Monster *mad* at him.
And then the Monster . . . runs after him
and *gobbles* him up.
And he goes into the mouth of the Monster.
And then he gets inside.
And there are the people.
There are all the people,
and there is everything.
And so he says,
"I've gotta get *out* of here!"

And then . . . he decides,
 "Wait, . . . this is the way to *kill* the Monster."
So he cuts out the heart.
 And the Monster dies.
And there's the Monster.
And Coyote looks around,
 and he says,
  "What will I do with it . . . ?
   A-a-h, from this Monster I will . . . create people."
So he takes . . . the leg,
 and he cuts out the leg . . . of the Monster,
  and he takes and *heaves it* as hard
   and as far as he can [voiced as if throwing something].
And the leg goes
 and goes.
  And it lands in Montana.
   And there comes the Blackfeet,
    the Crows.
     And *because* of that . . . they are tall,
      they have *lo-o-ng* legs.
       All of the people in Montana are now tall
       [laughter from audience].
And so he took the stomach,
 and he threw it,
  and it landed.
   And that is where we got the Gros Ventre.
    They all have large bellies [laughter from audience].
And then he took the hair,
 and he throws it,
  and it lands among the Nez Perce.
   And that's why you see them,
    they have long, . . .
     shiny, . . .
      beautiful hair.
       And they are very vain! [laughter from audience].
And so he distributes . . . all the parts.
 He throws them and he gets rid of all of them.
  And every time a part lands another tribe is created.
And so he takes the heart

and he throws the heart,
    and of course . . . naturally . . . here is where the Coeur d'Alenes come
    from [laughter from storyteller and audience].
        And so the Coeur d'Alenes have *real*, . . . *good* hearts.
And so one of the people says,
    "Coyote, . . . you left somebody out!"
And he says,
    "Who?"
And he says,
    "Well you have to get another tribe."
He says,
    "I have no more parts left."
So he takes his knife
    and he puts it on the grass
        and he just wipes the blood onto the grass.
            And he *grabs* a clump of grass
                and *throws* it.
                    And that's where the Spokanes came from.
                    They are poor![9] [laughter from audience].
(Transcribed from an audiotaped recording before a live audience in April
1991.)

Coyote and the Green Spot[10]

Coyote was going up the St. Joe River.
    He was enjoying himself.
It was *warm*,
    the weather was warm,
        he felt good.
He had no ailments,
    nothing was wrong with him.
        And he was in a very good mood.
He was going up the bank of the river,
    the St. Joe River,
        and he was *yelling*,
            and *shouting*,
                and singing,
                    and *happy*.

Because he was free,
  he was alone,
    nobody to bother him,
      and he felt real good,
        "*Yeh, yeh, yeh, yeh, yeh, yeh, yeh.*"
He was *running*,
  jumping,
    and having a lot of fun, . . .
      all by himself.
And as he went up the river,
  shouting
    and having fun,
      "*Yeh, yeh, yeh, yepy, yepy, yepy, yep, yep*" [jumping motion
      with left hand moving from left to right].
He was going along,
  and all of a sudden he stopped. . . .
He looked across the river,
  and high up on the mountains, . . .
    was an open spot [right hand and arm extended and raised, pointing
    to the right],
      and it was *green* . . . .
The sun was shining on it [hand raised in that direction],
  and he looked
    and he says,
      "That is pretty,
        that is *beautiful* . . . .
          I bet there are a lot of mice.
            I bet there are a lot of other Coyotes to play with.
              I bet you that there are a lot of things there that
              are really . . . good.
                I've *got to* get to that green spot!" [in a firm, deliber-
                ate voice].
So he runs . . . toward the spot,
  and all of a sudden he stops [right hand raised, palm out].
And there's the river . . . going by . . . [left hand motions, slowly moving
across front of speaker, in a slow, deliberate voice].
  The river is *swift* [pace picks up],
    and the river is *wide*.

And he looks, . . .

   and he . . . remembered, . . .

      he never learned to swim.

So he thought for a while,

   "How can I get across that river? [right-hand index finger quickly raised and lowered].

      I've got to get to that green spot!" [finger raised again].

So he goes, . . .

   running up and down the river,

      and all of a sudden . . . here comes Old Lady Mole, *Puhe-lee-ah-ha*. . . .

      [Mrs. Mole is often referred to as Coyote's wife.]

"Coyote, . . . " she says,

   "I know you. . . .

      You have that mischievous look on your face.

         I know you are up to something bad. . . .

            Tell me,

               what are you doing?"

And he says,

   "Don't bother me Old Lady,

      I'm *having* fun.

         I'm *enjoying* myself.

            Now I want to get across the river,

               and get up to that beautiful green spot up there" [again motions with left hand, to the river, and then with left hand, up to the spot].

So she looks and she says,

   "Well, . . .

      you should have learned to swim . . . when you were young.

         Now you can't get across [shaking his head as if saying no]

            unless you go downriver about six or seven miles,

               then you can wade across.

                  But otherwise, . . .

                     you can't make it!" [shaking his head].

And Coyote says,

   "*Oh, yes,*

      I'm going to make it, . . .

         somehow.

            I've *got* to get across that river [pointing his left hand across the river].

I'm going to do it *here*!"
And Old Lady Mole says,
    "No [shaking his head], no
        oh no you can't, . . .
            and you're going to get into trouble if you *try*."
He says,
    "Oh, Old Lady,
        you don't know *what* you're talking about."
He says,
    "I can get across."
So he says,
    "Just leave me alone" [hand motions].
So he starts running up the bank of the river again.
He was happy.
    Looking and looking.
When all of a sudden, . . .
    he hears something way off in the distance,
        and he listens. . . .
And then . . . all of a sudden he realizes,
    "That's a *Human* voice!
        That is not an Animal,
            that is a Human!"
So he says,
    "I have to listen,
        see what it is saying."
Then all of a sudden . . . from way in a distance . . . he can hear, . . .
    a boy singing [slow, deliberate voice, left hand motions off to distance],
        "*Shush taways talee, chacha taways talee,*
            Shush taways talee, chacha taways talee."
He says,
    "What does that mean?"
He thinks about it,
    "*Shush taways talee,* . . .
        chacha taways talee, . . .
            Go apart logs, . . .
                come together logs" [motioning with both hands, first apart, then
                together].
"What does it mean?"
So he goes to that bank

and he gets close,
and he can hear the voice, . . .
  coming loud [left hand points away]
    and clear across the water [left hand points away].
He pushes . . . the brush aside [hands move apart]
  and he looks out onto the river [leans forward].
And then in the middle of the river,
  is a little boy, . . .
    standing on two logs.
And he says,
  "*Shush taways talee.*"
    And the logs go apart [hands move apart].
      "*Chacha taways talee.*"
        And the logs come back together [hands move together].
          "*Shush taways talee, chacha taways talee.*"
And the Coyote looks and he says,
  "Gosh, . . .
    that is really something."
He says,
  "Now, . . .
    I wish I could do that,
      those are *magic* logs.
        I wonder how I can get them?"
He says,
  "I have to *get* those logs!" [right-hand finger points above].
So he goes back into the brush [right hand motions to back]
  and he starts yelling.
    "*Help!*
     Help!
      I need help!"
He says,
    "I know that the humans . . . always help each other [right-hand finger
    points above]
      and I know he wants to find out what's going on."
So he *screams,*
  and he *hollers,*
    and he *shouts,*
      and he makes *all kinds of noise* like he is in trouble.
        "*Help!*

I need help!"
The little boy is on his logs,
   "*Shush taways talee, chacha taways talee*" [motioning with hands].
     Logs are going back and forth.
All of a sudden he stops.
   "Somebody is in trouble. . . .
     I'd better go
       and see if I can help."
So he turns his logs to the bank [motions with hands]
   and he sings along,
     the logs go along [motions with hands].
       They get to the bank.
He stops,
   and he *runs* up the bank [motions with fingers],
     and he *goes* into the brush [motions with fingers],
       and he's looking for the Coyote.
And the Coyote comes around in the other direction [motions with hands].
   He runs as *fast* as he can.
He *goes*
   and he *jumps* on the logs.
     He *gets* on the logs
       and he *turns* them toward the middle of the river.
         And he looks down [looking down].
           "I wonder if they will work for me?
            They worked for that little boy!"
So he says,
   "*Shush taways talee.*"
     The logs start moving apart [motions with hands].
       "*Chacha taways talee.*"
         They come together [motions with hands].
         "*A-a-ah, this is good!*
          This is fine!"
So then he starts,
   "*Shush taways talee, chacha taways talee* [much faster pace].
     "*Shush taways talee, chacha taways talee.*"
       The logs are going back and forth [motioning with hands],
         and he's moving out to the middle of the river.
And oh boy he is happy,

"*This* is what I want,
　　this is how I will get across to that green spot. . . . "
So he keeps singing.
　He looks down,
　　"*Shush taways talee, chacha taways talee.*"
The logs move back and forth,
　and he is getting out into the deep . . . part of the river.
　　And he is *enjoying* himself.
All of a sudden he gets carried away.
　"This is fun,
　　this is really good!"
So he starts singing faster,
　"*Shush taways talee, chacha taways talee.*
　　"*Shush taways talee, chacha taways talee*" [very fast pace, with hands
　　motioning back and forth].
　　　The logs go back and forth,
　　　　back and forth,
　　　　　and he's going full speed.
He's going out into the middle of the river [points with hands],
　and he's just having fun.
And then he says,
　"*Shush taways talee.*"
　　And his mind snapped [snaps fingers],
　　　and then he couldn't think . . . of the words.
He says,
　"*Shush taways talee,*
　　Shush,
　　　Shush,
　　　　Shush?"
He got all mixed up [hands raised].
　He couldn't figure out the words . . . to bring them back.
So the logs kept moving out,
　and out.
His legs started to stretch.
　His legs went out farther
　　and farther [looks down with outstretched arms].
And he says,
　"What am I going *to do?*

What am I going *to do?*"
And the logs finally go apart,
  and he couldn't remember the words.
    And he falls *in,*
      and he *drowns* . . . [slow, deliberate voice].
        The poor Coyote is dead. . . .
His body goes *down* the river [motions with left hand].
  It floats
    it goes down
      it floats around the bend.
And there's a branch . . . sticking out . . . from the . . . .water [points],
    and it hooks onto the back of his neck
      and stops him.
So there lays the Coyote.
  No more Coyote.
In the meantime Old Lady Mole is going up.
She says,
  "That Coyote!
    He's going to get into *trouble.*
      I've got to catch him.
        I've got to see him.
          I know he's going to do something foolish."
So up and down the river she goes [left hand motions].
And she comes around this corner
  and there's the Coyote [motions with left hand].
    His body is laying in the water [motions with left hand],
      floating along.
So, . . . she goes
  and gets a stick
    and then she gets in there
      and she finally gets his body up onto the bank.
And then she looks up into the sky [looks up].
She says,
  "Oh, Great Animal Spirit, I know you have given powers to others . . .
  to bring people back to life.
    This worthless Coyote,
      he's no good,
        he's mischievous,

he does things that are bad [motions with left hand].
But he's a Coyote, . . .
and we have to have Coyotes on this earth.
Please help me so that I will be able to bring him
back!" [motions with left hand].
So she lays him on the ground.
Then she goes up to the body.
She looks down [looks down]
and she sings.
And she dances around the body [motions with right hand].
And she says,
"I am told,
if I jump over him three times, . . .
he will come to life."
So she goes with her song
and she *goes* around the body.
And then she *jumps* over once . . . [motions with right hand and in a
rapid voice].
She gets over to the other side,
and she turns around.
She says,
"What am I *doing?* . . . .
The Coyote is *no good.*
He always gets into mischief.
He doesn't listen to people [motions with left hand].
When you tell him to do something
he doesn't pay any attention.
He does whatever he wants! . . . "
And then she says,
"Well, . . . guess he's a Coyote.
We need him."
So she *jumps over* him again [motions with left hand].
And again it bothers her [motions with both hands].
"*No,*
no,
I can't do this.
Why do we need a Coyote?"
And she thinks again,

"Well we *do* need a Coyote."
So she finally *jumps over* him [motions with left hand].
She jumps over him a third time.
And the Coyote opens his eyes [looks up]
   and he looks up.
He sees the Old Lady Mole,
   and he stretches his arms,
      "*O-o-o-h. ka-seep-a-tee-chee-eetch* [outstretched arms],
         a long time I have slept."
And she says,
   "*Sleep* nothing!
      You've been *dead*. . . . "
And she says,
   "And I've brought you back to life again.
      Now you can be a Coyote again."
And he looks at her
   and he says,
      "Thank you, . . .
         thank you for bringing me back.
            And I promise I will be a different animal.
               From now on I will be *good*.
             I will do what I am told.
              I will be a good one.
                  I will not be the same kind of person."
And she says,
   "Well that's great,
      that's good.
         Now that you are a different person you will be okay,
            you will get along with anybody."
So he says,
   "I'm *new*,
      I am a new person.
      I'm different.
         You'll see!"
So he takes off again.
And again he runs up and down . . . the river [motions with left hand].
And then all of a sudden he stops,
   "Uh, that green spot [slow, deliberate voice, with a smile on his face],

ah, *that green spot.*
I'm going to get over there."
So again, . . .
he goes back to the river
and then he remembers,
"*I can't swim.*
Old Lady Mole told me that I should not do anything that
I'm not supposed to,
and here I am looking, . . .
here I am looking at that green spot again,
trying to figure a way to get across."
And then he thinks about it,
"*I'm a Coyote,*
I *don't* have to listen to that *old woman.*
The *heck* with her."
So, . . . he starts looking,
"*Where* is that little boy?
Where can I find those magic logs?"
So again, . . .
he goes back to the same old Coyote.
And so, . . .
to this day, . . .
we still have that Coyote,
mischievous, . . .
crazy, . . .
wise at times. . . .
But he is still the Coyote,
and he will always remain the Coyote [a big
smile on Lawrence's face].
(Transcribed from a videotaped recording made in April 1993).

CHIEF CHILD OF THE YELLOW ROOT

In light of Coyote's role among the First Peoples, it is important to appreciate the unique and pivotal role played by another of the First Peoples,
Chief Child of the Yellow Root. The narrative cycle surrounding this character is still remembered by Lawrence Nicodemus, who refers to it today
as the story of "Son of Light" (*Sp'ukhwenichelt*), a "Coeur d'Alene prophet"

who goes "around the lake" (Lake Coeur d'Alene) and "teaches the animals how to behave." Some twenty years earlier, Lawrence Nicodemus had similarly revealed to Gary Palmer: "Long ago, when the names of animals were also the names of people, *Sp'ukhwenichelt* taught every animal how to live" (Palmer, Kinkade, and Turner 1996:21). "When Coyote went to the moon, old man *Sp'ukhwenichelt* traveled around on earth, inspected Coyote's work and set right many things that Coyote had left undone. He was always helpful to mankind" (Palmer, Nicodemus, and Connolly 1987:69). In her own analysis of the narrative text "Chief Child of the Root," Gladys Reichard observed that among the Plateau peoples it is Coyote who is typically acknowledged as the key transformer, with the other First Peoples taking secondary roles (1947:63–68). And while Chief Child of the Yellow Root appears in the oral literature of other tribes—e.g., Thompson, Lillooet, and Sanpoil—references to his specific transformational deeds are not reported, and his eventual demise is only vaguely conveyed.[11] But among the Schitsu'umsh, as Reichard points out, it is Chief Child of the Yellow Root, along with Coyote, who played the central roles as transformers.

The derivation of the term for "Child of the Root" is of interest here. As mentioned previously, Lawrence Nicodemus refers to this culture hero as *Sp'ukhwenichelt*, "Son of Light." Using a phonemic orthography Gladys Reichard recorded Dorothy Nicodemus's employment of the same term, "*Spuxⁿäni'tcält*" (1938:607; 1946:173–201).[12] The first part of the term, *Sp'ukhwenich*, has been interpreted as "sun," the derivation of which is "light," *sp'i'khw* (Nicodemus 1975[1]:252); the ending of the term *elt* (*ält*), means "child" or "offspring," and in this context "son" (Reichard 1938: 607; and personal communication, Raymond Brinkman, August 1997). Hence the name Child (or Son) of the Sun (or Light), used by both Dorothy Nicodemus in 1927 and her grandson Lawrence in 1997.

This literal translation "Son of Light," refers, of course, to a particular plant in the Schitsu'umsh landscape. Throughout her transcriptions and analysis, Reichard identifies this root as "probably hogfennel," "a yellow flower somewhat like a sunflower but smaller" (1947:39, 57). According to Reichard, it "was not eaten by the Coeur d'Alene," but was "baked by the Spokan. The second wife of Dorothy's father was a Spokan who often prepared it. Dorothy tried to eat it but it was too strong for her. She was sorry she could not eat it because it was very nice-looking. When baked it split open and looked like a very ripe apple" (1947:39). What is occassionally identified as "hogfennel" actually refers to another plant, since hogfennel (*Peucedanum officinale* or *palustre*), per se, is not native to North America.

In the Reichard text (1946), Dorothy Nicodemus does refer to the specific root gathered by the boy's mother, and upon which he is raised, as "*spä͏ʷäntc,*" or, as written by Lawrence Nicodemus, "*sp'ekhwench.*" *Sp'ekhwench* is translated by Lawrence Nicodemus as "yellow root" (1975[1]:229). In their discussion of *sp'ekhwench*, Palmer, Kinkade, and Turner (1996:20) identify the root as "probably Desert Parsley" (*Lomatium macrocarpum*), a species related to cous. It produced an edible root, eaten raw or cooked into flat cakes. In addition, it had medicinal applications. "It is a yellow root; mother boiled it and mashed it up, put it on sores before bandaging; it was good for everything; they didn't drink it" (Palmer, Kincade, and Turner 1996:21).

Adding to the mystique, yellow root can also be identified as Indian helle-bore (*Veratrum viride*), a healing root used by the Schitsu'umsh. While this root is medicinal, when improperly consumed, Indian hellebore is poisonous, and can cause death. Thus it seems appropriate that Chief Child of the Yellow Root would be raised on such a powerful healing root, especially if the plant itself was normally toxic when consumed orally. But as Indian hellebore is not an edible food, it is the least likely of our yellow root candidates.

Finally, the root in question could, in fact, be *smukwe'shn*, or what is referred to by the Schitsu'umsh in English as the "sunflower." At least one of my consultants mentioned that the root of the sunflower could be eaten. Belonging to the sunflower family, the yellow-flowering, Jerusalem artichoke (*Helianthus tuberosus*) produces an edible yellowish root (similar in form to a three-to-four-inch ginger root) and is indigenous to the area. Palmer, Kinkade, and Turner also identify *smukwe'shn* as "probably Balsamroot" (*Balsamorhiza sagittata*), which has an edible root and can be used medicinally (1996:19). In either instance, the correspondence between the image of the yellow sunflower and that of the bright light of the sun is intriguing.

Whether "yellow root" refers to desert parsley, Indian hellebore, Jerusalem artichoke, or balsamroot, since Reichard notes that "*Spuxʷäni'tcält*" refers to a "name of a root" (1946: 174) and that the child is raised on this root, I will identify the hero as "Chief Child of the Yellow Root" in the narrative to follow. Prefacing the term *Sp'ukhwenichelt* is the label *ylmikhum* (Nicodemus 1975[2]:104) or, as appearing in Reichard's interlinear transcription, *y:lmi'xum* (1946:173–201), meaning "chief." The significance and usage of chief will become apparent in the narrative.

The story of Chief Child of the Yellow Root critically identifies the Schitsu'umsh with the roots and with the lake. In all his journeys Chief Child of the Yellow Root travels "the whole world" in his canoe made from a "monster fish" he had killed, and those journeys are over the lake and up the rivers of Schitsu'umsh country, "to where the river comes to an end." With Chief Child of the Yellow Root raised on "yellow root" and with his father named "Yellow Root," clearly his identity is associated with both the root foods of the Schitsu'umsh, such as camas, cous, and water potato, as well as the healing roots, such as Indian hellebore. Given Chief Child of the Yellow Root's elevated status, his story reiterates the emphasis the Schitsu'umsh place on the overall importance of the roots and the lake in their lives.

Chief Child of the Yellow Root[13]

There is a lodge where an old woman lives with her daughter who has a baby. Every day the daughter gathers yellow roots. She comes back with a great many of the roots. Then they would eat them. The boy grows tall. Every day she gathers the yellow roots. Then they would eat them. The family eats them. Then the boy grows tall. The mother always goes out alone to gather roots. The boy is with his grandmother. The boy grows tall.

Then he asks, "Where is my father?" "You are pitiful. You have no father." "Why have I no father?" he asks. "He has been dead a long time." "What was his name?" "He had none."

The boy takes a stick. He says, "If you don't tell me who my father was I'll kill you." "Yellow Root was your father," the grandmother says.

Then the boy is sad. Then he lies down and covers himself with his blanket there. All day he lies like that. In the evening his mother comes back and sees him lying as he was. She thinks, "I suppose his grandmother has been telling him tales." She says nothing. [The storyteller makes signs that the daughter is going to club her mother.] After she cooks the roots, she says, "Come, we are going to eat!" The boy pays no attention. Then she and her mother eat. The boy does not join them. Then the next day the same thing happens. He refuses to eat. Then the mother goes out to gather more roots. After she is gone the boy gets up and says to his grandmother, "I am leaving you forever."

Then he goes out. He goes to the edge of the water and sits down there. He sings, "Yes, then *yexiya* Chief Child of the Yellow Root *xeya, xeya.*" He

Coeur d'Alene River, c. 1912 (photograph by Frank Palmer; courtesy Northwest Museum of Arts and Culture and Eastern Washington State Historical Society, acc. no. L84-327.1528)

washes his face, his head, and his entire body. Then he reaches into the water and takes out the throat of a fish monster. He makes a canoe of it, gets into it, and rows away singing his song, "Yes, then *yexiya* Chief Child of the Yellow Root *xeya, xeya.*"

Then he hears someone who says, "Chief Child of the Yellow Root, give me a ride. We'll see the whole world even to where the river comes to an end." "All right, I'll give you a ride." Then the passenger, who is Pestle Boy, jumps up and down in the boat. "You might break the canoe. Here, I'll fix a paddle for you to sit on." He fixes it. Then Pestle Boy jumps up and down. Then Chief Child of the Yellow Root dumps him into the water. "You will no longer eat people. Don't be a man-eater anymore. They will use you for a pestle," Chief Child of the Yellow Root says.

The Chief Child of the Yellow Root goes on paddling around the lake. Suddenly he sees a tree burning there. Someone falls into the fire. He thinks, "That person will die." Then he finds Foolhen feeling for her eyebrows. They are all red and blistered from the fire. "What's the matter?" he says. "Ha uh-um, Chief, . . .I am getting this black moss," she says.[14] "Don't do that anymore. You might die. If you get hungry, fly to the tree there and eat the black moss raw. Don't live in a lodge anymore and don't cook your food," he says. "Thank you, Chief," Foolhen says.

Then the Chief travels on around the lake. He sees a lodge with smoke coming out there. He thinks, "That's where I'll eat." There is a good fire burning in the house, but the people are gone. He sees little Awls hanging all over the walls there. In the middle is a big one, nicely beaded. Then he goes over and takes it down. As he is going out with it all the Awls cry out, "He is taking our chief," and then go after Chief Child of the Yellow Root. They pierce him all over his body. "Don't do that," he says. He hangs the chief back on the wall, goes outside, and sets the lodge afire. The Awls are crying, "*Yar, yar, yar!*" "Don't be man-eaters anymore. You are to be used for making moccasins," Chief Child of the Yellow Root says.

Then the Chief travels on around the lake. He sees something that looks like a lodge there. He goes in. There is a good fire burning, but there are no people around. Then he sees Combs hanging all over the walls. A large one decorated with beads hangs in the center. He thinks, "I'll comb myself with that comb." As he takes the Comb, the other Combs cry out, "He is taking our chief." Then they all come after him and comb him. "Don't do that," he says. He hangs the chief back on the wall, goes outside, and sets the lodge afire. The Combs shriek like scared chickens. "Don't be man-eaters anymore. You are to be used for combing hair," Chief Child of the Yellow Root says.

Then the Chief travels on around the lake. He sees another lodge there. Inside is a fire, but no people. The walls are hung with Bladders. In the middle is a fine-looking large one. "I'll take it for my own use, put kinnikinick in it or my powder," he says. Then he takes it down and all the Bladders cry out, "He is taking our chief." They come down and bump him, and some of the Bladders blow in his face! "Don't do that," he says. He hangs the chief back on the wall again. He goes outside and sets the lodge afire. He hears the bursting of many tight skins. "Don't be man-eaters anymore. Hereafter you'll be used for storing tobacco," Chief Child of the Yellow Root says.

Then the Chief travels on around the lake. He sees another lodge there. A nice fire burns inside, but there are no people. All around the walls hang Lassos. A fine one is in the middle. Then he takes it down, and when he does, all the other Lassos rope him. "It's our chief. Don't do that." Then they tie him up. He puts the chief back and goes outside. He sets the lodge afire. "Don't be man-eaters anymore. When people want food they will use you to trap their game," Chief Child of the Yellow Root says.

Then the Chief travels on around the lake. He sees someone jumping into the water, coming up with clasped hands there. The person runs into the lodge, brings out a bucket, fills it with water, and goes back into the lodge to make a fire. The Chief looks on and sees him wringing the ends of his fingers in the pail. He comes to the person, Fishhawk. "Oh, Chief, . . . you find me humble, I am poor," Fishhawk says. Then he gives the Chief some soup. It is very good. "If it weren't for my fingernails I would have plenty to eat. I guess you saw how I catch fish," Fishhawk says. "Let me see your hands." The Chief makes the nails long. Fishhawk tries them out and comes back happy with a good fish. "Thank you, Chief. Stay and eat with me," he says. "No, I have eaten. You eat by yourself. Then fly. Don't live in lodges anymore. Don't cook your food. Eat it raw. Take only one fish at a time and eat it all," Chief Child of the Yellow Roots says. "Thank you, Chief."

Then the Chief travels on around the lake. He sees many people there. They see him coming too. "He is coming, Chief Child of the Yellow Root," they cry. Two men come forward and carry him in their arms. The chief of the people says, "I have two daughters for you to marry."

It is so crowded that Toad is pushed away and cannot see anything. That always happens to Toad because she is so ugly! She tries again to see, but cannot. "You are so ugly that what is the use of trying to see him," they say. "That might be true," she says.

Then Toad goes out for water. She sprinkled water from the sky. She goes into her own lodge and waits. It rains hard. Everybody goes into their lodges. It is so wet in the lodges that no one can lie down. Then Chief Child of the Yellow Root tips his canoe over and lies under it. Soon it is wet as well. Then he gets up and sees a light far off there. It is Toad's lodge. She has a nice fire and everything is dry and comfortable.

Then Chief Child of the Yellow Root goes to her lodge. "Why are you dry, my grandmother?" "Now I see you close up, even if I am ugly," she says. "Why are you dry, my grandmother?" "I am not your mother's mother." "Are you my father's mother?" "No." "Are you my sister?" "No." "Are you my daughter?" "No." He gets up and asks one last time, "Are you my wife?" "I am your wife."

Then Toad jumps up and lands above the Chief's nose, right between his eyes. He tries to pull her off, but cannot. The skin stretches. "Come, get this toad off me," he says. They try to cut off the toad, but with no luck. Toad stays on Chief Child of the Yellow Root.

Then Coyote calls all the people together. A great council is held. Coyote says, "We ought to have a sun during the day and a moon at night. I'll be the Moon." Robin says, "I'll be the Sun."

When the Sun comes up it is too hot. The people have to spend their time swimming. That's all they can do. When the Moon comes up, Coyote spies on all the people. He sees everything the people do at night and announces it to everyone.

Then the Chief says, "The Sun is too hot and the Moon, Coyote, is utterly no good!" They pull down Robin and Coyote from the sky and throw them away.

Then Helldiver's child, who has only one eye, says, "I'll be a good Sun to you. I don't see so well. I will not be too bright, not too hot." "All right then," they say.

Then Child of the Yellow Root says, "I'll be the Moon to you. I'll go far off there so you can't very well see this toad that's on my face!"

Then, the end of the trail.

Receiving the Gifts

The First Fruits

I think one of the most powerful things that I remember most graphically was when we got there, after we unloaded everything, and then my dad would disappear, and then nothing would happen. Nobody would unpack nothing. And pretty soon, he'd come back, and he'd have in his hands, maybe two hands, bushes, huckleberry bushes. He'd come back, and he would be singing, and then we'd sit there and he'd take those huckleberry bushes and rub them all over my brother and I, and dust us off, if you will, I guess is the best terminology to use, of those bushes. And then the berries on there, he'd hand them to my mother, and she would pick those berries off. She'd put them in a cup, and she would eat them herself. We never got to eat them. We would stand there and watch as my mother would eat them, and he would talk in Indian, and he would talk about reproducing human beings and the power of mothers, the power and the spirit of the mothers being like Mother Earth, needing nourishment. So she would take the first berries. It was the women in our family. When my grandmother was alive, it was my grandmother that took the berries and ate, while everybody sat there in the camp and watched her. (From an interview on June 4, 1996.)

A WORLD PREPARED

The First Peoples, such as Crane and Coyote, and Chief Child of the Yellow Root, brought forth and prepared the landscape. In their actions, the terrain of the Schitsu'umsh landscape was defined. From Tekoa Mountain to Mount Spokane, from the waterfalls along Spokane River at Spokane Falls and Post Falls to the various rivers and creeks draining into the lake, to Lake Coeur d'Alene itself, the landscape of the Schitsu'umsh world was given form. This transformation of the landscape is well illustrated in the example of Coyote's adventure with the Rock Monster. It became a landscape no longer plagued by "man-eaters" but inhabited by a multitude of Animal Peoples and endowed with "gifts." Among those who are often called the "Animal People," Deer would now await the prayers of a hunter and, in turn, might offer itself to feed a family. Wolf or some other Animal or Bird would await the suffering of a lone vision quester and, in turn, might grant a *suumęsh* song and make itself visible again during a Jump Dance. And Eagle would now inspire a song, a dance movement, or perhaps the regalia of a dancer during a Powwow. In their small ways, Rabbit and Jackrabbit have provided pitch, bitterroot, and camas on Tekoa Mountain, as well as something else vital to the Human Peoples: an important teaching.

Among the various gifts imbued within the landscape were venison, camas, water potato, huckleberries, and other foods that nourish the body, certain plants and roots that heal the afflicted, teachings that instruct the youth into maturity and reinvigorate the elders, and *suumęsh* songs that transform what it means to be Human.

In those teachings the Human Peoples were provided with knowledge essential for hunting deer and digging camas, and indispensable for the Jump Dance, Sweat House, and Memorial Giveaway. In those teachings the landscape was itself morally and ethically endowed. The landscape was rendered as "a book," a text whose ridges and ravines vividly tell the stories of kinship and sharing, of respect and equality. And when conveyed in the oral traditions and retold aloud, and when embedded in song and sung aloud by the Human Peoples, the teachings and *suumęsh* are reinvested back into the landscape, continuing to help contour and animate the world of the Schitsu'umsh. The First Peoples have thus given the Human Peoples the means to communicate properly with, relate to, and help perpetuate all the Peoples of the landscape.

The discussion in this chapter will focus on identifying the many gifts that continue to hold meaning or are remembered to have been significant by those I have interviewed and observed interacting with their landscape. To better appreciate the meaning of the act of receiving such gifts, the contextual relationships entered into between the First Peoples, Animal Peoples and the Human Peoples will also be considered. This relationship is marked by a particular land-use pattern, revolving around the Schitsu'umsh definitions of family, home territories, and partnership. The nature of communications between these Peoples, in the form of prayer and song, will also be considered. And finally, many of the specific methods used in the

Digging camas with the pitse', June 1996   *Camas bulb*

gathering, hunting, and receiving, as well as in the preparing of these gifts, will also be discussed.

It's Probably Better. . .

My father was in the hospital. Theresa Camel, . . . she brought some camas to my dad when he was in the hospital. She opened it. My dad had a good sense of smell but he couldn't see. He started eating it. . . . I was there at the time. He started eating it and the nurse came in. She wanted to grab it and take it away from my dad. She said, "He can't have that. It's not on his diet." My dad told that nurse, "I've been eating this stuff for over ninety

Flowering camas

years!" He said, "It hasn't killed me yet!" The doctor happened to come in. Theresa told the doctor. The doctor said, "He can have all that he wants. It's probably better than what we're feeding him now" [followed by a laugh]. (From an interview conducted on May 20, 1996.)

GATHERING

Among the plant gifts used as foods are the roots of the "black root," camas, bitterroot, cous, wild carrots, "wild onions," and the "water potato," the stems and perhaps roots of the "sunflower," the stems of "Indian celery," the lichen called "black moss," the berries from the chokecherry, elderberry, huckleberry, Oregon grape, serviceberry, soapberry (also known as "foam berry" or "Indian ice cream"), thimbleberry, and "thornberry" (black hawthorn).[1] Camas and bitterroot both continue to be served at some family gatherings, birthdays, Easter and Christmas, or just "when the grandmother would like some." At the passing of a relative, a little camas and bitterroot might be placed in a pouch to accompany and nourish the deceased on his journey to the Creator.

The Bitterroot

That's the first thing we dig in the springtime. Right after Easter we go out, go out down toward Spangle [Washington], in through there, up that way [pointing to the west]. Until then, that way. You know what bitterroots are? It's bitter. But they're good for you, and they've got pretty, little flowers, they're right next to the ground. And you've got to dig them just certain times of the year. . . . After they bloom a while, you can't skin it, and their skin tightens up. When you skin them, they're just white. And you have the little heart. They have a little heart right where their flower is, right in there, they have a little heart. It's the only root that I know has a little heart, it's bitterroots.

You dig [them the same as you dig] your camas, the same thing, *pitse'* [a digging stick]. You dig them out and skin them. When you get home, you will wash them and then put them out in the sun to dry. After they're dry, you just put them in the flower sack or in a can and they're good for a long time. Then you cook it, when you need a little bit of it, and boil it. Some put the drippings or whatever you want to put in there, to season it, and then you eat it with sugar, yeah. Some don't like it, but we all like bitterroots.

They're hard to pick [followed by laughter]. A lot of work, yeah. You've got to skin them and clean them, and it takes quite a while to get a bunch. And we go from there. A long time ago, we'd go on the wagon after Easter. We'd pack up and put our camp wherever we wanted to. You can't do that now. You can't put your camp just anywhere. They'll come chase you away [followed by laughter]. Now we have cars. We park our car and go in the fields. It's rocky where they're at, on the other side of Davenport, . . . in those fields, it's rocky. That's where you see the bitterroots. They've got pretty, little red flowers, like little roses. In the rocky places, where you dig. Then we'd go out there and spend maybe a week digging around until we get enough, because you can just wash and put them out in the sun, and let the sun dry them.

We'd pray all the time, especially Grandma, who prayed day, morning, and night. They'd pray for whatever they're going to pick. (From an interview conducted on February 11, 1998.)

What the Schitsu'umsh call *sqigwts*, or "water potato," is called "wapato" (or arrowleaf) by other lower Columbia River peoples. The water potato is the large root of a white-flowering, arrow-leafed plant. It grows in the soft mud under the water, near the shoreline, often where creeks and rivers flow into the lake. There are numerous locations along the shores of both Coeur d'Alene and Hayden lakes where the root was found. According to Schitsu'umsh elders, among the tribes of the immediate region the use and knowledge of the water potato is unique to their own people. The Yakama and Spokane, for example, apparently did not use it. The traditional method of collecting the root was by canoe or boat, paddling up to the plants, and then pulling them out by hand or with a forked stick. If the lake's water level was low, the water potato could be dug with a shovel in the soft mud.

Every fall, during the latter part of October and first part of November, several families have continued to harvest the water potato. The Tribal Council has designated the fourth Friday of October as Water Potato Day, an official tribal holiday. Often students from the Tribal School at DeSmet are taken to the lake for the experience of digging. Most elders coordinating the activity would offer a prayer prior to the gathering, asking "permission" to dig the bulbs, for good fortune, and for blessing to come to those who share in the feast.

The water potato is prepared "like a regular potato," by baking or boiling. "Keep the tails (the narrow segment of the root) on them; that's where all the favor is." A celebration and feast then follows, in which the prepared water potato and other foods are shared with all in attendance. Powwows celebrating the water potato have been held each fall over the last five years. Some families have also been informally celebrating the fall harvest of the water potato every year since before the reservation was established.

Both Felix and Lawrence Aripa remembered that the water potato was distributed and eaten during sporting events. During a fall high school

John Abraham digging water potatoes among the cattails, October 1997

Cleaning the water potato in the lake, October 1997

football game in 1939, for example, "sacks full" of cooked water potatoes were distributed to those in attendance. "One guy who'd never eaten any liked them so much that he ate almost half a sack" [followed by a big laugh].

Digging Camas

We'd gotten off the main highway onto the gravel road that ran along-side and occasionally intersected Sheep Creek. The elder periodically stopped her car, got out, and surveyed the adjacent fields and wooded areas. A moment later we'd continue our drive. Finally she found what she was looking for. We parked our cars and walked the short distance from the road, each of us with our own *pitse'* in hand, the traditional dig-ging tool. Only after pointing them out were the tall, blue-flowering plants distinct and seemingly everywhere along the narrow stretch of earth between the gravel road and the farmer's plowed field. The three of us gathered around the first camas we came upon. Gently placing the tip of a *pitse'* close to the base of the tall, flowering stalk, the sharped spiked tool was pushed down a foot or so into the moist earth. She then moved it about carefully, loosening the earth's grip. Revealed was a small, inch-and-a-half, white bulb. With care, the camas was pulled out and placed in a plastic bucket, the first of many the next three hours would provide. And as if in one motion, the tobacco from a cigarette was placed in the earth from which the bulb had come. In preference to tobacco, *qhǝsqhs*, a healing root, might have been offered as a gift of thanks. But the elder had none today. We were all standing silent. A prayer was then said, ask-ing permission to gather the camas, and thanking the Creator, the Father, for this gift and the nourishment it would provide. The camas gathered over the next few days and weeks would be prepared and served during this family's winter Jump Dance. Before going on to the adjacent plant, the flowering stalk of this bulb was placed back in the earth, beside the tobacco, and covered over. Having made this tobacco offering and prayer with the first camas dug, the act would not need to be repeated during the rest of the day's gathering.

As we were digging, a pickup truck pulled up alongside us and a local farmer asked what we were up to. He had always wondered about the name of that "blue weed."

After the narrow strip of land provided us with all the camas it could, we were on the gravel road again. The next sites were located in wooded and drier locations, with the camas not nearly as plentiful and the bulbs much smaller by comparison. Most of the good camas fields have now been taken over by wheat and barley cultivation. (From participant observations made on June 6, 1996, near Sheep Creek.)

During Gladys Reichard's research in 1927 and 1929, she observed that "several old women still gathered the old foods and baked them for a winter treat." The following description of camas baking, as conducted by Susan Antelope, was provided by Reichard.

Camas Baking

Susan Antelope who was over eighty was famous for her camas. She spent at least three weeks digging camas and wild onions and gathering the black moss (Alectoria) which are much prized. When she was finished she spread them neatly on the floor of the barn to dry and they were a lovely sight, the camas a silvery white and the onions a purplish pink.

After these things had been gathered Mrs. Antelope spent several days collecting big chunks of wood for her fire and pine bark which was used for the covering next to the last layer of earth. When she was nearly ready to construct her oven, she travelled a long distance to a place where a particular broad fleshy leaf was found. This leaf gives the final excellent quality to the cooked camas. Everything was now ready for the building of the structure. The entire family, mother, daughter and two grandsons, worked for three days from early morning (about sunrise) until dark cleaning, that is, skinning, the camas and onions. After all were cleaned they were packed in burlap sacks, each kind by itself.

A pit about three feet deep was dug in which a fire was built and kept very hot for several hours in order to heat the rocks which had been placed on the bottom of the pit. Then the work of constructing the oven was begun. Mrs. Antelope's grandson helped her with this part of the work. The coals were left in the pit and the wood embers were shovelled out. Then the workers arranged grass on top of the coals, on the layer of grass the sacks full of food, then the large fleshy leaves. The steam emitted from the whole thing when these leaves were put on smelt slightly sweet and very savory. Next came the bark and finally, earth covered the entire structure. The burning brands were now placed against a circular fortification of wood chunks and the fire was kept burning energetically. On the day chosen for the baking there was a strong wind and nice judgment was required to keep the fire sufficiently active to bake and at the same time to control the blaze so it would not become dangerously hot. The result was an error on the side of caution and Mrs. Antelope was much disappointed, two days later, upon cautiously sampling her camas to find it was not done. They thereupon gathered old fence rails and other fuel and in half a day more she was satisfied. . . .

The word went out when Mrs. Antelope's camas was finished. She made a special point of sending some to her many friends. Others were especially invited to the house. They all get hungry for the old food and Mrs. Antelope had the reputation of making the best. The "best" taste is due to the use of the fleshy leaves. Most of the old women, even Susan's best friend who helped her dig the roots, sprinkled sugar over their camas while baking it. It improves the taste but is not "quite as good" as that secured by steaming with the leaves. (Reichard 1947:38–39)

Among the healing gifts that continue to be used are lovage—*qhasqhs* (referred to by Teit as "*xasxas*" [1930:197] and pronounced *khäs-khəs*, with the *kh* a guttural, uvular sound), wild rosebush, mint, "cub ears" (likely wintergreen), chokecherry bark, the needles from the western red cedar and "a lone tree on St. Joe Baldy, only found there," the red "pitch gum" from ponderosa pine, and "yellow root" (Indian hellebore). Known by other terms throughout the Plateau, *qhasqhs* is a powerful "medicine root" used for a variety of purposes. "Cub ears" resembles the ears of a "bear cub" and ranges in size from a "quarter to a silver dollar." Like many other healing plants, such as *qhasqhs* and mint, cub ears is found in well-watered bogs and springs, as well as in shaded forest sections along mountain creeks and rivers.

Of the varieties of pine pitch, clear, white, or pinkish, the latter is considered the most medicinal. The needles from the "lone tree" and cedar are used to "smudge" the interior of a house or a Sweat House, spiritually cleansing those within. Found in the mountain meadows, "yellow root" is used for a variety of medicinal, typically external, applications, such as healing sores or skin rashes. The alkaloids of Indian hellebore can even slow the heartbeat and lower blood pressure. But yellow root must be administered properly and in the right dosages, as an external salve or poultice, or in a "tea" or a "bath," for instance. Excessive consumption of either the roots or the new shoots can be toxic and can lead to death. As with the other healing roots and plants, prayer would likely accompany the gathering, application, and use of yellow root.

It's Medicine

We were driving to the camp near Rosalia. The riders would be arriving later that afternoon and we needed to get the Sweat House ready in time for them. We talked about many things. Eventually the conversation moved onto the topic of "healing plants," and to one particular "root." Though I was unfamiliar with it at the time, the root is widely used. Singers at Powwows often use it to help their stamina and throats. Before a stick game, the "bones" used in the event are washed in a "tea" made from the root. This very morning before the riders began their all-day ride, they were given some of the root, "for strength." "It gets rid of bad feelings and touches your heart." And then he pulled a small piece of the root out of his shirt pocket and handed it to me. I thanked him, though not quite sure what I should do with it.

His daughter of five or so had been seated between us, in her own world, or so I thought. As I looked at the root, and before I could formulate my next question, she said in a confident, matter-of-fact voice, "Eat it, it's medicine!" So I took the qhǝsqhs in my mouth and ate it. (From a participant observation during the Hngwsumn Memorial Ride, May 25, 1996.)

Water itself is considered to have "healing" properties. When people got sick, they would traditionally take a sweat bath and then bathe in the waters of Lake Coeur d'Alene. When smallpox ravaged the camps, the "first thought" was to go into the waters of the lake: "It wasn't to flee into the plains, or flee into the mountains, to seek their medicine powers was [to go] into the banks and into the waters of the lake where they all went to save themselves. . . . Because that's where the *T'upye's* [grandmothers] had washed their babies. . . . Part of our *suumesh* is in the lake."

Then We Take Water

Well, last night we had a birthday dinner for my mother. And, as usual for any dinner, we started out with talking about what we're gathered there for. Since I was putting up the meal, I did the talking and kind of announced, it's my mom's birthday and how old she is. And we're glad to have a mom like we do. And if it weren't for her, we wouldn't be here. She gave us the greatest gift that anybody could give anybody else: our lives, our heritage, our history. Through her and her parents and grandparents, we have what we have to enjoy, . . . what we call our land and our people and our lan-

Flowering water potato, Benewah Lake, July 1998

guage, our heritage, from her. And thanked her. Mother's love is kind of one of the most powerful forces in this world, like my grandparents would say, second only to the Great Spirit's love that He has for His people. And we kind of went through what it means and thanking her and happy birthday and many more and good health.

And I turned it over to my younger brother—he's the baby, he's her baby—and she still thinks of him that way like the way mothers do. So I had him praying for her. So he got up and prayed for her life and tried to tell the Creator what she means to him and to us and wished her well, and ended it.

Then we drink water. In our family, we drink water after you pray, before you eat, that water and that food go together. As you take that water, that food will go down good. And together they're going to make up that they've got life-giving or life-sustaining properties. So you'd first drink that water, just a little bit. And then you can eat your food or with your coffee or pop or whatever you have. And then just pass it around while they're eating.

Somebody might want to get the attention of everybody and stand up and say, "Can I have your attention." And they'll say a few words and they did. And what it means to have a mother and thank you. And here's a birthday gift from us and a card and whatever token they want to use to express their feeling. And then our way, gift giving isn't a, . . . the way my grandparents said, it's not a kind of responsibility or burden. It's a chance to represent what you're saying with more than words. This is to convey what I'm saying and I want you to know that I really mean it. You don't have to say that, but that's kind of between the lines. And so you try to symbolize or represent your expression in some kind of a gift. So they do that. Then at the end then, after all that, when to cut the cake and let everybody sing "Happy Birthday," blow out the candle. (From an interview conducted June 12, 1996.)

HUNTING AND FISHING

Among the animal and fish gifts consumed are white-tail deer, mule deer, elk, moose, black bear, porcupine, grouse, robins, cinnamon teal, Canada goose, mallard, the anadromous chinook and sockeye salmon and steelhead trout, the resident mountain whitefish and cutthroat trout, freshwater clams, and crayfish. Some remember that salmon were once caught below Spokane Falls and along Hangman Creek, though they are no longer today. The clams were gathered along the sandy beaches of Fighting and Lake creeks.

Stand There and Wait for You

The deer, especially, are really smart. People that don't hunt don't know that. They have a great will. They're kind animals. The way my parents talked about it, they're kind of like God's favorite pets. They're very, very kind. They wouldn't harm a flea and they have to be taken care of just right.

Fawn (photographed near Benewah Lake in 1998)

You're not supposed to wound them and then not find them. You're not supposed to wound them at all. But if you do, you better find them and take care of them right, pray about it and try to get it all right as best you can. You have to practice being a good shot. You can't just go out there and shoot around and wound them up and then not care. You find one, you try to work yourself to a place where you can get a good shot, which is hard to do. They are really smart. They know you're there. The way my grandpa talked about, "They know you're coming after them. Sometimes one will . . . one will be picked out. Stand there and wait for you."

Also, they're going to make you work. Not easy like going to the store or something. They're going to make you respect them and care enough to work for it. . . . They'll circle and they'll jump off of their track. They'll walk back over their own steps. All the neatest tricks that Indian trackers and people knew, they learned them from the deer. They're the ones that have all the tricky things they can do to fool you. (From an interview conducted on May 24, 1996.)

Mariane Hurley vividly remembers how her grandmother would always have "dried meat" hanging above the kitchen cook stove. "When we were kids, we'd run through the kitchen and pull some down, just like taking cookies." At least three extended families continue to rely on the deer and elk as their primary source of meat throughout most of the year. Deer and elk meat, smoked and served as dried meat, is an indispensable part of any meal served at Schitsu'umsh Powwows and community celebrations, such as the annual Pilgrimage to the Cataldo Mission and the *Hngwsumn* Memorial Ride. It might also be "served at one's place of employment." For example, during the hunting season one employee of the Coeur d'Alene Housing Authority, an avid hunter herself, always keeps a cardboard box of dried meat on her desk to give to clients and friends who stop by.

Dried Meat

It was morning, around eight or so. It would take most of the day to smoke the meat from the four elk brought in by the "designated hunters." The "dried meat" would be served to over a thousand anticipated at the Powwow later that afternoon. The Powwow was part of the annual Pilgrimage to the Old Mission at Cataldo, the Feast of the Assumption.

We dug the pit the width and length of the single-framed bedsprings, some three feet by seven feet, and about five to six inches deep. The bedsprings were raised above the ground some twenty-four to thirty inches, and secured to metal fence posts at each corner. A heavy-gauge screen was laid over the springs. A fire was then built of pine logs, burning them down to provide the bed of hot coals. Cottonwood, cut to lengths of two foot and ranging in diameter from a couple of inches to eight-inch logs were laid on the coals. While very hot, the fire produced only minimal flames. The meat was to "cook from the inside out."

The stakes of deer and elk were cut into long, thin strips, some two to three inches wide. Cutting with the grain of the meat, the strips were a quarter to three-eighths of an inch thin, and could extend as long as two feet in length. If took a sharpened knife and great skill, as a potential slip with the knife called for a box of bandages to be kept close by, even for

Smoking elk meat during the Hngwsumn Memorial Ride, May 1996

the most expert of cutters. Salt is generously sprinkled over all the strips, as the only seasoning.

The strips of meat were laid on the bedspring rack, covering its entire surface. With a careful eye to ensure the meat did not completely dry out, each piece was turned and cooked for some thirty-five to forty-five minutes, depending on the thickness of the strip. "You can just tell when it's ready. When you poke the fork into it it doesn't give much."

As the first pieces were being pulled off the rack, inevitably an elder close by would "know it's ready" and stop in for a piece. If the aroma doesn't attract them, one of the women preparing the meat would take a few pieces around to the other camps and make sure all the elders had some of the still-warm dried meat. (From a participant observation made in August 1997.)

HOME TERRITORIES, FAMILIES, AND THE SEASONAL ROUND

Access to camas, deer, huckleberry, and water potato is bound into a particular land-human relationship. Each Schịtsu'umsh family has its own "home territory," generally an area inclusive of certain deer and elk populations, as well as specific berry and root plants. The social group designated for such a territory prior to Euro-American contact was probably the "band," an association of several bilaterally related families (Joset 1838–77:JP 36; Teit 1930:162; Reichard 1947:42).

While it is certainly true that the contemporary residential pattern on the reservation, with a housing style structured along individual nuclear-family units, has tended to isolate members of the traditional family from one another, the fundamental defining features of the Schịitsu'umsh family have, nevertheless, not changed significantly. They remain those of a bilaterally related, extended family, made up of both one's father's and mother's kinsmen, of sibling-defined relations extending beyond one's biological parents, and of multigenerational members, grandparents, and grandchildren. While family membership is bilaterally defined, the family name is typically patrilaterally oriented, with children taking their father's last name.

One indicator of the size of the bilaterally defined family may be in how many relatives are regularly provided deer and elk meat by their "designated hunter." One designated hunter, for example, considers the size of "my family" to include "some sixty to seventy people"; the families of ten other hunters range in size from "twenty to thirty individuals." In all instances, the Schitsu'umsh family is clearly much larger and more inclusive than the typical Euro-American nuclear family.

Leadership responsibilities within the family are situationally driven, alternating among the eldest or most accomplished in the family who can best conduct a deer hunt, organize a birthday celebration, or sponsor a Jump Dance, for example. Gender roles and privileges are marked by their social equality. Today, women are elected and serve alongside men on the Tribal Council, for instance.

The Indian Family

Inside the tribe, the families are very big. And they say the words of a relationship meant more or closer than just first cousin or second cousin. In the modern society, that sounds kind of distant or almost kind of not really related. Whereas in the Indian family, your first cousins were so close and the word for them meant so close, that today oftentimes you hear them called "brother" and "sister" as a more accurate translation of the relationship, how it would be or should be translated from Indian to English. And then, second cousins and beyond, they might say, "That's my cousin." And maybe even the parents' first cousins, they might call them "uncle" and "auntie." And your grandparents' first cousins, you'd call them "grandma" and "grandpa." You wouldn't call them "great uncle" or however they do that.

Because in the Indian way, your immediate family goes beyond your brother, sister, mom, dad. It includes all your aunts and uncles. All your first cousins, second cousins, who maybe were kind of raised by someone in the family. People weren't shy about taking their relatives' kids and raising them, then becoming an immediate part of the family, and all the relatives' cousins of your grandparents, . . . those are all your grandparents. . . . Immediate family is kind of big. I think our system was based upon bands. . . .

The way I view family it should be all together. . . . And we kind of all take each other's children as our own children—care about them, raise them, nurture them, help them, be there for them. In my particular household, I've got my wife and I and our children. We've got a lot of people coming and going. Sometimes my uncle will come and stay with us. And sometimes one of my sister's boys might come and stay with us for quite a period. And go back home again. Probably any given month for a week there'll be somebody there for a month or two. Sometimes my uncle will come around for a month or two. Then he'll go back home. (From an interview conducted on June 12, 1996.)

Traditionally, and continuing today for many Schitsu'umsh families, each family had continuous access to particular hunting, berrying, and root-digging territories from generation to generation, "since time immemorial." The family's territories would not necessarily be contiguous, but rather distinct areas scattered over a wide range of ecological zones—mountains, rivers, lakeshore, and prairies. One family today, for example, hunts deer and elk near Grassy Mountain and in certain areas in the Minaloosa Valley, whereas they berry and offer prayers in an area along a high mountain creek that flows into Lake Pend Oreille. While there were distinct family hunting or root-digging areas, several families might also gather together at a specific camas site, or collectively hunt deer using the "drive" method. The roots and meat obtained would then be distributed among all participating families.

Make a Drive

He was one of the good hunters around here. He knew all the deer trails, game trails. He said, "Look, come on you guys. Let's go. We go hunting." Four or five of us young guys go out with them. He tell us, "You go there, you wait there, go there." Then have some of us guys make a drive. He tell us, how far to go, where to go, a certain place. Then we drive all the deer to these guys up on the certain areas where you could tell where the deer will go. By God, it never failed.

But what they call "widow hunting" is what deer [we] would get, would cut it up and give it to the needy people or a lady who lost her husband and had a bunch of kids. We would pass the meat out to them. That's why he called it "widow hunting" [followed by laughter]. (From a interview conducted on May 20, 1996.)

While individual home-territory patterns have continued for many families, the total areas of home territories have been significantly reduced. Access to the northern regions, in particular from Liberty Lake east into the Coeur d'Alene River drainage and north into the Coeur d'Alene Mountains, has been curtailed because of historical, legal, and environmental factors.

So They Won't Fall Down

For deer, some of the older ones still enjoy their hunting. . . . They go to certain area, they say, "Well, this is a trail here where the deer are going down towards the lake or go to get the water, or they're coming back to feed. During the day they'll find a place to lay down. But in the evening they'll come and. . . ." So they study the area. They'll put their salt lick . . . and they'll put their hut in the ground and then they'll cover it and just have the hole for the rifle or bow and arrow. So deer can't smell them. . .

A lot of times, my dad says, when they had a camp up in the flats between Benewah Lake and St. Mary's, there's a little lake out there that the deer used to come down. They'd have a certain tree right next to the open, . . . that's all open field by that lake. They get up in the tree. They'd wait all night. . . . They take buckskin or rope or canvas and wrap it around themselves and tie themselves to a tree up there, so in case they fell asleep, they won't fall down [followed by laughter]. That's how they get some of the elk. They want to save their ammunition because it was hard to get. They only used ammunition when they had to, like when they couldn't do it in the wintertime. (From an interview conducted on May 3, 1996.)

The families' access to their distinct home territories is based on the "readiness" of the various plants and animals within the seasonal cycle. Given the changes in residence and subsistence patterns, the Schitsu'umsh of today are no longer reliant on transhumance for their survival. Nevertheless, animals and plants remain important, especially as supplemental sources of food, as healing medicines, and as spiritual links to the Creator and the Ancestors. Meat is critical for meals served at wakes and funerals, at community and family gatherings, and at Powwows and celebrations. And while winter camps are no longer established each year, deer and elk remain the primary sources of meat within many Schitsu'umsh households.

Thus the pattern of the seasonal round, while greatly abbreviated, is generally observed. Today a family might spend an "extended weekend" camping at a summer camas or a fall huckleberry site, instead of making such sites their residence for several weeks. The hunting of deer and elk continues, and while still done mostly in the fall and winter, now takes place over a weekend or after work. Today's seasonal round varies from year to year, given changes in the weather and rainfall. It also varies for individual families, depending on the location of their current residence relative to their home territories. And for many families, berrying, hunting, and root digging continues in their lives only as memories of bygone days.

After the Bitterroots

See, I was raised by Grandmother. I never had a mother, because she died when I was four months old. Grandmother raised us, my sister and I. So we had to pray, therefore, and be thankful for what we get.

We canned a lot of bitterroots first, and when that's done, we wait for the camas. After they've bloomed and they're ready, then the bulbs are ready. And they're solid. Then we go pick them. Then also, we wait for elderberries. . . . We'd pick them. Oh, I didn't like to pick them. Too much stems and stuff like that to clean. Then there's serviceberries. We'd pick them and dry those in the sun. We always had lots of Indian food, because that's the way she [Grandmother] was raised, and lived on it, and if you don't, you'll starve. Then, the last is the deer meat, after you get all this. We had to do all that, picking our bitterroots. Of course, they eat sunflowers, too, before they bloom, then they're easy to pull, and they eat them like celery. Then there's chokecherries, too. They used a rock, a flat rock. They'd find some there and they pounded them, you know, to break the seeds. Then they dried, put it in patties or just dried it. But now we have the grinders, and we use that to grind up the chokecherries and then dry it. Or, you can leave it home, dry it, they seldom use it that way. Then huckleberries. That's something. [We'd go] probably August. And sometimes it's earlier, in late July, or around the Fourth of July sometimes. It depends on the weather. Sometimes it's early. So we wait for the weather, how it is, and then they go check it, and it's ready, and everybody goes to get their share. Yeah. (From an interview conducted on February 11, 1998.)

PARTNERSHIP

The relationship of any family to its home territory was, and remains, fundamentally one of partnership rather than ownership. The territory embraces kinsmen in partnership with one another—Animal and Human relatives. Following the teachings set forth by the First Peoples, everyone enters into certain kinship and sharing patterns. The Animal Peoples and the landscape offer to their Human kinsmen foods, medicines, *suumesh*. In turn, the Human relatives respect their kinsmen, never taking more than they need, offering gifts of tobacco and prayers of thanks, and not abusing the land and water. During tough winters, for example, families might hold off on the hunt until the deer and elk populations grew stronger. Together, the Animal Peoples and their associated Human family provide and nurture a home for themselves in that territory. Home territories "belong" as much to the Human as to the Animal Peoples. The right of access to that home is only assured as long as these kinship and sharing patterns continue.

Dumb Birds

When you're up in the mountain, there's elk, bear, and deer. Mostly up in the higher elevations, they had, . . . not white-tail, but the other species, . . . other type of deer. Occasionally, they'd eat porcupine and blue grouse. They had another species, . . . they call them "pool hens." They're dumb birds.

It was the last time that my grandmother went up there. She was getting up in years and she could hardly see, but we were going up the mountain and here were some of these pool hens that flew up in a willow tree. They were all perched up there. My brother got off and was going to shoot them with this .22. My grandmother stopped him. "No, no, no. Don't, don't. Shells are too expensive. You're just wasting it." She told my brother, "Go get me a long stick." She took the stick and cut a piece of her moccasin. She made a loop on the end of that long stick. Then she took that stick and put it right over the head of that grouse and pulled him with that thing. She pulled it down. She had a little pack and she put that grouse in there and then pulled down another one. My older brother said, "Damn, my grandmother is smart!" [followed by a big laugh]. (From an interview conducted on May 3, 1996.)

By extension, Lake Coeur d'Alene and its associated rivers, mountains, and prairies are the home territory of the entire Schitsu'umsh family, to be used and respected in the same manner as the specific plants and animals in a given family's territory.

You Don't Own It

These things are just . . . lent to you by the Creator, . . . because He knew that you needed meat for your family. . . . It doesn't belong to one person. You don't own it. You can't put up signs. You can't put a fence around it, try to fence these elk in. . . . Everything is just borrowed from the Creator. . . . I'm not abusing it, so you'd be able to give back. (From an interview on July 2, 1996.)

Each Schitsu'umsh family respects the integrity of each others' home territory by generally hunting and berrying only on its own territory. But access to another family's area is certainly not prohibited, as long as the same respect is extended to all the kinsmen of that territory as would be extended to the Animal Peoples of the family's own territory, and as long as there is a genuine need. The story "Little Muskrat and Otter" provides an example of a family's territory that is not respected. Little Muskrat was told by his grandmother not to eat the grass in Otter's territory, but he would not listen and suffers the consequences. The sharing of a home territory can occur at the invitation from an elder in one family to the members of another family. Today, when a large quantity of meat is needed for a wake and funeral dinner, or a Powwow celebration, for instance, such an invitation may go out to other hunters. Teit noted that the "whole country was considered the property and food preserve of the tribe," and that the "'home ground' of each band was free for any member of the tribe to use, as long as the chief of the band was notified and his regulations followed" (1930: 162–63). Today, when a particularly large wake-funeral meal (in which dried meat is typically served) is anticipated, a designated hunter might invite other hunters to his territory, knowing of the approximate location and size of an elk herd. The meat obtained from the efforts of all the hunters would be used for the intended meal.

You Ought to Come There and Pick

I used to go up to Lewiston and I seen a woman there, a Nez Perce, at Goodwill store. . . . There was a sack, flour sack, and I took it and I threw it at her. I says, "Here, you better buy this for your camas." She looked at me; she threw it back at me. She says, "You don't even dig your camas." "You're wrong." I says, "I still dig it" [laughing]. She says, "Where do you go?" I said, "I go up towards Cheney, . . . wherever we can get the camas." And she says, "Well, we have a place to pick, Musselshell" [a Nez Perce site northeast of Kamiah]. She says, "You ought to come there and pick." She says, "It's nothing but camas." She says, "It's just like a lake." Well, . . .

it's way up in the mountains. It's Musselshell. Well, she showed me how to get up there. I said, "Okay, I'll go up there." She said, "Don't bring your *pitse'*," you know what we dig with. She says, "You use potato fork." She told 'em. I said, "I'll go up there."

We made it up there. My sons-in-law, we all went and had a picnic up there and the men folks were diggin' and us women on the ground picking the camas. One they'd turn over maybe three, four of them on one turn, over, and I'll tell you they are thick, thick. It's when the flowers are blooming blue, and when the wind blows it's just like waves of water. They really look like a lake. Just nothing but camas. It don't take long and we have a sack full. Some that big [two inches]. . . . Big ones up there. Then there's a few little ones, but we pick the big ones [laughing]. . . .

There was nobody around when we went up there. But we seen old camps where they used to camp. And it's really nice, but when it gets evening, feels spooky; I felt spooky. . . . Last time . . . . I went up there and we got stuck and that's where we got stuck and we stayed there until the evening and I sure felt spooky. Lot of old camps there, that's left where they used to come every year, you know, and put up their camp and stay there, probably bake it there, because there's lots of wood, . . . a good place to bake it. So . . . went across to some people to come and help us pull us out and we came home. . . .

That's the best place to get camas in a hurry. Yeah, I know people dig around here, it's hard work. It's really hard with a lot of roots. . . . So I'd go up there if we're going to get camas and drive up there. (From an interview conducted on July 11, 1996.)

Patterns of interfamily sharing of home territories extend also to intertribal territorial use. When a Schitsu'umsh family goes to the Kalispel, Nez Perce, or Spokane reservation to gather roots or pick berries, they do so respecting that area as they would their own, leaving it the way they found it, and waiting until local families are not using it. It is important to note the extensive degree of actual kinship relations between Schitsu'umsh families and Kalispel and Spokane families, their close historical ties, and their sharing of Salishian-based languages. As a result, seldom is formal permission obtained prior to territorial sharing.

This may not be true for the Nez Perce–Schitsu'umsh relationship, however. As shown in the vignette above, a Schitsu'umsh woman was invited to dig camas in Nez Perce territory, and has been going to the site every year since. But she only goes when there are no others around, and she is respectful of the area. And still she "feels spooky" when "it gets evening." In like fashion, the Nez Perce have a "designated hunting area," "rich with elk and moose," just south of Chatcolet Lake on the Coeur d'Alene Reservation, having acquired formal permission to access the area. Those who are only distantly related should first seek permission from those associated with the home territory before entering it. And then they should treat this home of another as they would expect others to treat their home.

The Dove

I watched my dad sing songs and walk up to a Dove that was in a bush in Lovell Valley [south and west of Plummer on the Coeur d'Alene Reservation], singing to him, holding his hands like this, . . . touching his fingertips together like a prayer hands, but . . . he bowed them, so there was a hole like this. And he'd go up and he'd sing like this to that Dove, and . . . my mother and I and my brother sat there and watched him. We sat in a car as he got out and went over to this Dove on a tree and walked up to him and sang like that. He sang, and put his hands around it like that, and picked it up off of the tree. He talked to that Dove, and he reached over and he took one feather from that Dove, and then we went like this, and he put him back in the tree like this. He got in the car and we left. Nobody said nothing. Nothing. I sat there. . . . I was thirteen, my brother was fifteen. I said, "What do you say to your father when you see him do something like that?" [tears in the eyes of the interviewee]. And it's so powerful [tears continue throughout]. It's so powerful to see him do that, that you know all of the things that he had told you were true. Were absolutely the truth, because he could do that, and he could sing to the Animals, and he could go and grab them and capture them and take one little thing and put him back, and to go on. That was truly the spirit of us Indian people. (From an interview on June 4, 1996; the Dove was the *suumesh* of the interviewee's father.)

FASTING, SONGS, AND *SUUMESH*

In addition to the gifts of venison or camas, gifts of "song" also emanate from the landscape. The songs, also known as *suumesh* (pronounced sü-mesh), derive from a special relationship established between a Human individual and his or her Animal spirit.[2] The song is the voice of one's spirit guardian. Once bestowed, the song can become a primary means of communication between an individual and the Animal Peoples around him. "It's a way of prayer, of asking for something." But it can be something more.

A *suumęsh* song is also a source of power that can help one succeed in a stick-game tournament, animate the dancers at a Powwow, give a blessing to a small child, or heal the sick. While *suumęsh* songs are considered powerful in themselves, they are a source for transformative power only as long as they are linked to the associated Animal spirit and, ultimately, to the Creator. In this sense, the songs are like "channels" through which the healing powers transpire. Great care and respect are thus shown not only to one's *suumęsh* song but, critically, to one's associated Animal Spirit.

Where the Songs Come From

I asked my grandpa, . . . "Where do these songs come from?" He told me, he says, "You can't turn on a radio or you can't go out and buy them." He says, "Those songs come from [my] dad and from [my] dad's dad, and from all of our people, from the beginning. Those songs, they're handed down to each one of the men in the family." So you have to go out and get your song, either from a vision, or you go out and if you think you have to go out and look for a song. You listen to the Trees, you listen to Mother Earth, and that's where you get your song from.

He says that some guys go out and sing other people's songs and stuff, but he told me, you should never do that. You should go out and he said the songs that I learned from him, those are the songs that he learned from his dad. So I teach them to my boy. And that's the way you keep it. It's just like our history, all of our history in our family is all oral history. He said, "That's where your songs are. You just pass them on orally to your children." (From an interview conducted July 30, 1997.)

Formerly, all boys were expected to acquire a spirit guardian, and with the spirit guardian generally came a song—one song per spirit (Teit 1930:169). In fact, almost everyone had a guardian spirit, both men and women (Teit 1930:192). Medicine bundles, or "bags," were assembled, which may have included "skins, feathers, bones, or other parts of his guardians, and also charms of stone and herbs," symbolically demonstrating the relation of the individual to his Animal Spirit (Teit 1930:193). While certainly not as pervasive today, the seeking of *suumęsh* songs remains important. A song can be received while in the Sweat House or while asleep, as a dream, or while at a "prayer circle" on a distant mountain overlooking Lake Coeur d'Alene. A *suumęsh* song may even come when not expected or sought, as a young child or while sick, from a dying relative, or while "living in an apartment building in downtown Chicago."

If a *suumęsh* song is deliberately sought, an individual may go to a special site on one of the nearby mountains. While at this prayer circle, the individual enters an intense period of prayer and fasting from food and water. The fasting may last from a couple of days to four days. In his prayers the individual must speak from the heart. In one instance, a man received a powerful *suumęsh* that would be used to help the sick. In his later years he traveled extensively to other reservation communities "to doctor." When his "Animal *suumęsh*" first came to him, he was told not to be scared, that he would be taken care of. The Animal told him what he needed to get for "his bundle," and when he obtained all these items, he would be ready to use the *suumęsh*. Once received, the song will guide and nurture the life of a young man, and the well-being of his family and potentially others.

Gift from the Cougar

It comes, spiritual. It comes to you. I don't know how; you can't explain. It just comes to you. Sometimes in their sleep, in your dream, it comes, and it tells you what to do. Or maybe, like my husband, . . . he was a good Indian doctor. When he was small, and his folks was drinking, and they got in a fight. And he grabbed his little sister and went under the wagon, you know, because they were afraid of the fight, and he says, they cuddled up under this wagon. He says, "I don't know if we fell asleep or what, when this Animal came to us, Cougar, and told us, 'Do not be afraid.'" He told me. He told me, he says, this big Cougar told me, "Don't be afraid. I come to see [you]." And he says, "I'm going to give you some songs," and he sent the songs to him. He says, "Remember these songs I'm giving you. When you get old, when you start turning gray right there [pointing to the middle portion at the front of her head], then I'll come back to you."

It was right here [pointing to the front of her head] that it started growing, and he used to tell me to take them off, and I'd take tweezers and I'd pull them off, because it was just a little bunch right here. It was a little bunch of white hair. I didn't know it, he didn't tell me then. He told me after he got the song, you know, and surprised me with what he could do.

So that went on and finally, one night, it came back to him. That's when he got turning gray, and we couldn't keep up with it. That's how he got his song. This Animal comes to him in his dream and tells him what kind of song. And these songs are from way back, his ancestors' songs, and it just comes back to the sons, to the close relative that they think can take care of it. And this Animal comes to them in their dream. And they always come and tell you what to do and what not to do. They've got to do it, just what they said, or they'll get hurt. And he was a real good doctor, . . . a real good doctor. His dad was a good doctor. And some of that went to him. . . . And he got all his songs through different Animals that comes to him, Birds and Animals. Each one has different songs and give to him. So he had quite a few different songs to dance with or to doctor. . . .

But he wouldn't tell me until that night when we came to that Jump Dance. . . . And [this man] went out, he Blue Jayed [along with another man]. The two of them went out, the two leaders on this Jump Dance, they both went out. . . . That's when my husband went and took the cane and he says, "Well, I'm going to bother you a little bit," he says, "and I'm going to sing and see what I can do to bring them back in." Because they left, they went out. They're Blue Jays, these two who went out. So he sang. He sang, and he told them that he got this when he was a little boy. He told them all how he got that song. He told us how he got it. It came to him when he was scared, he was a little boy, and he had a little sister. He said, "I don't know if my sister knew about it or heard it or not, but I know I did, and this is what he told me." He explained everything, what he was told that he can do, to doctor the people. He's doctored many people.

The Cougar appeared to him in his dream, and he says, "And you're going to have to collect certain things," and he had to collect, when he gets all this collected, what he's supposed to collect, then it'll be ready to sing, and to help the people. That's how he got his. . . . Yeah. He's got a bundle where he keeps all of what he's supposed to. And his dad helped him to get what he had to get. So that was special. He took care of that in his bundle. . . .

My husband said, "I don't charge. Don't give me it as a pay. I don't charge nobody when I doctor anybody. This is a gift to me, to heal people that needs to be healed." He don't take pay. My husband never took it. He's healed a lot of people. (From an interview conducted on February 11, 1998.)

To seek a *suumęsh*, a song, one typically goes to the mountains, the places of the prayer circles. The mountains are the abode of the spirit world, the place of the Creator and of the Ancestors. Father Joset related how a boy of twelve went to the mountains and on the evening of the second day received his "somesh" (1838–77: JP 69). He was told he "will be a great hunter." Someone today might pray on the mountains that overlook the lake. Each morning, during the fast, he would come down to the waters below and bathe, without drinking, and make offerings to the Water Spirits.

Prayer circles are located throughout aboriginal Schitsu'umsh country. Many guesting sites are indicated by their "standing stones" and rock "windbreaks." One of the publicly recognized mountains used for its prayer circles is called *Tch'mutpkwe,* "One who sits by the water" (Palmer, Nicodemus, and Connolly 1987:xix, 130). It overlooks both the lake and rivers below and is considered the source of the St. Joe River. Prayer circles are also in the hills overlooking the southern end and western sides of Lake Coeur d'Alene, as well as on a hill near the site of the Sacred Heart Mission at Cataldo. At many of these sites the "powerful Skitswish," or medicine people (*t'ek'wilsh*) once performed their ceremonies (Nicodemus 1975 [2]:260).

Send All Your Animals Back

My husband died in 1974. Forgot now what he had. He had something that couldn't be taken care of, and he just dried up and blowed away. He died in a hospital. He told me, he said, "Well, I'm going to leave you," and he asked me if I wanted part of his power, and I said, "No, I don't want it, because," I said, "who's going to take care of me? Somebody's got to take care of me, if something goes wrong. Maybe I'll turn into Blue Jay. Who's going to get me back? Who has the power to do these things? Nobody has it. Everybody's gone." I says, "Just send them back. Send all of your Animals back to where they belong, and they can go wherever they want." That's how I didn't take his. Otherwise, I'd have the power. I don't have that big power. I have some power, but not that much. Not like him. (From an interview conducted on February 11, 1998.)

PRAYER

Prayer is an essential component in the acts of gathering camas, hunting deer, and seeking a *suumesh* song. In addition to song, prayer is a primary means of communication between the Human Peoples and the Animal Peoples and Creator. Take the example of deer hunting. Understood as "brothers," the Deer have the capacity to "offer themselves up" to a hunter and can even "laugh at you if make too much noise. . . . They are really smart. They know you're there." And they need to be acknowledged and "spoken to." Before the deer hunt, prayer is given and a sweat bath might be taken, asking for a good hunt and giving thanks to the Deer and the Creator. While hunting in the Minaloosa Valley, a Deer will inevitably and voluntarily come out of the trees and offer itself up to the hunter, if the hunter has hunted with skill and has shown respect. "You say a prayer when you . . . kill your hunt, after the hunt's over, and then you continuously pray when you're skinning him out, cutting him up, just show total respect to him."

Deer, Rock, and Earth

Every time you shoot one of these Animals you give a prayer, you say a prayer for them, and thank the Creator for giving you your brother, the Deer or the Elk, and you always leave an offering of tobacco or something. You just scuff the ground and you put the tobacco in the ground and cover it up right where you got your kill. And you respect that Animal when you're skinning him, when you're cleaning him out, when you're preparing him to cut him up, you respect him all the way. Even when you eat him, you respect him. It's nothing to play around . . . . You be humble about it, because he's giving himself up so you can nourish your body, . . . your family. . . . And you continuously pray, . . . show total respect to him.

That was taught to me, that was taught to my grandpa by his dad, now I teach that to my boy, and my boy is three years old, and I take him hunting with me. So he knows about it; he knows about the prayer, and about the song [sung just after every kill] . . . . I was taught that the same Creator that created me created that Deer. So he's my brother, we're related. One species doesn't dominate another; they give each other respect. I was taught to treat all Animals like that. Everything is alive, even a Rock. . . . You can take a Rock and you can heat it and take it into a sweat lodge, and it comes alive, it creates steam, creates heat. Those are our Ancestors in those Rocks. . . . You don't do anything that will hurt the earth, like throwing garbage out on it. Because it's like throwing garbage out on your mother, that's Mother Earth. (From an interview on July 2, 1996.)

As with hunting deer, upon gathering camas, bitterroot, huckleberry, water potato, or *qhasqhs*, prayer is offered, "thanking the Good Lord and the Great Spirit." Lucy Finley vividly remembers how her family gathered water potatoes when she was a child (circa 1920s and 1930s). A camp of tipis was set up near Rocky Point, and she would hear the different prayer songs sung in each lodge in the morning hours before the gathering would begin. Most families offered a prayer prior to the gathering of any type of root or berry food, asking permission to take it, and requesting good fortune and blessings for those who share in the feast. Picking the berries by hand or "combing" them out directly from the bush have remained the preferred methods of gathering (Teit 1930:91).

Even in the collecting of cedar bark to fashion a basket or cover a canoe, prayer would be given as the bark was pulled from the tree. As I have observed, when camas is to be dug, gifts of tobacco or *qhasqhs* are first made, and permission is sought from "the Father" to acquire the camas. Other offerings left behind might include beads and colored pieces of cloth. Elders frequently voice the concern that non-Indian hikers might inadvertently discover these offerings left in berry patches or cedar groves and, not understanding their purpose, remove the items. "The offerings are supposed to be left."

TEACHINGS

In addition to the gifts of venison, camas, and song, the First Peoples provided practical knowledge, "the how to," as well as teachings and moral lessons. These gifts of "wisdom" convey the knowledge of how to catch salmon successfully, how to use the Sweat House properly, and how to behave toward kinsmen—a grandmother, an in-law, a brother—appropriately. The ceremonial knowledge of the Jump Dance and the Sweat House came from the First Peoples. An elder related to me how the First Peoples "taught us how to live, how to get along, how to take care of our children, how to deal with each other," and to illustrate his point he followed his comments with an abbreviated telling of the "Hawk and Turtle" story (see p. 113). As part of his family's oral traditions, this elder also referred to a story involving the archetypal Memorial Giveaway, the story of Bird. Upon his death, the feathers of Bird were pulled out and distributed among all the other Bird Peoples. The sorrow felt by an immediate few was therefore shared among all his family members, "lifting the burden." Then the Bird Peoples "flew to the wind," allowing the deceased Bird to "fly forever." The rationale for Memorial Giveaways, and the manner in which they are to be held, were thus set forth and established by the First Peoples.

The teachings of the First Peoples have been handed down from each generation to the next, conveyed primarily through the oral traditions. The entire body of Schitsu'umsh oral traditions is divided primarily into two genres, *meymiym q'esp schint* (meaning, figuratively, "he/she/they are telling stories and learning about the time before the human beings") and *meymiym łu' schint* ("he/she/they are telling stories and learning about the human beings") (Frey 1995:12–13).[3] In the former, which entails far more narratives than the latter, are the essential creation accounts of the Schitsu'umsh. These narratives are ingrained inexorably within the land-scape: Rabbit and Jackrabbit with Tekoa Mountain, and Chief Child of the Yellow Root and Coyote with Lake Coeur d'Alene. As Gladys Reichard observed in her analysis of Schitsu'umsh narratives, every story "has its local setting even if it is not mentioned in the tale" (1947:34). These sto-ries have been used as important "teaching tools," disseminating the teach-ings and moral lessons to the young and reiterating them to the adults. "Usually, non-Indians think of the stories as being stories told only for children, and they were not. . . . The stories were told to a mixed audi-ence, and children or the adults took the meaning out of it at their level of understanding."

The stories also have a critical spiritual and integrative role. In the act of telling the narratives, the stories help bring forth and vitalize the world— the lakes and mountains, the animals and plants (Frey 1995:171–77). Summarizing the importance of the oral literature, Henry SiJohn stated, "We survive by our oral traditions, which are our basic truths, our basic facts, handed down from our elders. They are the basis for our songs, our vision quests, our sharing" (Frey 1995:13).

The world traveled by the First Peoples is a world endowed and ani-mated spiritually. With his *suumesh*, Crane can successfully hunt deer, bun-dle vast amounts of venison under his belt, and even kick down a tree, causing it to burn. On the other hand, while Coyote can break the dam on the Columbia River, releasing the salmon to go upriver to feed the people, he can just as easily move great boulders, creating impassable falls and pre-venting salmon from coming into Lake Coeur d'Alene. And when he does "something crazy" and dies, Mrs. Mole can jump over Coyote, bringing him back to life. A spiritual transformative dynamic permeates the Schitsu'umsh landscape.

As modeled by the First Peoples, an all-inclusive kinship binds the Peoples. In the narrative "Crane and Coyote," Crane is a son-in-law of the village chief and a brother-in-law of Little Squirrel and Chipmunk. The women of that story are all related as grandmothers, mothers, daughters, and granddaughters. Even Coyote has a wife and children, and is related to the village chief. In the story of "Rabbit and Jackrabbit," each is related as cousins. It is a kinship inclusive of all Peoples. The world is inhabited by relatives.

The ethic of sharing is also clearly articulated in the oral traditions. Crane shares deer meat with Little Squirrel and Chipmunk, as well as with an entire village of hungry in-laws. Camas, brought by Jackrabbit, and pitch, brought by Rabbit, are intended to assist the other, who is thought to be in dire straits. The critical role of sharing is again reiterated in the narrative "Coyote and Woodtick," which shows what may occur when one becomes selfish and no longer wishes to share.

In the larger sense, the results of the actions of the First Peoples in "preparing the world" are seen as gifts for the Human Peoples. Camas and pitch are now found at Tekoa Mountain, and salmon now swim up the Columbia. The model is established. As the First Peoples shared with the Human Peoples, the Human Peoples, in turn, are to share with all the relatives in need (just as Crane, Rabbit, and Jackrabbit did with their relatives). The camas, bitterroot, and pitch left by Rabbit and Jackrabbit, and the manner in which Deer is related to by Crane—all are understood as gifts to be shared with those in need.

The sharing of the gifts comes "without strings attached," without either obligation or expectation of reciprocity. Crane simply gives to those in need, as the First Peoples gave to the Human Peoples. This feature is given particular clarity when one considers the character of Coyote. Many of his actions represent the antithesis of the norm established for kin-based relations: Coyote acts selfishly in anticipation of gaining something in return (Frey 1995:63–66). Story listeners laugh when a request for help is made and Coyote responds by saying, "What's in it for me!" The humor is found in the inappropriate behavior exhibited by Coyote.

In the actions and character of Coyote (often in the inappropriate fashion) along with the positive examples set by the other First Peoples, the proper etiquette and respect due to the giver of gifts (for example, the host of a meal) are illustrated. In the context of the ethic of sharing, while the host freely gives to the needy, without thought of reciprocity, the recipient of those gifts must demonstrate proper respect toward the host. In the story "Coyote and Woodtick," Coyote clearly violates the proper etiquette due to a host, and, in so doing, he helps illustrate what *should* occur. When he is disrespectful of his host, he loses access to what the host can offer. Thus one should not ridicule and abuse one's host, calling her "one who doesn't have a neck," and certainly one should not, as Coyote did, "kill" her.

Following in line with the respect due to a host, the First Peoples provide the model for the general respect that should be given to all gifts. While on the hunt, such respect toward gifts would be manifested in not "taking too much" and, in following Crane's example, in hunting "only two adult deer." In other words, the number of deer to be hunted—whether for an individual hunter (e.g., two deer) or for a collective hunt (e.g., 180 deer, as reported by Father Point in 1842)—is predicated on the needs of the entire community and not upon personal gain. Coyote continually suffers the consequences of his disregard of this etiquette. "We must not be a glutton," as Henry SiJohn stressed, and he elaborated by telling the story of Mosquito. "Mosquito was a glutton," he explained, "and he drink and drink and drink. He got real big, until a pine needle pricked him and he bled all down the river."

In Coyote's examples we also find important markers separating kinsmen from nonkinsmen, demarcating the boundaries of the Schitsu'umsh family. When Coyote engages in competitive games of artful deception and trickery to win advantage among his relatives, he generally fails and is the focus of laughter. Kinsmen should not compete with one another, since sharing is the norm. However, such behavior is deemed appropriate when directed toward potential adversaries. Thus, when Coyote engages in the same competitive games for the benefit of his family, and succeeds in those games, he has likely done so by engaging nonkinsmen. The boundaries of the family are thus delineated, with Coyote offering a model for behaving toward competitive and aggressive nonkinsmen.

Important teachings are thus established by the First Peoples and conveyed through the oral traditions. Among the teachings identified here are an all-inclusive kinship defined by its ethic of sharing and respect for gifts, with competitiveness marking the boundaries of nonkinsmen, all within a world that is spiritually endowed and vibrant.

Teachings

The First People, the ones with the wings, the ones with the four feet, the hoofs, the ones who crawl on the ground, they were the First People and they were the ones who taught us how to behave. . . . It was the Bear who came to us to teach us how to fish. It was the Badger who came and taught the Indian people how to dig for roots into the ground because that's where the food was. It goes on and on. It was the Fish who taught us how to do many things in the water—the swimming, the living in the water, the People that were in the water, the things that they gave. . . . It was *Amotqn* and the Animal People who came to us to build the Sweat House, to show us how to make the Sweat House in a certain way and which rocks to use, to put them into the fire. Those special rocks, when they're heated, come alive. They will talk to us and sing to us. (From an interview conducted on July 3, 1996.)

Sharing the Gifts

Gift of Berries

Getting the berries was a great honor, it was just like hunting. . . . Gathering food not for yourself, but for your family, your extension of your family, and the peoples of the community that ain't able to make it up there, and to see their faces when you come up and knock on the door and say, "Hey, we went up to Buckhorn or Clark Fork or up to Trestle Creek [on Lake Pend Oreille] and picked berries and we brought you some berries." And just the look on their faces was really satisfaction. You knew it was hard, hard work, hot, dusty, dirty, fun, but it was really good to see the old peoples' faces. . . . It was something that was instilled in me, was to take care of the people that need to be taken care of, the old people, treat them with respect. . . .

Sometimes they [the elders, upon receiving the berries] would give you dried meat or sometimes they'd give you a blanket, a Pendleton. Whatever. It wasn't the case, well, since I gave you huckleberries, you've gotta give me something. It was just, they were just so happy, they wanted to share or give something to you, and show their appreciation. . . . You would retain a lot of respect from the tribal elders. (From an interview conducted on July 7, 1996.)

The First Peoples have prepared the world for the coming of Human Peoples, endowing the landscape with gifts of food, medicine, *suumesh*, as well as with their teachings. It is a landscape inhabited by the Animal Peoples, who might give of their own bodies, as food, or bestow a *suumesh* song, to help nourish and heal those among the Human Peoples in need. In turn, those who have received these varied gifts freely share them—the foods, the healing songs, and the teachings—with those among their own family in need. The example set forth by Crane and the other First Peoples has continued in the lives of the Schitsu'umsh people today. In this chapter we will explore the many ways that gifts, bestowed in the landscape by the First

Peoples, are, in turn, redistributed by the Human Peoples and shared with those in need.

The example set forth by the First Peoples, in fact, intersects at many critical life stages of a Schitsu'umsh person. As the First Peoples had prepared the seasonal round, from spring through summer and fall, into winter, and back to spring, so too had they prepared the life-cycle round, from birth and infancy, through childhood and adulthood, into old age and death, and finally return to the Mountains. In so doing, the First Peoples have provided the means not only for successful travel over the landscape but for successful travel through the changing seasons of one's life. Those Schitsu'umsh oral and ceremonial traditions that have continued into the present are the essential vehicles through which a uniquely Schitsu'umsh identity is imparted and perpetrated in the lives of the Schitsu'umsh.

Among infants and children, the oral traditions, as well as the song, dance, and regalia of the Powwow, are among the primary means by which the teachings and the meaning of Schitsu'umsh identity are first instilled. Growing into adulthood, a body and soul might become nourished by the venison and *suumesh* song offered by the Deer. Throughout one's life, the berries picked and camas dug, the oral traditions retold and reheard, the song, dance, and regalia of the Powwow, the heat and prayers of the Sweat House, and the song and dance of the Jump Dance, all combine to provide the sustenance, enrichment, and renewal needed as a Schitsu'umsh. In times of particular distress or ill-heath, a special root or *suumesh* song, the Sweat House, or perhaps the Jump Dance might again be called upon for a healing. And then, at the completion of one's life, the wake and Memorial Giveaway could help assure that the "sorrow is lifted," and that the one who traveled among the Human Peoples now returns to the Mountains, among the Spirit Peoples.

THE ORAL TRADITIONS

The oral traditions, embedded in the landscape traveled, brought forth by the deeds of the First Peoples, and handed down from generation to generation, "since time immemorial," are themselves essential gifts. For within them are conveyed the fundamental teachings upon which the lives of the Human Peoples depend. And in their retelling, something indispensable is "given back."

The vitality of the oral traditions certainly continues today in the lives of the Schitsu'umsh people. The stories may be told during a family gath-

*Passing the stories and songs to the young
during the Hngwsymn Memorial Ride, May 1996*

ering, an evening of song and drum, at a birthday celebration, prior to a sweat, during a wake, in a school classroom, or at an academic conference. Handed down orally from generation to generation, the narratives themselves have a resiliency that is most profound. When the story of Coyote releasing the salmon on the Columbia River is told by a contemporary storyteller, for example, the basic plot and the characters themselves are fundamentally unchanged from that conveyed by Croutous Nicodemus in 1904 (Teit 1917:121) and his wife, Dorothy, in 1927 (Reichard 1947:101–3). In addition, for many Schitsu'umsh today the stories are first encountered and read in published versions offered in elementary, high-school, or college classroom settings, often in the native language with interlinear translations or as free-translations in English. The most important of these published accounts is Gladys Reichard's 1947 "Analysis of the Coeur d'Alene Indian Mythology," accompanied by her unpublished 1946 "Coeur d'Alene Texts," available locally in photocopied form. Critically, those accounts come alive when the stories are given voice and retold aloud to fellow classmates and friends. The oral narratives thus continue to be heard among the Schitsu'-umsh, shared in the company of others. However, increasing numbers of Schitsu'umsh encounter these stories first not in the voice of a grandparent but in the literacy and privacy of a book.

Their Footprints Were in the Earth Forever

And when he would tell me this story he'd begin to cry, and he'd talk in Indian, and he'd say how important it was for us to remember these people because their footprints are the one's that had walked in the mountains and the real trails, where the trails were filled with dust this deep—of moccasin tracks. . . . Their footprints were in the earth forever. And that's where we begin, and to remember those people.

So storytelling time was an educational time for us. Storytelling was taking a piece of our people and opening it up and looking at it, kind of like, from page to page. And we were told of our connection with the Christian world, and to remember over here the Bible and the Good Book and all the Angels and all things in the pictures in here. And on this side of our Indian religion, what was our bible, was the Salmon and the Deer and the Elk and the Bear and the Goats and the smallest Insects, the Rocks in the creek and the Wind and the Sky, the Thunder and the Lightning. That's what we were given. And how important it was for us to stand in the middle of these two worlds and reach back and forth and utilize those things every day to guide us. (From an address given by a Coeur d'Alene elder at the Lewis-Clark State College Native American Awareness Conference, Lewiston, on March 16, 1998.)

The particular and vital significance of the oral traditions is found not only in *what* is said—the teachings—but in *how* those teachings are told, in the act of telling the stories. While there is a certain degree of variation in the styles of telling the narratives, the various techniques employed by raconteurs generally all coalesce in an attempt to draw listeners into the story as participants (Frey 1995:147–54). Some storytellers will use their skills in hand and body gesturing, whereas others will be more adept at alternating their patterns of voice intonation for each character. But both techniques can have the same effect.

As I was told by Jeannette Whitford, "The story is like a person." Each narrative has a "skeleton, with muscle and flesh." When you tell the story, "you have to keep all the bones together; you can't add new ones or take away some. They all have to be there." This quality is certainly reflected in the resiliency through time of the plot structures and character personalities. A general comparison of the story texts—as collected by James Teit (1917) in 1904, Gladys Reichard (1947) in 1927 and 1929, and the more contemporary texts in Frey (1995) and here—reveals this sort of continuity.

On the other hand, the muscle and flesh of the same story can take on a different texture and feel, depending on who is telling that narrative. Each storyteller will add his or her own style of telling stories. In the act of telling the story, the storyteller will draw upon particular techniques in an attempt to animate the "bones of the story." Whether in the use of hand and body gesturing or through voice intonation, for example, each raconteur seeks to bring the story alive and facilitate the listeners' participation with the characters of the story. As Cliff SiJohn, an accomplished storyteller himself, once said, "When you tell the stories, you've gotta go inside and become the Coyote, or the Bear, or the Mole. Feel it as they feel it. And tell the story with your heart" (Frey 1995:216).

Coyote's Eyes[1]

He began in a low, though confident, voice. As the narrative continued, the storyteller's hands and eyes moved, and the pitch of his voice modulated, placing emphasis on Coyote's particular actions, identifying the direction he traveled in, or contrasting his character with that of other First Peoples. Despite the narrative's numerous and seemingly disjointed sub-plots, the rhythm with which the raconteur told the story did not vary. It was a story remembered, not memorized. The narrative came "alive," and for many of the others present, who moments before had been listeners, they now traveled with Coyote. All eyes were now seeing through Coyote's eyes. The twenty-five-minute-long story ended as it had begun, with each of the fifteen college students, Indian and white alike, quietly returning to the "reality of the classroom." (From an observation made in a course I was teaching, March 1997.)

A common linguistic feature used by storytellers are deictics, such terms as "here" and "there." In their application storytellers can make "visible" to listeners specific locations or objects, as well as locations relative to the storyteller himself. For example, in the sentence "The Coyote ran *there*," listeners are situated spatially relative to Coyote. The effect for the listener is to gain a greater sense of being part of the story's landscape and of witnessing the unfolding of an adventure. Deictics help anchor the story and its listeners in a spatial immediacy.

We have an excellent linguistic record of the spoken Schitsu'umsh phrases used in the narratives told by Dorothy Nicodemus (Reichard 1938, 1946). In these texts there is frequent use of such deictics as the demonstrative adverb $x^w i$', meaning "here" in reference to the storyteller, and the article *lä*, meaning the subject or object is remote in relation to the speaker (using Reichard's orthography). Also used are the article $x^w a$, meaning "this," near to the speaker, the demonstrative pronoun *ɫw'ä*, meaning "that," which is near the storyteller, and the demonstrative adverb *ɫu'ʉ*, meaning "there," distant from the storyteller (Reichard 1938: 694–95). Nicodemus also liberally used the adverb *hɔi*, or *kum'*, which translates "then." In the telling of the story the deictics help to contextualize specific locations or objects referred to by the storyteller. Thus, as you hear the story of Crane or Rabbit told in this manner, you feel a part of the action and the specific locale.

In the narrative texts presented here, I have included some of these deictic features. Their inclusions are based upon the general pattern found in the interlinear transcriptions of the Nicodemus texts (Reichard's 1946 "Coeur d'Alene Texts"). For much of American Indian oral literature, such attributes and contextualizing information are often lost when rendered in a printed, literacy-based publication. Deictics are editorially removed, and specific locations and objects referred to in the narratives are not noted in the transcribed texts.

Skilled and purposeful use of body language, hand gestures, and voice intonation further help animate the stories. Grizzly Bear inevitably is voiced and gestured with a big roar and wide-open arms. The storyteller often points with a hand, or gestures with the turn of the head, in the direction of Coyote's travel or to where a village is located, further anchoring the unfolding story to its landscape. Lawrence Aripa was adept at altering his voice to take on the qualities and characteristics of the First Peoples he was presenting. To add drama to a sequence in which Coyote was talking with the Creator, for example, Lawrence used a deep and deliberate voice when the Creator spoke to Coyote. In addition, the vowels might be extended to emphasize a particular action in the story: "Coyote, you weren't sle-e-e-ping, you were de-e-e-ad." Such attributes of storytelling are difficult to present in printed formats.[2]

Gladys Reichard suggested that the Schḷtsu'umsh formerly did not tell stories during the summer months, adhering to the general pattern followed by other tribes of the region (1947: 5). This point is reiterated by one contemporary elder: "The traditional way was for stories to be told only after the first snowfall." Among the neighboring Flatheads, the Coyote cycle was traditionally told in conjunction with the Jump Dances, held in January and February. As is true also of the Jump Dance, the telling of the Coyote stories involves the transforming and revitalizing of the world, a dimension of the oral tradition to be considered presently. But during her 1927 and 1929 field studies, Reichard seldom observed the Schḷtsu'umsh following a winter-only "rule," as most stories were told year-round. While growing up, one seventy-year-old elder remembers hearing the stories told year-round. And certainly today, the Schḷtsu'umsh rarely follow the winter-only rule. As Lawrence Aripa was fond of saying, with a big smile on his face, "As long as someone wants to hear them, I'll tell them any time of the year."

Little Muskrat and Otter[3]

Little Muskrat and his grandmother live together at their lodge. Then in the morning before she goes root digging this grandmother sees the Little Muskrat about to go to a particular area to eat some grass. She says, "When you go out to eat grass, do not go over there." The next morning grand-

Lawrence Aripa telling of Coyote, October 1997

mother says, "When you go out to eat grass, do not go over there." Then Little Muskrat thinks, "Why did she forbid me from going there? I'm going there." Then Little Muskrat goes there. There is a lot of grass. He says, "That is why she had forbid me. Now I know." He eats the grass there.

The Otter is there and sees him. He says, "I drive people out." Little Muskrat says, "I don't think its your land." Otter says, "It isn't your land." Then he punches Little Muskrat all over the head until it is flat. He punches him all over the head. Then the Otter throws him into the canoe.

Then the grandmother returns to their lodge. Little Muskrat is gone. Then at dark she hears him coming, saying, "*Änä änä.*" Then she sees the Little Muskrat paddling his canoe. He is lying down in it. His head is all swollen. His eyes and ears are just small beside his cheeks which are so big. The grandmother says, "I told you not to go there. It's your own fault you got beaten up so badly." Then she takes him into their lodge and lays him down. "*Änä*, sprinkle my little head," he says. Then in a few days he is well.

The Little Muskrat says to his grandmother, "Get the canoe ready. I am going there to kill the Otters." "No, you might get killed. Then I would be alone," she says.

Then the Little Muskrat gets into the canoe and paddles off quietly. He sees only Otter's sister, who is Mink, about to bathe. She makes a hole near the water. She had the hole made just big enough to sit in. Then a fire is made and the rocks are made hot. Then she puts those hot stones in the water. She has a baby. She lays it there. Little Muskrat quietly paddles ashore there. Then he shoots her right then and there. She fell into the water head first. The Little Muskrat paddles home as fast as he can.

Then the grandmother is watching for him. There, suddenly he comes into sight. "I am glad that my grandchild is alive," she says. "I killed their sister," he says. "What will happen to us now," she says. Then Little Muskrat says, "Make a hole through the brush [like a tunnel] beginning where you are sitting. Then go through there as far as the woods there. You will see a lake. Then come back." She did this and came back. "Now tie up my little head, Grandmother, and, *änä*, keep sprinkling it for me," he says.

Then the Otter brothers look for their sister everywhere. Then they hear her baby cry, "*wä'ä wä'ä.*" "Why doesn't she take care of her baby?" they say. Then one found her. "She's dead." She is shot with an arrow sticking in her. "She's dead." "Little Muskrat must have done this," they say. Then the eldest brother says, "I am going to kill the Little Muskrat." Then he sets off paddling.

The Otter arrives. The grandmother is quietly sprinkling Little Muskrat's head. He is lying there with his head all tied up. Otter comes in with that stick. "You must be the one who killed my sister," he says. "No, no, he is small and helpless. Why, how could he be the one? He just lies there like this," the grandmother says. "Who could it have been who did it?" Otter says. "*Änä*, sprinkle my head, Grandmother," Little Muskrat says. The Otter thinks, "It must not be him. He never gets up." Then the Otter leaves and paddles off.

Little Muskrat says, "Keep watching him. When he is out of sight, give a war whoop and dance." Then grandmother watches. When he is out of sight she lets out a war whoop, "*Uhu ' uhu' '*, the Otter's sister is killed by a little arrow. Then she fell headfirst into the water."

Then the Otters think, "Who could it be? It must be Little Muskrat." Then the Otter paddles back. The grandmother is singing and dancing here. Little Muskrat and his grandmother run into the hole there and pull a blanket over it. Then the Otter searches the lodge. No one. Then he finds the hole and reaches into it. He fails. Where there are bushes they are gone.

Then, the end of the trail.

During the telling of this story, there is also extensive use of word, formal phrase, and sequence repetition. Key action phrases are repeated. Little Muskrat is warned twice by his grandmother not to eat grass from a particular area; then, when Otter attacks Little Muskrat, the speaker repeats the action phrase "punches him over the head." This pattern also holds true for Coyote's challenges. They may be highlighted by repetition of key phrases or actions. In his effort to free the salmon, Coyote needs several attempts to break the dam erected by the Swallow Sister or Snipe and her sisters. When Coyote has done something particularly foolish and "dies," it takes Mrs. Mole three attempts to jump over him to bring him back to life, whereupon Coyote says, "Oh, I've been sleeping a long time." And Mrs. Mole says, "You haven't been sleeping, you've been dead!"

The number of repetitions in a story often depends on the dominant number pattern found in a particular tradition. Among the Schitsu'umsh, three and four seem to be the primary number patterns. As Reichard observed, "Four helpers belong to Coyote, the man who lost his wife was given four needles and later four feathers to help him get to Thunder. Coyote had four sons; there were four mosquito brothers and one little one with strong power. The purification ceremony of sweating and bathing was carried out on four different days; Waterbird slept four days by mistake. . . . Among the Coeur d'Alene this unit [the dominant number pattern] was four" (1947:27). This four pattern stands in contrast to most of the other Salish and Sahaptin speakers of the Plateau region, where the dominant number pattern is either three and/or five, and does not typically include the number four (Frey and Hymes 1998). In the narratives told by Lawrence Aripa, I have observed his consistent use of a three and five number pattern, however (for example, in his extensive use of five in the story "Smallpox and the Five Peoples").

Many of the repetition sequences, as noted in the interlinear transcription of the Dorothy Nicodemus texts (Reichard 1938, 1946), are presented here. As with the "here" and "there" adverbs, these attributes are often removed by editors in narratives published for general distribution.

During the telling of a narrative, participation of the story listeners is actually monitored. In a traditional setting, as the story unfolds, the listeners acknowledge their participation by periodically saying aloud, *"hey"* or, in the Salish tradition, *i...´*, meaning "yes." Among the Pend Oreille, one hooks the index finger and draws it in toward the body—the sign for "I got it"—confirming participation. As long as the "yeses" are heard, the story continues. But should there be only silence, the story ceases, regardless of the storyteller's location in the story. When there are no longer any participants, there is no need to continue the telling.

Chipmunk Talking

The First People come alive in the story. . . . They swirl around you as the Turtle is saying his thing or as the Chipmunk is saying something. . . . They swirl around you and you feel the Indian medicine. . . . This is Chipmunk talking to you. This is Coyote talking to you. This is the Elk and the Deer and the Eagle, and this is Hawk. . . . All these things suddenly come alive. They are just as alive as they were a thousand years ago. (From an interview conducted October 3, 1997.)

As observed by Reichard, narratives ordinarily concluded with the phrase *"hoi hinxux*ʷ*a'tpalqs,"* a "variation on the theme 'I have come to the end of the trail'" (1947:28) or "then, the end of the trail."[4] In light of the previous discussion, the meaning of this ending is made more clear. The phrase itself is a formal ending to stories, "an old phrase used only in this context" (Reichard 1938:707). If a story is understood as a vehicle through which story participants travel the landscape, over the "trails" set forth by the First Peoples, then to finish a story is to complete a journey and thus come to the end of the trail. Or, as Lawrence Nicodemus, the ninety-year-old grandson of Dorothy Nicodemus, has said in reference to this ending, "The story is like traveling on a trail." A similar notion is expressed by other Plateau peoples in their use of the "canoe" metaphor. To participate in the story is to travel in a canoe, and includes "staying on course" and "tying it up" when you finish for the night (Frey 1995:172). The stories provide the trails necessary to travel the landscape. In the act of retelling aloud the stories of Crane and Coyote, Rabbit and Jackrabbit, Hawk and Turtle, and Chief Child of the Yellow Root, listeners are made participants in the story and travel the unfolding landscape on the trails prepared by the First Peoples.

Animation of the story is, in fact, fully realized when the power of the oral tradition is itself brought to bear (Frey 1995:154–58). Words have a transformative power on the world. They are not simply descriptive of it. When Coyote sang the specific utterance, *"Shush taways talee, chacha taways talee,"* the logs he stood on moved out and in, allowing him to cross the river, that is, until he forgot part of the phrase, fell into the river, and drowned (above; p. 140; Frey 1995:165).

This transformative capacity is potentially realized whenever words are given voice. Having ritually received his or her "Indian name," a person will hear that name in prayer spoken in the Sweat House and during the Jump Dance. And the child will grow to become the words of his or her name. One does not speak of a particular sickness out of fear of manifesting that affliction. When raconteurs weave the fibers of words into the fine tapestry of stories, the spoken words bring forth that which they portray. Phenomena are spoken into existence. At the end of the storytelling session, having spoken the names and brought the First Peoples into being, the storyteller tells the animals, the fishes, and the birds to go to the mountains, the rivers, and the sky (Jacobs 1959: 73). What was witnessed in the telling is now set free to travel the landscape.

The following Schitsu'umsh story illustrates the understanding of the power of words. As gleaned from the account, I suspect that this narrative was told during the early spring of each year, especially if the winter had been hard and cold, in order to help bring about a desired result.

Chipmunk and Snake[5]

Chipmunk and Snake live together there. Their fire is one long, burning log. Each of them has a stick which he uses to poke the fire. They are sitting there. Then Chipmunk pokes the fire, says, "U ya ha ya ha—spring."[6] Then Snake pokes it, says, "Winter." Then Chipmunk pokes the fire, says, "Spring." Then Snake pokes the fire, says, "Winter." Then Chipmunk pokes the fire, says, "Spring." Then Snake pokes the fire, says, "Winter." They argue like this for some time. The only time when the words are not heard is when they sleep at night. Then at dawn those words are spoken again. They poke the fire here.

When the log burns through the middle, the last word spoken is "spring." Chipmunk says, "I'll go outside, take a look." Then she goes outside there. The ground is clear of snow. Small blades of grass are coming up. Then she nibbles it.

Chipmunk goes back inside their lodge. Snake says, "Is it clear yet?" "No, there is still snow on the ground." Snake says, "Winter!" Then Snake suddenly says, "Do you smell green grass?" Chipmunk says, "No, it's the mat you smell. I just turned it over." Snake says, "Winter." Then Chipmunk says, "Spring!" She runs outside. Then Snake says, "My! It does smell of green grass!"

Then Snake goes outside. All is green. The sun is shining. Then Snake eats grass, curls himself up on the ground here.

Then, the end of the trail.[7]

PERPETUATING THE WORLD

The telling of the stories reveals that which was originally established by the First Peoples (allowing discovery of what is most meaningful in the landscape), as it also integrates those traveling the story with that landscape (a landscape itself newly revitalized and rendered meaningful by the act of telling its story).[8] Certainly the young require the practical and moral guidance the stories convey, just as their parents rely upon the reinvigoration brought by these lessons. Through their stories the First Peoples offer "an order and meaning to birth, life, suffering, laughter, death, and the spirit world." The example of Crane and Rabbit and Jackrabbit, for instance, offers a model for behaving toward one's kinsmen. The stories impart a prescription for the great ceremonies as well as for a simple handshake—in short, a prescription for how to travel the landscape successfully. And the stories are imparted with "feeling." To appreciate a good story is to crack a smile or shed a tear. Stories speak to the "hearts" of the people, offering a sense of drama and suspense, of humor and tragedy. Through the retelling of their deeds, the First Peoples and their perennial teachings are thus brought to bear and shared directly with those in need.

The Children or the Adults Took the Meaning Out

Grandmothers were considered teachers, and so they would tell stories to children, maybe to entertain, or to keep them occupied or whatever, just about any time of the year that they had time to do this, to sit down and chat and tell a story. . . . Usually, non-Indians think of the stories as being stories told [only] for children, and they were not. . . . The stories were told to a mixed audience, and children or the adults took the meaning out of it at their level of understanding." (From an interview conducted on February 5, 1998.)

In addition to the comic relief a good telling of a Coyote story can bring, something else is to be discovered in the stories of Coyote. After he completed the telling of the story "Coyote Devours His Children," one elder would tell his listeners, both young and old, to "take care of your children, clean your children. Don't let someone devour them, hurt them, cripple them in their minds. If you do, you'll be humped up all your life, crippled in your mind." In those many examples in which Coyote's self-serving schemes end in failure, moral teachings on *how not to behave* toward one's own family members are found. In his deceptions and trickery, Coyote's actions point the way to proper behaviors by spotlighting their antithesis. As the elder would say, "Don't be the Coyote."

Coyote Devours His Children[9]

Coyote and his wife were on the mountainside. They put their tipi up and she says, "I'm going to get some berries, pick some huckleberries, going to fish a little bit, and come back. Then we'll have supper. You take care of these kids when I'm gone." He said, "Okay." He was laying in the tipi. She said, "Clean up around here. Don't just lay around here all day." And he was laying with his back propped up with his legs crossed like this, with his foot going like this [storyteller crossed his own legs and rocked one of his feet up and down]. "Okay, go on, don't worry about me. I'll clean up." He always needed guidance. So his wife left to go get berries and stuff.

And he was sitting there, looking out the tipi door, laying there. Sees his kids rolling around, playing with each other, rolling in the high mountain grass. He got to looking at them and his stomach started growling. He looked at them and he says, "I'm kinda hungry. I sure could use some berries, fish." So he looked at those kids and called one of them little kids in. And he had a little stick. And he called the little girl in and when she wasn't looking, he stuck the stick in her, through her hind end. He held it up and ate that child. And he laid down and [storyteller rubs stomach] his stomach. "Pretty good. I think I'll have another one." So he called another one in and did the same thing to him. Nobody could see, he was in the tipi. Ate that child. He kept doing it, doing it. Finally there was just one running around, lost, looking for the others. He says, "I better get rid of this one because she'll be coming home pretty soon. She'll want to know where her kids are." So he went outside and told that one, "I think they're over there." Pointed them out. The coyote child looked over there. And when he had his back turned, he stuck his stick right in him and ate him real fast.

Pretty soon he sees his wife coming down the trail, basket full of berries. Came back down there, and says, "Where is our children?" "Oh, I don't know. They run around, and I think they went over the hill this way and that way." She looked at him. His stomach was protruding. She says, "You've eaten our children, haven't you?" He stood there with a dumb look on his face, you know. And she kicked him. She started kicking him in the hind end. Kicked him all around the tipi, and every time she would kick him between the legs, one of them kids would come out. Kick him again, and come out again. All dead, six of them. She says, "Look at them. Look at what you've done. You've devoured our children. You've killed our children. Aren't you ashamed. Just so you can feel full, so you can relax. They are destroyed." He hung his head in shame.

She went over and jumped back and forth over them and sang her song. Pretty soon they started breathing, coughing, breathing. They are all wet from his saliva. She rubbed them off. One of those kids was all crippled up. She took a long time to straighten his legs. They sit up and say, "Hi Momma, hi Momma. We're hungry, Mom." "We'll feed you children. We'll feed you kids."

She turned to him and went to the stick he had. It was in the fire. And she took that stick and started hitting him. Coyote would howl, and howl, and howl. And she would hit him over the back. Just really beat him really bad. Crippled him up a little bit so he kinda humped up. She told him, "When you run you're going to run humped up." She says, "Nowhere in our world, that we live in, should you be doing these things to children, devouring them. When you devour them like that, they are broken, crippled."

When she got this all done, and he asked for some berries. And she kicked him again. "You go lay down. I'm going to feed these children first. You're not going to eat for a long time. You're going to be skinny. You'll no longer have a big belly on you anymore. Always going to be hungry. Because you ate your children." (From an interview conducted on October 3, 1997.)

In this example of Coyote we have a very compartmentalized, though generalized, model for behavior. Typically, when Coyote's intent is *self-effacing*, to the extent that he can be, and his trickery is directed at an adversary, he triumphs and thereby benefits the Human Peoples (hence his endeavors at successfully subduing the Rock Monster and releasing the salmon from the man-eaters). In Coyote's actions we find a model of *how to behave* while interacting with competitors and aggressors in the world outside the Schitsu'umsh family. Wit, intelligence, pretense, tack, agility, calculation, prowess, vigilance, and occasionally deception all predominate.

On the other hand, when Coyote's intent is *self-serving* and/or when he directs his deception against relatives, his greed usually results in failure and he is duped. Hence his foiled attempts to get the mice in that certain "green spot," to obtain a wife from the Schitsu'umsh, and to devour his own children. Together these stories convey a model for *how not to behave* toward one's family members, which, in the context of all the oral traditions, is complemented by such examples as Crane and Rabbit and Jackrabbit on *how to behave*. Where greed fails, sharing succeeds. Contrary to what might be gleaned from this discussion, Coyote's model, as set forth in any given story, is certainly not always neat and tidy, and exceptions to the rule can be discovered by story listeners. But, of course, at the moment of discovery, predicated on the recognition of "exception," there is necessarily a reiteration of Coyote's archetypal model.

In addition to their didactic and emotive qualities, the oral traditions provide a vital integrative and creative role. The First Peoples not only "prepared the world for the coming of the Human Peoples" long ago but they continue to do so. In the act of retelling their stories, the journeys of Crane and Coyote are continued into the present, bringing forth, forming, and manifesting those meanings in the world. In the telling of these stories, listeners become participants in the unfolding events and deeds of the First Peoples. The listeners go "inside and become the Coyote, or the Bear, or the Mole," and the First Peoples "come alive" and "swirl around you as the Turtle is saying his thing or as the Chipmunk is saying something. . . . All these things suddenly come alive." Thus participants are placed in a landscape revealed through the stories. The essential connections—the kinship—with the First Peoples and all the animals and plants of the landscape are reiterated and renewed. The participants of the storytelling are thus defined within the all-inclusive, perennial landscape of the First Peoples.

Listeners' participation is not only felt during the telling but also carried forth as the trails in the surrounding landscape are traveled. To walk the slopes of Tekoa Mountain is to hear the Rabbit and Jackrabbit exchange greetings. To look out onto Lake Coeur d'Alene is to see Coyote hang from a cliff as the Rock Monster splashes in the water, creating the "blue of the lake." To sight a hawk is to see Turtle "win the race." And then the moral importance conveyed in such deeds is remembered and engaged: One remembers to share the camas and to provide protection and safety for those in need, and one recalls that "everyone is equal." One's identity is thus linked inexorably with a landscape endowed with the teachings, in a geography rendered morally significant. As Keith Basso, who has worked most of his life with the Western Apache, so aptly phrased, "Selfhood and placehood are completely intertwined" (1997:146). To travel the landscape of the First Peoples is to reaffirm one's identity and to assure one's well-being; it is to have an existence. The Human Peoples and the landscape they travel are given definition and moral import.

And not only is the reality of the Human Peoples made certain, but in the act of retelling the stories, the existence of the First Peoples and the landscape they have brought forth are secured. The telling is itself a creative act. "The world is made and rendered meaningful in the act of revealing Coyote's story of it" (Frey 1995:214). Each time Lawrence Aripa retold the story of Coyote and the Rock Monster, the "blue of Coeur d'Alene Lake" was re-created and perpetuated. The creation of the world is an ongoing process. In the retelling of the oral traditions, something indispensable is thus "given back" to the landscape. The landscape, the phenomena of that landscape—Lake Coeur d'Alene and Tekoa Mountain, the camas, deer, and hawks, *suumesh* song—and the Animal Peoples themselves, all are given form, meaning, and life, are "set free."

As Crane had shown the way, the Human Peoples, in turn, share with and give back to Crane and the other First Peoples, helping to perpetuate and vitalize the First Peoples and the landscape. While the First Peoples have "prepared the world for the coming of Human Peoples," the Human Peoples must help continue that preparation. The camas and deer are readied to be received. The landscape and all its Peoples are given animation.

The "real," then, is *participation* in the perennial landscape traveled by Coyote and by Crane. Contrasting Euro-American and Navajo narrative performances, Barre Toelken and Tacheeni Scott (1981:92) observed that Euro-American "audiences are said to *suspend disbelief* in watching a play, while Navajos [and Schitsu'umsh] can be said to *intensify their sense of reality* by watching Ma'i [Coyote]." The landscape encountered while walking on Tekoa Mountain, or through participation while hearing the story of Rabbit and Jackrabbit, are thus indistinguishable, both imbued with the value of kinship and an ethic of sharing. The story and the landscape are as one.

In preparing the Schitsu'umsh landscape for the coming of Human Peoples, the First Peoples have invariably and ultimately become the Animal Peoples, dissolving any temporal distinctions and dichotomies between a world in preparation and a world prepared. The First Peoples, in the guise of the Animal Peoples, offer the gifts of venison that nourish, the plants that heal, and the *suumesh* songs that transform. In the stories the landscape is made and given definition, and in their retelling that landscape is perpetuated. To "go inside the stories" is to go out into the world. To view the lake or the mountains of that landscape is to hear the stories of Crane, Coyote, Hawk, and Rabbit.

THE PLANT AND ANIMAL RITUALS

In the rituals associated with hunting deer or gathering huckleberries, for instance, the First Peoples have offered a means and an opportunity to reiterate thanks for what has been received, and to celebrate and ensure the sharing of those gifts with those in the community who are in need. Both James Teit (1930:185) and Verne Ray (1942:133–34) noted the importance of what they termed "First-Fruits Ceremonies" or "First-Products Rites" among the Schitsu'umsh. The patterns of sharing are expressed in a number of distinct and varied occasions, all involving the ceremonial sharing of the gifts of venison or berries with the entire family and community. They include the rituals associated with a boy's or a girl's first successful hunt of an elk or deer, those associated with designated hunters, and those associated with the gathering and distribution of camas, water potato, and huckleberries, for example.

For plant foods such as camas, water potato, and huckleberry, the sharing rituals are essential. Teit described how, prior to the gathering of camas or berries, prayer and an offering of some camas or berries, placed on a mat or in a basket, were made in the direction of the highest mountain and to *Amotqn*, telling him that his children were now about to eat them. Then the assembled families likely danced and feasted on the berries or roots gathered (Teit 1930:185).

These sharing rituals have continued into recent years, as illustrated in the gathering of huckleberries. As we saw in the vignette "The First Fruits," upon arriving at the family's huckleberry camp, the father's and mother's actions replicate the roles of the Creator and the Mother Earth—the father's role of providing life and the mother's role of nurturing that life. After the gathering of the huckleberries, and just before leaving their huckleberry camp, the father would take a small basket, partially filled with the berries, and leave it in a nearby tree, giving thanks to the *Amotqn*. Likewise for the water potato, prior to their gathering in late October, a *suumesh* song would first be sung, asking the Creator for a good gathering and giving thanks. Those gathering the water potato are instructed to "take at least one of these and give it to an elder, one who could not make it down here today, someone in need of this water potato."

In recent years the Schịtsu'umsh have been holding the Water Potato Powwow and Dinner as a community-wide celebration. On October 28, 1995, it was held at the Tribal Elementary School at DeSmet. As with all Coeur d'Alene Powwows I have attended, this celebration was open to all in the surrounding communities. Everyone, Indian and white, was encouraged to share in the food and dance. The feast, which preceded the dance, often includes salmon, beef stew, dried meat, an assortment of fruits, salads, pies, and cakes, fry bread, and the water potato, all in abundance. The women who organize the meals on these occasions typically prepare food in excess of the anticipated attendance, e.g., a meal for 1,800 in anticipation of 1,500. As people departed from the evening's celebration on this occasion, they carried plastic bags full of fry bread, apples, and salmon steak.

Its Life Was Fulfilled

My boys, . . . they didn't get their first deer until we came back home here three years ago. What I did then, we had a big dinner. We cooked up a lot of it. Made some stew, froze some steak and invited people over, family and friends. Before we eat, then we announce, my son got his first deer, what it means to our people, that story about the deer giving up their life for us. You ask nature for one. They know that you're after them. All the things about how to hunt that they learned all that when they were little. Now we want that deer in spirit to be happy. Its life was fulfilled. Part of its purpose for us people have been fulfilled. In spirit we want it to be happy. We want the food to be blessed. We'll have strength that our children will have good health and all of us who partake of it will have good health. Our son, he can't eat any of it, the one who shot the first one. From it, the strength of the deer is going to be with him. Have good eyesight, have good instincts, a good mind and then after dinner, we distribute it all out. We don't keep any of it. (From an interview conducted on May 24, 1996.)

In a young boy's "first kill" of deer, elk, or "even porcupine," all the meat from the kill is usually distributed to others—to his family members, to elders, to those in need. This sharing may even extend beyond the hunter's own family, as meat from a first kill is sometimes given to "widows, families without men in the homes." Some families continue this pattern of ritual sharing following the first kill of each fall hunting season. In these instances, while the hunter may butcher the animal, he does not consume any of the meat. The act reiterates his "honored role" as a "provider," and the importance of sharing with those in need. As with the first kill, in all subsequent hunting occasions it is understood that the deer or elk "offers itself up" to the hunter only if the hunter exhibits great hunting skill and shows respect to his "brother."

In the actions of the designated hunters, also formerly known as widow hunters, we see a continued and essential expression of the sharing behavior of the Schitsu'umsh. The term "widow hunters" referred to those hunters who, upon the death of a hunter, would bring meat to the widow of the deceased. This generalized pattern was reported by James Teit and corresponds as well with Father Point's 1842–43 observations (1967:180). Deer hunters typically kept the "brisket and one sidepiece" of their kill for members of their own extended family, and then distributed the rest of the meat among "neighbors or friends" (Teit 1930:162). In the instance of buffalo meat, "each hunter owned all the meat he killed," but "whatever was left was the property of whoever wanted it, and all could help themselves without restriction" (ibid.). As related by an elder, when families used to gather into the fishing camps during the fish runs, a sharing distribution took place. At the completion of the catch, camp leaders would redistribute the fish based upon the needs of individual families, not on how much effort each of those families contributed to the fishing.

Like the widow hunters, the designated hunters of today are generally young men with a "skill at hunting." In addition to their normal subsistence hunting of game animals for their immediate household, these hunters provide venison and elk meat to members of their extended family, including elders (parents and grandparents, as well as uncles and aunts), who no longer hunt for themselves, and sisters and younger brothers, who may not have the skill to hunt for themselves. The term "designated" refers to the hunter who hunts for someone else; the "designated hunter" is not hunting for his personal needs. In fact, all the meat acquired while hunting for someone else is given away to that person. It is considered inappropriate for a hunter to keep for himself any of the meat that has been designated for someone else.

In one instance, a family's designated hunter provided game meat for the members of seven separate residential households, in addition to his own, all of whom he considered his family. These individuals are related

Frenchy SiJohn, a designated hunter, and son Victor, May 1996

to him as father, sisters, and brothers-in-law, nieces and nephews, and uncles and aunts. Thus some sixty to seventy people directly benefit from the meat secured by this single hunter. This hunter estimated that the game brought in during a single year typically amounts to ten to fifteen elk or deer, with "maybe a bear" as well. A bear might not be obtained more than once every three years or so. "You don't go out and hunt a bear, but if you're out, one may come to you." He personally loves bear meat, but commented to me that "nobody likes to eat bear hardly anymore. It's too greasy, they say." But "if you try it, you'll crave it."

The amount of venison and elk this particular designated hunter usually acquires during the year provides up to 80 percent of his own household's meat consumption, with the rest coming from store-purchased beef and an occasional hamburger from a "fast food" restaurant. "I really don't care for beef that much. I don't have a taste for it," he said. The children of this thirty-year-old hunter "don't have a taste for it either." This 80/20 breakdown is true also of at least two other Schitsu'umsh families I have observed. While the other designated hunters may not be responsible for as large a family as this hunter, the ten active designated hunters of whom I am personally aware may provide fresh meat for up to twenty to thirty individuals within each of their respective families.[10] However, it must be noted that this level of reliance on venison and elk meat does not encompass all Schitsu'umsh families and their households. Many families have become dependent on store-purchased beef for their day-to-day needs.

Besides the meat provided to those in his own family, various designated hunters are also called upon to bring in meat for meals served at the community-wide Powwows, such as the annual Cataldo Pilgrimage (Feast of the Assumption) in August, the Water Potato Powwow in October, and the Graduation Powwow held in June. At the Cataldo Pilgrimage held in 1997, four elk were brought in by hunters and then smoked for dried meat. Designated hunters would also likely be called upon to provide meat for the meals held in conjunction with the wakes and Memorial Giveaways held throughout the year, and for the Jump Dances held in January and February. In addition, there are always individual tribal members "down on their luck," or an elder with few relatives, who will also become recipients of the designated hunter's meat. "A roast or something will be dropped off"—something done "out of respect."

At the Powwow and wake meals, the dried meat is always served in abundance. Toward the end of such meals, plastic bags are distributed and the remaining meat given to the elders and needy families. One designated hunter has observed the rise of two types of hunters on the reservation today: those who "beat the bush" and those who hunt with their "Glad zip-lock bags!" He followed his comment with a big laugh. During the breaking up of the 1997 Cataldo encampment, I observed the woman who had smoked the dried meat rush over to various elders and give them a large handful of dried meat to "take along for the ride home."

Gladys Reichard observed that "much stress is laid upon the dispensation of food. A stingy person was despised. It was proper to have enough food for the guests to eat to repletion and to take some home, perhaps enough for their families. Chiefs were expected to share food with the whole village" (1947:51–52). This was expected of the chief for the meat given to him by Crane in the narrative "Crane and Coyote," for example.

While certainly not all Schitsu'umsh families rely upon venison and elk for their daily needs, because of the level of participation by Schitsu'umsh at the various meals held at the numerous Powwows and wakes, at least two interviewees estimated that up to 90 percent of the Schitsu'umsh con-

sume, at various times during the course of a year, meat brought in by designated hunters. These estimates conform to my own observations of meat
consumption over the last few years.[11]

It is not just that the dried meat is served and consumed at the Powwow
and wake meals; it is "expected." "It really isn't a Coeur d'Alene meal unless
dried meat and salmon are served." As we will discuss in the following sections, "The Jump Dance" and "The Memorial Giveaway," while the
Schitsu'umsh certainly enjoy the "taste" of venison and elk, the significant
spiritual and kinship meaning attached to both necessitate their being served
at the meals.

Gifts are used not only to nurture growing and healthy bodies but also
to heal those bodies and souls when they become sick or "wounded." For
instance, chokecherry bark is used to make a "salve for cuts and sores,"
and "cub ears" is used to treat skin rashes. The red "pitch gum" from the
ponderosa pine tree is applied as a poultice to the eyes, "both in the eye
and over it," to assist in the healing of "snow blindness." In the application of *qhasqhs* ("*xasxas*"), James Teit observed that it "was dried and pow-
ered fine, then mixed with animal grease and used as a salve on sores"
(1930:197). Found along the mountain streams and rivers of the St. Joe
and Coeur d'Alene rivers, *qhasqhs* continues to be relied upon. It might
be boiled to make a tea for a sore throat or upper respiratory infection,
or singers might chew the root, helping them to maintain their stamina
and preventing them from losing their voice during a Powwow. Mint is
gathered along streambeds and made into a tea for "colds." As Blue Jay,
Hawk, and Badger first instructed, the "whole tree, the roots, bark, and
leaves" of the cedar are to be used to heal the sick, make baskets, and purify
the impure. The roots are pulverized and made into a tea for a "blood-
cleansing thing." The fibers of the cedar are made into storage and carrying baskets. In the Sweat House, entire branches of cedar are tied to
the ceiling of the lodge. "When you come out, the cedar has cleaned your
head, eyes, and throat." Cedar boughs might also be hung in homes, "to
protect."

The rosebush and "rose tea" (boiled from its bark) are also used for spiritual cleansing and protection. In preparing a body for burial, the corpse
might be washed in rose tea. Rose tea might also be used to pour over the
hot rocks during a sweat and, by a hunter, to wash over his rifle to improve
its accuracy. Branches from the bush might be hung in the living room of
someone's home or around their windows for protection from "spiritual
invasion or bad spirits."

Yellow Root

The yellow root was used for medicinal purposes. They boiled it, and you could drink it as a tea. . . . I was playing with my cousins and it could have been nettles, whatever it was, gave us rashes, and we thought we had the "seven-year itch," because we didn't know what it was. When we got back to my aunt's house, she boiled this yellow root and she made us bathe in that water and rubbed us down with the yellow root. And that rash, whatever it was, disappeared, and then she washed and boiled all our clothes before she gave them back to us. We didn't know what we had gotten into, and we ended up with this itch and rash. She used the yellow root to instantly cure whatever was wrong. I never forgot that experience. (From an interview conducted February 5, 1998.)

SHARING THE VENISON

Designated hunters continue as the critical and primary source of meat for many families. *Qhasqhs* is still gathered and used by the Powwow singers, or to relieve the suffering from cold or flu. Many of the grandmothers love nothing more than to have bitterroot or camas prepared and served to them at a birthday celebration. While deer, huckleberries, and camas are now supplemental to an overall contemporary diet, their significance has not diminished. And while the inventory of medicinal plants is greatly reduced today, the importance of the healing plants continues.

The ritual acts associated with deer and camas, water potato and *qhasqhs*, embrace and reflect the essential teachings of the First Peoples. In hunting deer or digging camas, a respect for the animal or plant is shown, as expressed first in song or prayer asking permission to hunt or gather the animal or plant. In prayer the Creator is addressed, and there is an understanding of participating in a "spiritual world." The water potato consumed at a Powwow, the smoked meat chewed at a Memorial Giveaway, the camas eaten at the conclusion of a Jump Dance, and the small pouch of bitterroot tucked in the coffin beside a deceased relative, all reiterate an essential, perennial, and expanded kinship. In partaking of the plants and animals of the landscape, the Human Peoples reclaim their affiliation with and identity in relation to that landscape, the lakes and mountains, and the Creator and the First Peoples. Even in picking only "a handful of berries" and eating them, "you are connecting to the old people and to the spirit world and to our ancestors, to my grandmother, asking for strength, and from them through the earth, through Mother Earth, to grant us those things." In providing the dried meat or camas to those in need, the people are sharing, just as "the Creator wanted the people to do with these things."

While no longer physically able to hunt deer or dig camas because of his age, Felix Aripa mentioned that he often finds himself the recipient of gifts of venison and camas. In one interview session he spoke with great appreciation of a jar filled with camas root recently given him. The central role of "sharing with all peoples in the community," an attitude of generosity and inclusivity, is reflected in the feasts held during the Water Potato Powwows, Jump Dances, and Memorial Giveaways.

In the character and actions of Crane is found the archetypal designated hunter. As Crane had provided for the needs of Little Squirrel and Chipmunk, and for an entire village, so too today do the designated hunters generously provide venison and elk for those in need, without thought of receiving anything in kind. Thus in sharing the venison and water potato with the children and elders, and the yellow root and *qhasqhs* with the sick and ill, the Schitsu'umsh reiterate what was first demonstrated by the First Peoples and continued in the actions of the Animal Peoples.

THE POWWOW CEREMONY

The singing, drumming, and dancing of the Powwow provide opportunities for the Schitsu'umsh to express prayer and give thanks, renew family ties, and "just have fun." And in the regalia worn, the dancer's movements, and the songs sung, the Powwow is also an important means to celebrate and share with others the images and sounds that emanate from the Animal Peoples. The sounds of a *suumesh* song or the sight of an eagle feather inexorably link singers and dancers, and all those engaged in the Powwow, with the Animal Spirits of the mountains. In solidifying this link, the health and well-being of the entire Schitsu'umsh family are thus renewed.

It's a Prayer, It's a Ceremony

Like if you go to a Powwow, you might see the dancing, and then the people watching. It's a prayer. And everybody that goes to Powwows, or maybe somebody that may be going there out of curiosity, maybe some *Suuyapis* [white people] go just out of curiosity, they might think of it as entertainment at first, but I think they see it's more than that. It's like it's a ceremony, is what it is. It's a ceremony, a gathering of people, the strength of

Intertribal encampment near Spokane Falls, August 1995

Indian people. That's what you see out there. Pretty soon, they start feeling it, and they want to participate, and at some of the Powwows they do let them go out and participate and dance, which is, I mean, they can feel the energy and feel the Spirits. I mean, it just starts moving them, and they want to get out there. (From an interview conducted July 30, 1997.)

Certain gatherings are held throughout the year: the Casino Powwow and Celebration in March; the Graduation Powwow, which honors graduates from all levels of education, elementary through college, in June; and in July at Post Falls, the highly successful intertribal gathering, *Julyamsh*. Each August two important Powwows are held: the large Intertribal Powwow at River Front Park, near Spokane Falls; and, on the fifteenth of the month, the annual Powwow and Pilgrimage to the Cataldo Mission. The North Idaho College Powwow, Veterans Powwow, and Water Potato

Powwow are held in the fall. In addition, occurring throughout the year, Powwows are held in association with an elder's birthday celebration or Memorial Giveaways. In fact, song, drum, and dance might spontaneously come together for any number of family occasions, as, for example, following a Saturday evening meal.

The Family Drum

It was after breakfast, and the family, numbering some twenty adults, gathered around their drum near the tipis. Many others, with their children, looked on, seated on folding chairs. When the first beat was heard echoing through camp, it immediately caught the attention of the children, and they began gathering around the bass-sized drum. The drum was "calling the family together." There they found a warm reception, not turned way, but welcomed in. With adults guiding their arms to the beat of the song, young and old voices were raised. A young parent would hold his three-year-old son on his lap throughout most the morning hours, as he too drummed. From the doorway of one of the tipis, looking on, a great-grandmother held a small child in her arms, at times motioning the child's arm to the beat of the drum.

All morning long family songs were sung. Between songs, someone would tell a story. As it unfolded, complete silence engulfed the entire camp; all listened intently. Some stories were recounting events in the family's history—hunting stories, war stories—while others were, . . . well, just "events," which were inevitably followed by tremendous laughter from all. Then song would commence again, the beat and voices in perfect unison. The voices sang with an energy and emotion, with heart. A little later the sword taken at the *Hngwsumn* Battle by one of the great-grandfathers was brought out and each member of the family, young and old, given the opportunity to closely view and hold the war trophy. As they did, they were inescapably linked to and made part of those who had traveled and fought for this land and its peoples so many years past. During that morning's singing and storytelling, the heartbeat of a family beat strong, and, with care, the world of the great-grandparents, and of the Creator, was being shared and passed on to the children. (From participant observations made at the *Hngwsumn* Memorial Ride on May 26, 1996.)

Typically a Powwow is preceded by a meal provided for all in attendance—the dancers and drums, as well as the guests and onlookers. Following the

The family drum during the Hngwsumn Memorial Ride, May 1996

meal, the "emcee would begin the Powwow." A few "warm-ups" might first be sung, just to get the drums prepared. Then the emcee calls for the Grand Entry. The host drum, or "lead drum," sings the grand entry followed by the "flag song." The host drum also provides the final song of the evening, "the retirement, when we retire the colors." The emcee coordinates the evening's events. He informs the drums when each is "up," and he announces which drum is providing which type of song. He also adds commentary throughout the Powwow, pointing out a special elder in attendance and asking for applause, or remarking on the significance of a particular dance, for example. He might also bring a laugh by teasing a "sister" or telling a joke. He is often assisted by the "whip woman." She looks after the young dancers, helping to quiet a noisy few during a prayer or showing the proper way to dance during a particular song.

The Drum

The drum is a heartbeat. It's a heartbeat. It's the center of our people, Coeur d'Alenes. We've always been taught that everything is in a circle. Everything comes around. From birth, from the day you're born, you're young, and when you come out of the womb and you're wrinkly, you have no teeth, no hair, and you're just fragile, and you make that loop, and then, when you get old, when you get real old, you lose your teeth and you lose your hair, you get wrinkles. That's what my grandma used to tell me all the time. You just make that circle of life, and that's the way a drum is, it's in a circle. Because that's what we've always been taught, is everything is in a circle. It takes a life-cycle.

A drum is a very, very highly respected thing in my household. With my boy, as young as he is, four years old, he sits at the drum when I practice, and he knows it's time to practice. It's something that's taken serious. As young as he is, he's like four years old. He knows it's not a plaything. You don't bang on it. You don't crawl on it. It's just something of respect. That's where the heartbeat is of our people, every time we drum. It's a very respectful thing. (From an interview conducted July 30, 1997.)

With all the onlookers standing in respect, the Grand Entry of all the dancers is led by the "flag bearers." Made up of veterans with "combat honors" and elders, they parade the "Indian flag," a fur-and-cloth-wrapped crooked staff upon which eagle feathers are attached, as well as the U.S. and perhaps the Canadian flags. Upon entering the dance arena, the procession dances clockwise around the dance floor, with elders followed by the younger dancers and men, followed by women. "They'd enter with dignity and purpose, very stately." With all the dancers on the floor looking toward the flag bearers, the "flag song" is sung. "You'd feel the pride; it was spiritually uplifting. The flag told the story of sacrifice." This is then followed with an opening prayer offered by one of the elders. "Sometimes it's Father Connolly, sometimes it's Lawrence [Aripa] or the chairman. They'll have someone that will lead the opening prayer, to offer up the evening to the Creator."

After the Grand Entry but before the evening's dancing gets started, the dance area might be "prepared" with a Sneak-up Dance. Male dancers, often veterans, move about the area as if crouching to "sneak upon and scout out an enemy." The way is prepared for the others. The main body of dances are Intertribal Dances. Participants dance counterclockwise around the arena, and as they do they exchange handshakes and smiles and renew acquaintances. All, including visitors, are encouraged to participate, whether in full dance regalia or not.

There could be anywhere from a single drum to a dozen drums at a Powwow, depending on the occasion. In addition to the Schitsu'umsh drums, groups from the Spokane and Nez Perce reservations are often present. Each drumming group may have up to eight singers, men and women. To be "invited to the drum, to join in the singing, is a honored position. It means you have listened and learned, learned the prayers. The songs are prayers, are to be done with humility."

The lead singer begins a song by singing the first line or verse of the song, with the others members of the drum following in a repeat or chorus, and with a slight variation of that line. The repeating of the entire line and chorus four times, or four "push-ups," constitutes an entire song. By accentuating the speed and volume of the last five beats of a song, its end is signaled, and the dancers are prepared to stop on the proper drumbeat. A "tail," or final chorus, is sung and the song ended.

The lead singer must be well versed in the various types of dances, for when his drum is called upon, he might have to lead, for example, a fancy dance song, a shawl dance song, a traditional, or an honor song. Most songs are sung without words, though "word songs" are more frequently heard today. The songs are composed of vocables, vowel sounds such as ya, hey, hi, lay, and so on. These are sounds that came originally from the First Peoples, such as Coyote and Badger.

Throughout the Powwow, specific etiquette governs the behavior of dancers, singers, and onlookers. During an Honor Dance, for instance, everyone is supposed to stand "respectfully," neither recording nor photographing this special event. Should an eagle plume or feather accidentally drop to the floor from a dancer's regalia, a Pickup Dance is held. Male Traditional dancers, often war veterans, immediately circle the feather, protecting it from the other dancers. The feather lies on the floor just as "a warrior had fallen." After the dance floor is cleared, one of the veterans, likely "a spiritual man," may then publicly recount a "war deed" and offer "a wish for good fortune." The "restored" feather is given to the dancer, who reciprocates with a gift to the veteran for his blessing. The dancer is made whole again, able to resume dancing. The Pickup Dance acknowledges the preeminence of the Eagle for the dancers.

Alternating with the Intertribal Dances are a number of specific types of dances. Men's and Women's Traditional are two such dances. A Men's

Skip Skanen dancing at Cataldo, August 1997

Traditional dancer can be identified by his regalia, which includes a single eagle-feather bustle at the waist, a porcupine-hair "roach" headdress with one or two eagle tail feathers standing upright from it, beadwork, breast-plates, necklaces, leggings, anklets, and moccasins. The roach headdress is said to represent the "top knot of a male prairie chicken." The dance style is "earth-bound" and reserved, but can include active head and upper-body movements. The action mimics hunting, tracking, or fighting.

Women's Traditional regalia usually includes a full-length buckskin or cloth dress, a fringed shawl wrapped over the shoulders or folded over an arm, extensive beadwork (belts, capes, crowns, hair decorations, braid wraps, leggings, moccasins), a choker, and a handbag. Female dancers do not wear bells. Women's dancing is done in very modest steps. Women often dance in unison, two or three or four women side by side, with only subtle foot movements, or they may dance in place in a vertical movement. Both men and women may have an eagle-feather fan, a mirror, or some other hand-held object. Within these generalized patterns, tremendous individual variation occurs, as each dancer takes his inspiration from his own family traditions and personal experiences.

Sometime around 1870, a women's Round Dance was introduced at the intertribal gatherings. It may have come from the Crow or Cree. Dancing sideways and in a large circle, women take a male partner, holding his hand, and dance "a limping step." It was said that she presents a gift to the man she sought to dance with. Like the Round Dance, women seek out their partners for an Owl Dance. Each couple then dances together, hand in hand. In the Rabbit Dance, the men take their turn seeking out female partners.

Brightly colored dresses with large "jingles" sewn in a line or chevron pattern characterize the Jingle-Dress Dance, a women's dance. The metal lids from chewing-tobacco containers are rolled into cones to make the best jingles. Unlike the Traditional Dancers, Jingle Dancers do not use a shawl. The distinct sound of the jingles is often a highlight for many elders.

The Fancy Dance and the Grass Dance are dances of exuberance and stamina. In contrast to the stately Traditional Dance, the regalia of the Fancy and Grass Dancers is more colorful and expressive. The Fancy Dancer wears two large feather bustles, one at the waist and the other on the shoulders, with plenty of long fringe adorning the arms and legs. The dancer swirls and twists with elevated feet and elaborate leg movements to the rapid beat of the drum. Lacking bustles altogether, the long, vividly-colored yarn fringe of the Grass Dancer's shirts, pants, and aprons flows with his contorted body movements and the sound of ankle goat bells. Often found in judged

Lucy Finley dancing at Cataldo, August 1997

contests, Fancy and Grass Dancers attempt to avoid missing a beat of the drum and, most important, the final beat of a song, as the drummers try to confuse them.

An Honor Dance might be held out of respect for a particular person or family. It could be given for a veteran who had distinguished himself in combat. An honor song would certainly be heard during an elder's nineti-eth birthday celebration, or during the "naming ceremony" for a nine-month-old infant who is receiving the name that will "protect" him for his entire life. And following a Memorial Giveaway, a honor song might be sung, helping everyone remember the deceased and as a way to "welcome back" a family who has been in mourning for the past year. It is custom-ary for all to stand in silence and respect during an Honor Dance.

SONGS FOR HEALING AND PRAYER

The songs and dances of the Powwow are the most overt and public expres-sions of what it means to be Schitsu'umsh. In song and dance, both of which are acts of ceremony and prayer, the values of family and sharing, and the unique heritage of the Schitsu'umsh are disseminated to the young and reaffirmed in the old. The Powwow is also a means for simple enjoyment of company, a time to laugh, visit, renew friendships, and start new ones. While no longer able to ride against the colonels of the nineteenth century, today's Schitsu'umsh use the Powwow as a kind of "battlefield" on which to express their resistance to the onslaught of Euro-American culture.

Powwows also reiterate and strengthen the Schitsu'umsh connection with family and landscape. The drum is the "heartbeat of the people," and the songs come from "listening to the Trees and Mother Earth." The dance regalia itself, made up of feathers, quills, and buckskin, celebrates the Eagle, Porcupine, and Deer. In dance, the people become extensions of these Animal Peoples, and the kinship of the Schitsu'umsh family is reinvigo-rated. In song and dance, the people hear the voices of and move with the Animal Peoples of the Schitsu'umsh landscape. The Powwow is thus an important opportunity to express and demonstrate to the world what is most cherished by the Schitsu'umsh.

The Songs Are For . . .

Some songs are used for healing. Some songs are used for praying. There are certain songs for different ceremonies. There's the Powwow songs.

And the Jump Dance songs. There's a lot of songs that I know that are for different things. And I just use them for myself, too. Like for a hunting song, before I go hunting, or a prayer song, or I sing for my kids. I've got certain songs that make me feel good myself inside. Even coming to work, a morning song or an evening song. There's always a song that I sing like when I wake up in the morning, or before I go to bed, I sing those songs, because that's what my grandfather taught me. All the times.

It might get monotonous or whatever you call it, but you pray a lot. Even when you're driving down the road or riding your horse. Like I said, in the morning, I just sing. There's a special song that I sing in the morning, called the morning song. I sing that song for the Creator. I sing it for my kids. I ask the Creator to take care of my kids when I'm not with them. To give me the strength, to give me the courage to come to work, to work for the tribe.

Because every day, our tribe is under scrutiny by the federal government, state government, all the time. In today's society, like myself, I look at it as a warrior. I'm working for the tribe, I'm a young man. I go out and tap into these different resources to help better the tribe and help better our people. I might not see these benefits as an old man. And it's going to be my boy, when he's eighteen, nineteen, twenty years old. The things that I do now is going to affect him, maybe it's going to affect his boy. Things have changed a lot from a long time ago, but they haven't really, if you really think about it. I know they always sent the young guys out to protect the people, to feed the people, to feed the tribe. And that's what I am. Not just me, but other young men that work for the tribe.

So I just kind of pray for things like that. And I have certain songs, and not only pray for myself and for my family, but for the tribe as a whole, and all the Indian people, to help perpetuate us and help move us forward. (From an interview conducted on July 30, 1997.)

THE SWEAT HOUSE CEREMONY[12]

Despite the efforts of the First Peoples in preparing the world, ridding it of Monsters of all sorts and rendering it with gifts, the Human Peoples are still afflicted with "sickness" and find themselves wanting and in need. In the ceremonies of the Sweat House and Jump Dance, people are afforded a means, through prayer, song, and dance, to convey the desires of the sick and needy, and through song and intense heat, they seek to bring to bear the healing *suumesh*. This could be a healing sought for a physical ailment,

Nicky Pakootas and daughter, Olivia, dancing at Cataldo, August 1997

or for the "wounds" from an interfamily rift or from "a lack of understanding of the Coeur d'Alene ways." In addition, the Sweat House and
Jump Dance offer an opportunity to give back to the landscape. In the inten-
sity of the heat generated from "jumping hard," and from the heated rock
and steam of the Sweat House, participants can give of themselves to help
assure the health and well-being of the gifts—the camas, huckleberries, deer,
and *qhasqhs*.

Sweat with My *Sile'*

I was fortunate enough to sweat with my *Sile'* [grandfather], who was a
medicine man. My *Sile'* never talked English in the sweat. He never did. He
just talked Indian and saying and praying. It was a time to cleanse ourselves
and to purify ourselves. Maybe go to, I'd say the Church, but to go to a
Jump Dance or go to Medicine Dance. He used it to purify himself, to get
ready to heal somebody, to try to find out what's wrong with them. But
it's definitely a spiritual mode. You can meditate, get outside of yourself
and look inside yourself. You have to be there. It's not a time to show off.
It's a time to really be humble and really pray and get one with your sur-
roundings and the Maker. Visions come at that time, they come. If they
don't, that's good, too.

I find that it's a little like, in the Catholic Church, they have a time they
go to renew themselves. They call it a retreat. Nowadays, they go like three
days, . . . during that time they would be fasting and praying. You can go
do a sweat, in a night, and come out feeling the same way. You feel high
and one, and at peace. You come to terms with yourself. (From an interview conducted on February 12, 1997.)

Addressed as "the Grandmother" or, as stated by Paschal George in 1938,
the "Great grandfather of grandfathers" (1938:16), the Sweat House is constructed of willow saplings, some ten to twelve feet in length, each planted
a few inches into the ground and in a circle ranging in diameter from six
to eight feet.[13] The saplings are arched over, attached, and secured to each
other to form a domed-shape structure, some four to five feet in height. A
blanket and, in the past, an animal-skin door might face south, as toward
an adjacent creek (as I have seen in one instance) or face east toward the
mountains and the rising sun. The entire willow-sapling structure is covered with a thick layer of rugs, canvas tarps, blankets, and quilts.

Paschal George noted that in the "olden days" the lodge structure might be "covered with cedar bark" and "dirt," and the ground inside covered with "some dry grasses of different sorts" (1938:16). The covering of earth on these particular lodges would be from "5 to 12 cm" thick (Teit 1930:62). Today a typical lodge could comfortably accommodate four to six adult men, each seated within. Teit noted that most of the Sweat Houses he observed in 1904 "were small, and could accommodate only one or two persons" (1930:62). On the Coeur d'Alene Reservation, the Sweat House might be located at a remote site, along a stream, or even in a town, such as Plummer, perhaps in someone's backyard.

The Womb

Well, you go in the door, it's supposed to be like going in the womb of the Mother Earth. That's what you hear a lot of our people say. And you go in there and they dig a pit in the sweat lodge and they bring in the heated rocks. They're usually red hot when they bring them in. And they call the rocks "Grandpas." They're part of this Mother Earth. And they have life. And that heat with that fire is in them, the spark in them, the spark of life, they have life. You bring them in with the water that has life. It has the power to sustain life with the other elements, the earth, and air and the fire. Together they have the power to create the miracle of life itself. We all have all the elements of the land in our body. Whether it's calcium or zinc or whatever. In every cell of our bodies, it's there in the earth. There's nothing different that we have in our bodies than there is in the earth. And whatever it is, 90 percent of our body is water. And the air was blown into us by a higher power when we took our first breath. And we have that heat in our body like that, that flame, the fire.

And, so they use that, those rocks, the Mother Earth. They use the fire and they put on the water. The steam that comes out is like a medicine. First it gently comes over you and soothes you. You can breathe it in. It's supposed to be like good medicine. When these elements combined together, they made this good medicine come forth. You breathe it, it's going to make you have good health. It's going to clear your senses, your mind. It's going to make your vision, hearing, stronger and better. And you're going to sleep good. You're going to wake up feeling strong. All like that.

So they begin it that way. They put on that water for, . . . depends on which family you go to. It might be a little bit different. The way they inherit it from family to family. That water on for the Mother Earth. And the four directions. They might put on some cedar and tobacco and sage. Kind of like cleanse out the sweat and everybody there and put their hands through the smoke and touch it to their body. And they might use tobacco; one kind or another to put it on there.

Then they'll pray in there. They'll pray about everything. Always remember the elders and the children and the needy. They'll pray about what they came in for. Things they might need in their job or home. Trouble they're having in the family. One of the teenage children are running off a little bit and having a tough time. Bring them in there and just pray for them from there. That they're going to be all right. They're going to be protected and watched over.

Then as they finish their prayer, they'll sing. Different families have different songs. So songs have meaning. They've all been handed down one generation to the next. They can't sing just any old kind of song, a social song or funeral song or something. It's got to be a song appropriate for that ceremony and that prayer. But they'll know which one to use. And they might sing a song or two, usually it's two, and after that, they'll take a break. They'll open the door and people can go out if they want to. Or sit inside and catch their breath a little bit. Drink water. And they'll come back in again and kind of repeat that procedure.

And when they go out, it's totally dark in there [inside the Sweat House]. When they go out they open that door and whatever doors have been closed to them, whatever obstacles may have been put up before them, they'll be swept away and those closed doors will be opened. They'll kind of arise from the womb of the Mother Earth. Kind of renewed, reclaimed like a newborn baby. Mentally, physically, and spiritually. And they'll greet that light of our Creator. They say that sun is the Father, the Great Spirit. So I've come from the darkness of the womb to life again. They'll put their hands to that light and kind of touch it to themself and greet that world again. That's all spiritual, all deeply religious to the people. They really believe and practice it. It's actually pretty simple. It's just the way I described it. It's that simple. (From an interview conducted on June 12, 1996.)

In addition to the willow-constructed Sweat House, the Schitsu'umsh traditionally used a pit-house sweat. While no longer used today, Paschal George described it as "a hole three feet in diameter which they fill with water, mix it with all kinds of herbs, then they throw this hot rock into it until it starts to boil. After it is cool enough for a person to get in, the[y] sit in there and just sweat" (1938:16). The pit-house sweat is also referred to in the narrative "Muskrat and Otter." According to Reichard's consultants, "it was customary for everyone to take baths like this" (1947:48). It could provide a "remedy for various ailments like rheumatism and so forth" (George 1938:16).

Unlike the Jump Dance, sweats are taken year-round, during the summer's heat as well as the winter's cold. The lodge structures are sometimes built or rebuilt, replacing a lodge "worn down with use" in the spring, "when the willows grow long, straight, and tall." When a sweat is to be held, rocks are first piled on top of pine or cottonwood logs, which are then set afire. Up to an hour is needed to obtain the desired temperature. The most prized rocks are volcanic, since they seldom "explode on you when heated."

With a pitchfork, each rock is placed in the pit, located just to the right of the door within the lodge. The pit, approximately a foot deep and eighteen inches across, is completely filled with rocks. In the past, instead of a metal pitchfork, a forked stick was used to roll the rocks into the hole (George 1938:16). A bucket of warmed water, and formerly a watertight basket of water, was placed near the rocks, along with a ladle. Upon entering the lodge and with the door closed, the glow of the hot rocks is clearly visible. Each participant, completely undressed, enters in a solemn fashion, sitting around the perimeter of the lodge. The last man who enters typically pours the water over the rocks, and leads in the ritual procedures. Just before the door of the Sweat House is closed, he dips his hand in the water, sprinkling the rocks with a few drops, just to "warm things up a little."

Both men and women sweat, but they do so separate from each other. At the *Hngwsumn* Memorial Ride encampment in 1996, which included more than sixty adults, a Sweat House was prepared for the riders and for "all who wanted to sweat." At sunset the sweating began. The men who elected to sweat did so in shifts of some six or so. Once all the men had completed their prayers, the women took part, again in shifts. A man kept the fire going, periodically adding more heated rocks. It was well into the early-morning hours when the Sweat House finally cooled down.

With the door closed, the ritual proceeds with the *suumesh* songs associated with the man pouring the water, with periodic prayers spoken aloud, with the ladling of water over the rocks, all marked by a four-quarter cycle. "You pray in complete darkness, to direct your communications. It is like the cycle of a day, with tomorrow's daylight bringing a new start, a better day." Paschal George noted that once the sweating began, the men would sing, "Great grandfather of grandfathers, I respect you" (1938:16). Sweet cedar or "sweet-smelling herbs from the forest" might be sprinkled over the hot rocks. Smudging serves to further "cleanse" the participants. The herbs might also be rubbed directly onto the bodies.

Between each set of pourings, a short break is held, in which the door is opened for a breath of cooling air. The heat generated by the water applied to the rocks is intense. Depending on the length and nature of the prayers, the entire sweat might last up to an hour. If built near a creek, when the sweat ends, the participants might plunge into the cool water, washing themselves off. And if taken during the winter, a hole in the iced-over creek could be chopped open. When the men came out, they plunged into the "ice-cold water. When they came out, icicles form on their hair" (George 1938:17). But since few backyards have creeks running through them, buckets filled with water are now usually used for washing. Today, sweating can occur on a regular basis, every couple of weeks or so, and, for some individuals, even more frequently.

You'll Hear a Song

The Sweat House . . . was given to us. My father told me when we were inside the Sweat House that this was like a womb and you crawl into the womb, our Mother Earth. And *Amotqn* will come to see you, along with your relatives in there because that's the most sanctity place for us to go to, the Sweat House. Because then when we strip off and we're like we came into the Earth, when we were born, with nothing and we go in there to see the *Amotqn* and to feel him.

And to take something as dead, as some people might look at, a rock, that's just dead, just sitting there in the creek or just sitting there on the ground. It doesn't do anything. But yet it was *Amotqn* and the Animal People who came to us to build the Sweat House, to show us how to make the Sweat House in a certain way and which Rocks to use, to put them into the fire. Those special Rocks, when they're heated, come alive. They will talk to us and sing to us—a Rock. And when I'm blessing it with the Water, . . . that Rock will suddenly come alive and it will glow. It will show light. You'll go inside the Sweat House and it will be so hot, it's just glowing and it's dark and you can see. . . . The Rocks are so hot that they'll show you light. They make you feel good. You sit down and you get ready. Now I'm ready.

It's your first glimpse at this light, of the *Amotqn* 's world. You start using Water to put on there and his light goes out, . . . and what comes in is this whole new light of *Amotqn* and he'll come to you and he'll bring to you your grandmothers and your grandfathers and all those people and all the songs will just start coming to you. You don't even have to close your eyes. You just sit there. It's dark and the significance of the heat, the significance of doing some suffering to pay for this. It's not free. You have to give something of yourself. The pain that you have in your body, that you just want to cry and run out of there. The purpose of that is you have to pay for this so when *Amotqn* comes to you, and this world comes to you and it cleanses you and it finally does come to you, then you begin to receive his special messengers, the *Amotqn* 's messengers—the Hawk, the Ant, the Weasel, the Beaver.

    That's why there's such a powerful, powerful kinship with this. When he starts sending those Animals to us, whatever it might be, maybe there's one he keeps handing to us, handed to us, handed to us. You'll hear a song, you'll hear a song. When you first hear it, it's so far off with this Animal, . . . and it might take you ten, fifteen sweats, the whole year waiting for him because he'll come to you each time a little more, a little more. Finally he'll bring a song to you. When he does, that song is like a gift. (From an interview conducted on July 3, 1996.)

HEATING UP THE ROCKS

The Sweat House rocks can be heated and the lodge prepared for use on any number of special occasions, such as a birthday celebration, in anticipation of travel to another part of the country, or prior to a Jump Dance. When guests, either family or friends, arrive for an extended stay at one's home, the first thing that might take place is a Sweat. "We use the Sweat House to rejuvenate our lives." The Sweat is thus an occasion for "cleansing" and "purifying," not only physically cleansing the body but also spiritually renewing the individual. As an extension of the maternal character of the lodge, in entering the lodge the participants enter the "womb." While taking in the heat and steam, "you get in an embryo position." When the door is opened and you emerge from the lodge, "you are reborn." "You are rejuvenated, become stronger to help our people." And as one is reborn from the Grandmother, in the entire act of sweating the participants seek to renew their kinship with their grandmothers and grandpas, as well as with the *Amotqn*.

Sweating is also done at the beginning of and in conjunction with the hunting season. Paschal George remembered hearing the men inside the Sweat saying, "O merciful great grandfather, have pity on me, your child. Make me clean, so I [can] kill my game, so my children have plenty to eat" (1938:17). Many hunters rely upon the prayers given by all the elders who sweat at the start of a hunting season. The prayer and song, given throughout, are requests for assistance, as well as offerings of thanks for "good fortune." But it is not only requests for a good hunt that emanate from the lodge. In the "suffering" during the intense heat, "something is given back." The sweaters give back to the Animal Peoples, and to all of the landscape, helping to maintain their spiritual life-force, their *suumesh*, and thus the well-being of the deer herds and camas fields. "You have to do some suffering."

Prayers of Healing

We just stopped off in DeSmet on our way to the Sweat House. We drove up to a house, midway down the block. The driver of our car, an elder, got out and went into the house. A few minutes later, the two of them came out and we were back on the road again. A young boy sat quiet in the back seat. By the time we arrived at the Sweat House, the early evening's light drew our eyes immediately to the fire, in its final stage of life. The rocks were well embedded in a bed of red-hot coals. The others there were all Schitsu'umsh, seven of us in all, and one young boy, maybe thirteen or fourteen years old. It wasn't long before we entered the tarp- and blanket-covered domed-shaped lodge, entering in only our "birthday suits." The Rocks were now alive. In the dark, the glow of the Rocks shown bright and soon the lodge was filled with steam and song, and the voices of all the grandparents.

I soon discovered that the shared relationship these men had with one another was more than being Schitsu'umsh. They were all elders and close relatives of this particular boy. It was his first Sweat, and, as would be expected, he was noticeably nervous and even reluctant. But there was something more to his uneasiness. For all the prayers said and songs sung were, in fact, being directed at and for this young boy. I learned that he had been "running around with the wrong crowd, getting into trouble and disrespecting his parents and grandparents." This Sweat had been specifically set up for his purpose. Well into the Sweat ritual, one of his elders turned to him and asked the boy to pray aloud. The boy's fears and tentativeness were replaced by tears and emotion. As he cried, he shared his heart that evening with those who deeply cared for him and for the welfare of his family. He shared his heart with the Amotqn and this Sweat House. In the heat and the prayers, this boy was forced to confront himself and what he was doing to others. (From participant observations made in the summer of 1993.)

As brought out in the four vignettes included in this section, the Sweat House can be used as a vehicle for healing sick and "wounded people," and as a potential means for receiving the gift of a song, a *suumesh*. As George stated, for "very nearly every ailment, . . . the sweat house was the Indian[s'] main doctor" (1938: 17). The healing is not only sought for those with some physical ailment, such as a backache, but also for those who might be "lost," abusing drugs or booze, those who are sometimes called the "wounded." The wounded people are also those who have lost touch with their cultural heritage, with the teachings of the First Peoples and the Ancestors. They are in need, and, like Crane, the Grandmother Sweat House, along with the elder relatives, seek to give to and heal them. In participating in the songs and rituals of the Sweat House, many attempt to regain a sense of their Indian identity. And sometimes even more is given. Following this same pattern of sharing with one in need, "the Amotqn's messengers—the Hawk, the Ant, the Weasel, the Beaver"—might bestow a *suumesh* song on one in need of guidance and healing. The song given could help guide an individual for his entire life.

Wounded People

The songs . . . and all the ceremonies and things are for taking care of the people. . . . When you see a family, their traditions are fractured, their spiritual touch with the Ancestors has been interfered with, their hearts . . . are laying on their back, so to speak. . . . When their heart is laid down there like that, it's kind of flat, it's kind of lopsided, it's kind of deflated in certain areas. But it's still beating, but it's not as round and robust as it should be. . . . I look at it like these people are wounded. They're wounded. And sometimes they don't know it, and sometimes when they look and they turn, and they say, "I need my spirits, I need my Indian people, where's my Indian people? I need them to sing songs. . . . " They can't do it, because it's been removed from them, so they have to turn and look, and then they see us over here, and they'll call us, "Come help us, come help us. Sing those songs. We like to hear those songs." (From an interview conducted on June 4, 1996.)

For several Schitsu'umsh families, the Jump Dance represents the culminating ceremonial expression of their most important spiritual desires and endeavors. Held each January or February, the Jump Dance—sometimes referred to as the Medicine Dance, Stomp Dance, or Winter Spirit Dance— occurs typically over two and sometimes three consecutive evenings, generally from sunset to sunrise.[14] "We dance til daylight." The Jump Dance is a family-sponsored event, often held in the home of one of its members. It is also typically, though not always, an open event, with individuals from other families welcomed and in attendance. This was true of the 1996 Jump Dance I attended. There were approximately forty-five men, women, children (not more than ten), and infants (not more than six) in attendance. In 1994 I attended a Jump Dance sponsored by and including members of two families, with other families also participating. In this instance, the event was held in the Worley Community Hall and included some seventy participants in all. As in the past, when the Jump Dances were often organized along band affiliation (Teit 1930:187), the dance today is based upon extended-family sponsorship and participation. Because of the particular needs of a family, sometimes it is announced that a Jump Dance is limited to the participation of family members, and is not an open dance.

Whether in a home or community hall, all windows of the facility are covered and taped with black plastic to prevent the outside lights (from cars passing by and streetlights) from disturbing the dancers, and to help keep the dance "secret," in remembrance of the days in which the dance was forbidden. If held in a home, most of the furniture, such as tables and sofas, is removed from the designated dance area, leaving a dance floor as large as possible.

In the past, and as recently as the 1950s, the Jump Dance might also be held in a specially erected "big tipi." The area on which the lodge was placed was first cleared of snow and then dug down below the frost level, "a foot or so." The poles from three to four big tipis would be used to erect a longhouse structure. Suspended from the crotch of the overhead poles and extending the length of the lodge would be "a special pole from way up the mountains." Once cut, "the pole would not be allowed to touch the ground." From this pole the powerful Blue Jays would "hang," and, from their perch, "they can just go right out through the top" of the lodge. As recently as 1995, at least one of the Jump Dance sponsor told me that "he'd love to do it the old way," and contemplated once again erecting a big tipi to hold his family's Dance.

Then We Jumped . . .

It must have been around 2 or so in the morning; I'd lost track of time. We had been "jumping" hard for some time. Throughout the evening, several men, each in turn, had come forward, and talked from their "hearts." Particular challenges needed to be faced, challenges that affected their families. After each completed his talk, he would then begin his *suumesh* song, and soon we'd be "jumping." With the echoing of his words and family needs still clear, we would all be brought into the unison of song and dance. Heat, sweat, and exhaustion enclosed the room and covered each of us. We "suffered." And in doing so, I was told that it was an expression, "a desire" on the part of those who "jumped," to give something to the man who had just spoke and to his family.

When the song ended, another man came forward. As he stood there, he specifically thanked members of a particular family that stood before him for coming this evening. As he continued, he spoke of a misunderstanding between the families, and the hurt it was causing. Someone in the community had unfairly attributed the source of the tension to him. "It was not true." The resulting conflict was "hurting our families needlessly." He prayed for a healing between the families, and for the elders and for the children. Then we "jumped" to his *suumesh* song.

In this instance and with all those who spoke from the "heart," there was a clear intent on bringing people together, on healing old wounds, and on nurturing the health of the family sponsoring this Jump Dance and of all Schitsu'umsh families. (From participant observations made on February 10, 1996, in a home in Plummer.)

Upon initially entering the dance area, participants proceed to greet those already present with a handshake or hug, moving counterclockwise around the dance floor. Participants come prepared with a blanket and perhaps a pillow to rest upon while not dancing, and each establishes a place around the outer perimeter of the room or hall from which he or she will dance. Individuals were dressed in regular street clothing, blue jeans and shirts for men and dresses or slacks for women, though most wore moccasins.

Those with *suumesh* might also wear a sash or necklace adorned with the symbol representative of the power—a certain type of feather or animal skin, for example. Some might also bring a "dance stick" with them. These dance sticks sometimes have rattles attached to them, and, during the dancing, are tapped on the floor to the rhythm of the singing.

As the dance is about to start, all overhead lights and lamps are turned off. Eyes soon become accustomed to the dim light of a few candles placed throughout the hall or living room of the home. The dimming of the lights is a signal that the dance is supposed to begin. Once the dance has started, a designated individual is responsible for not allowing participants, or "Blue Jays," to leave the dance area, and for preventing late arrivals from entering the building. Sometime around midnight, a "little rest" period occurs. Participants can take some water, use the bathroom facilities, and late arrivals are allowed to enter the dance.

Singing one's *suumesh* song and what one family calls "heart talk" are central to the Jump Dance ritual activities. A participant steps forward and publicly talks about the difficulties or good fortune he and his family may be having. For the Schitsu'umsh, the "heart" is "the seat of thought and right-doing" (Reichard 1947:4). To speak from the heart is to speak with "sincerity and truth." The individual who steps forward might give thanks for a prosperous year or ask for good health for himself and his family in the year ahead. The individual might relate how a *suumesh* song came to him, and for what purposes it is to be used. As in the past, the various winter gatherings have always been an important time for elders to encourage proper conduct and to emphasize the teachings of the First Peoples.

Following the heart talk, the participant then sings his "Jump Dance song," and, with most in attendance following his lead, begins the "jump" dance. The actual dance step involves hopping with both feet together, moving in a counterclockwise fashion on the dance floor or in place (if, such as in someone's home, space is restricted). No drum is used. As the young people "jump," they are encouraged to "think about their mothers and grandmothers," or about someone who is ill. The jumping becomes a prayerful act. When the song is completed, the dancing ceases, and another participant comes forward.

Suumesh songs are particularly important. When sung, the power of the Animal spirit associated with the song is "close at hand," directed at whatever might be sought in the accompanying prayer. *Suumesh* songs are understood as having tremendous transformative powers. When properly used, their power can "watch over a family," heal the sick, and even transform a Human into an Animal being, and back again.

During the Jump Dance, as a dancer sings his song, his movements and voice may take on the characteristics of his *suumęsh*. The dancer is understood as having "become his Animal spirit, maybe a Bear or a Wolf or some Bird." James Teit related that during the "Medicine Dance" of old, the "participants sang the songs obtained from their guardians and imitated them by cry and action" (1930:186). But if the *suumęsh* songs are disrespected, they can also bring ill-fortune. Some understand that if the *suumęsh* songs are not sung during the Jump Dance, they can cause "spirit sickness."

It is at the moment when the dancers become their *suumęsh* Animal spirit that the human dancers "jump back into the world of the First Peoples." As one elder, active in Jump Dancing, described it to me, "Certain First Peoples, such as Eagle, Rabbit, and Turtle, the ones that could speak with the other First Peoples and showed the way, they are the Animal Peoples. When you sing your *suumęsh* song you go into, jump back into, this world of the First Peoples. And when you come out, the power lasts for several days. It's very high, very high!" Not quite sure I heard him correctly, I asked, "So the First Peoples and the Animal Peoples are one and the same?" He replied, "You've got it." While on a Mountain, Wolf, as one of the Animal Peoples, can bestow a *suumęsh* song on a Human, and then, while in a Jump Dance, Wolf, as one of the First Peoples, can lead that same Human into the world of the Eagle, Rabbit, and Turtle.

They Blue Jayed

And [this man] went out, he Blue Jayed [along with another man]. The two of them went out, the two leaders of this Jump Dance, they both went out. . . . And the mother wanted to go out, too, you know, Blue Jay. So they cornered her and kept her in. Finally, well, they "black out," no lights. We calmed her down, and that's when my husband went and took the cane and he says, "Well, I'm going to bother you a little bit," he says, "and I'm going to sing and see what I can do to bring them back in." Because they left, they went out. They're Blue Jays, these two who went out. . . . Yeah.

Well, they're outside. Maybe they're gone out in the mountains or where, I don't know. They're gone. . . . They go right through there [the top of the "big tipi"], just like Animals, when they're Blue Jays. I seen that. . . . Yeah. During their dance. It's part of the night, and they say, "Well, they're going to black out, blackout night." See, we had fires in those big tents. One fire over there, and one fire over here, and they have lamps, lights, to light up the room. And when that night comes, they call it "the blackout night." All of them lamps and the fire, all of them lamps are gone. They're out, it's dark. That's when they turn, the ones that turns Blue Jay, and they're gone, and when they put the lights back up, they're gone. They go up through the top. . . .

And [my husband's] dad was a Blue Jay, too. He was a big man. Boy, he can just climb through there like nothing, go out. One time there was a tent, we all have tipis and they had a tent, and they had a stovepipe. They have a little stove in this tent, and it was smoking, and this Blue Jay got on top of this tent on that pole. Well, the pole ain't very big, and two of them got up there and danced on that, and they run out. They'd thought for sure they'd break that. And they were getting that soot, that smoke, because they are painted with black, the Blue Jay. . . . But they come back. . . .

You've got to have a power to protect your people that comes to your house, to your [Jump] Dance. You've got to protect all of them. That's the way my husband was. Anybody that came, it's just like he puts a cover over them, everybody that's there. . . . Blue Jay is good for them to go out, and they get more power. And he gets them back.

When they Blue Jayed, they're not themselves. They're Blue Jays. They're not people. . . . They're light on their feet and they will not drink or eat. But they will come and bless your food, when they do come in, . . . at midnight. . . . We have midnight dinner, and it [Blue Jay] comes in, and he has his little rattle, and takes care of all the food, so you don't get sick, or nothing. Then they go away. Then they pick him up before daylight, and fix him, and they come out of it. . . .

The one that takes care of them, like [my husband], takes care of it, . . . he knows they're coming. And you'd see him and tell them if they're coming in. . . . And when they come back, they'll have a little stick, and they pound on the doorway. "You come in," and they can't open, you can't touch them. Nobody is to touch them, or they don't touch anything. But with this little stick, and you open the door for them, then they run in and fix everybody up, doctor them all. Yeah. It's something. I'll never forget it. I was there. . . .

They open the door and they'll come running in. And they're not themselves. They're Blue Jays, . . . a human being turn into a Blue Jay. . . . So when they catch [them], they have to hurry and take everything off and wash them, and dress them up, and they fix them. . . . Yeah. He [the medicine man] sings his song and uses his rattle and hooves, deer hooves. I don't know what else is on that, what he uses. He gets them out of that. They're okay, they're back. It's something great. All that time they don't know, they have their own language. They don't speak this language. . . . And they come out of it, and then they tell us what they seen, what's ahead. And what we're to do and what we're not to do.

You were the first one I ever really told how this turned to Blue Jays, how this human being turned to Blue Jay, and they have the power for the good, not bad. It's not to destroy people. The power they have is for the good. Some has the power to be mean. Some has the power to be mean, and maybe destroy people, destroy things. They do have some, in some other reservations, they have bad, bad people. But these people are just for the good. Anything good you want, you need, you go to them, and they'll take care of you. Especially for the sick people. Or, their mind is leaving. They can bring it back. That's great, I think. (From an interview conducted on February 11, 1998.)

The most dramatic and spiritually powerful transformation occurs when a dancer becomes a Blue Jay.[15] While dancing and during the "blackout night," when the lighting within the dance area is extinguished, a dancer might "Blue Jay" and "want to go out." He or she becomes the Blue Jay, no longer human. He disdains human food and drink, speaks his "own-language," and is "light," able to fly up to and perch on the "special pole" suspended within the big tipi. The transformation is completed, when, as an "Animal," he leaves the lodge and returns to his abode for much of the night, to the surrounding trees and mountains. "Painted in black," the Blue Jay merges with the surrounding night landscape. However, the transcendence is not permanent. The medicine man, a "doctor with the power," will attempt to bring him back. But without that medicine man's *suumęsh*, the Blue Jay would remain in the mountains as an Animal.

The Blue Jay announces his return by knocking at the door. Still an Animal, the Blue Jay is not to touch or be touched by people. With his enhanced *suumęsh* powers, the Blue Jay "blesses the foods" of the midnight meal to prevent "sickness," and later foretells the well-being of the dance participants and recommends any cautionary action that should be taken. The Blue Jay thus brings to bear among those he left behind that which emanates from the landscape. At some point "before daylight" the medicine man, one "with the power," will sing his own *suumęsh* song and use his "cane" and "deer hooves" to "fix" the Blue Jay and restore him to his human self.

Steller's Jay

While still sought by Jump Dancers, in recent years Blue Jays have not appeared among the Schitsu'umsh. The last four medicine men who led Dances among the Schitsu'umsh, and who were generally recognized by others as having "the power to bring back the Blue Jays," passed on in 1974, 1981, 1988, and 1993. Without such power available to call upon, one current Jump Dance leader said, "It wouldn't be safe to Blue Jay." Thus, when he puts on his family's Dance, he stations a younger brother at the door, preventing anyone, but especially a Blue Jay, from leaving. Hoping that someone will succeed in receiving the power to "fix" Blue Jays, one eighty-five-year-old elder said, "There's so many that's trying. . . . It would be a great thing, if it did. A lot of them are really trying. They're going to Sweat House, Sweat House, and praying. And it might come back. That is, I hope it would, for the good, to help the people. . . . They're doing their best. So I hope someday, I hope it comes back." In any case, the Jump Dancing continues.

In addition to prayer acts given while one is dancing, each individual also has an opportunity to deliver his or her prayers directly to the landscape. During a pause in the Jump Dance, an elder might come forward, placing a blanket or cloth on the floor before himself. He then announces that all who want him to pray for anything should place a "scarf or necklace or something personal" on the blanket. At some point following the Jump Dance, days or even weeks later, the elder takes these items into the nearby hills and mountains. In prayer, he asks for that which the others are seeking. The items are then left at a special site—a particular tree or rock outcropping—or are buried, so as not to be disturbed.

In the early-morning hours of the Jump Dance, the participants are "doctored" and blessed by an elder. "If the medicine man is going to be able to help the sick, he must have gotten his power from the Creator." Each dancer, in turn, comes forward, standing with his or her back to the elder, as the elder fans that individual's body with his eagle-feather fan. Infants are held by their mothers. The *suumesh* powers of the Animal Spirits are made available to those in need.

The Jump Dance is ended with a "certain song," signaling that participants are "free to go outside." Following this song, a morning meal is shared by all in attendance. This might include camas, along with sandwiches, cakes, pies, and coffee. It is not unusual for some of the participants to fast from food and water during the entire two- or three-day event. The fasting helps to focus the dancer's prayers and, as an act of sacrifice, acts as an offering for that which is being sought in prayer. After the morning feast, all the participants return to their homes to rest until evening, when they reassemble to continue the Jump Dance.

At the 1996 Jump Dance I attended, a "naming ceremony" was also held during the early-morning hours. Either held or escorted by their parents, the children of particular families were called out. An "Indian name" was then ritually bestowed on each of these infants and young children by one of the elders. The name, often descriptive of a particular animal or of an animal quality or characteristic, is understood to help protect and nurture the child throughout his or her life. The parents of each child receiving a name then follow with a small giveaway, in which all the participants of the Jump Dance receive some gift item—for example, a woven belt, a hand towel, or a scarf.

Song Is the Hoof Glue of Our People

While in an encampment someone would start singing. People would hear, come over to that camp, see who's singing, . . . [and say], "That's a nice song. Where did it come from?"

That song came from the First People or from the spirit world; that song came from sitting and laying in the huckleberry mountains. In your camp, you hear the wind blowing through the trees and it starts singing a song to you. It will come to you. Up on the high mountain, sitting there, the grass moving next to you, will sing to you. It comes from that spirit world or it comes from the messengers who stand up. The Groundhog will stand up and he'll look at you. All of a sudden he'll start singing to you. That's where that song comes from. . . .

So it is important for us to continue to make drums, continue to have our kids sing, to continue to have them feel that power of song that comes from the spirit world, the Animal world. It is like the hoof glue. That's what the Indian people used for seams and stuff like that. That glue they made from hoofs, that holds things together. . . . The song is the hoof glue of our people. (From an interview conducted on July 3, 1996.)

AND THEY DANCED

When an individual participant gives voice to his *suumesh* song, he comes to know his *suumesh* spirit better. He reiterates and renews in song and dance his kinship linkage with his specific Animal spirit, and thus with the Mountains and Creation time from which the *suumesh* came. The landscape of the Animal and First Peoples is made intimate. In the example of the Blue Jay, this essential kinship with the landscape, and the bringing to bear of its healing powers, is made even more immediate and vibrant. To dance and sing one's *suumesh* songs helps to heal afflictions or to assure one's own well-being. Thus one becomes a stronger contributor to the health of one's own family.

This individual healing can be expressed in the overcoming of "spirit sickness." Some Jump Dancers feel that if one's *suumesh* song is not sung during the Jump Dance, he may be stricken with what is called spirit sickness. In singing the song the sickness is held at bay. "When you sweat and get exhausted, you get rid of all the bad things in your system, and sacrifice for the other sick persons." The doctoring and naming rituals that might be held during a Jump Dance have the same purpose, that of strengthening the individual and thus his or her own immediate family ties, as well as reiterating his connections with the Animal spirits and mountains. It may be physical ailments or spiritual wounds, resulting from loss of a relative or from lack of understanding the Schitsu'umsh traditions, that are treated. Working among the Schitsu'umsh in 1904, James Teit stated that an essential component of what was then called the Medicine Dance was to allow the people "to learn . . . [who] had received songs from their guardian spirits and the nature of their powers," "to learn who had powers over certain things, such as the weather; and who could through their powers be of most service to the people when help was required at any time," and "to make life easier and drive away sickness" (1930:187).

Healing transpires not only for individual dancers but for the community as well. The Jump Dance seeks to address and eliminate interfamily tensions, and to strengthen and renew the entire community and Schitsu'-umsh family. This purpose is expressed in what is often spoken aloud during the heart talk, and in what is implicit in the singing and dancing of the participants. In sharing the meal following the dance, people feed their bodies and, in so doing, strengthen themselves for the sake of others in their family and community. The meal also literally brings members of families together in solidarity. Through the eating of traditional foods, such as camas and bitterroot, the people are linked to world of the Animal Peoples and the Creator, strengthening that critical kinship link. As Teit stated from his 1904 observations, the dance sought "to bring people together in a friendly way and induce closer fellowship between them and their guardian spirits; to bring the people as a whole in closer touch with one another, with guardian spirits as a whole, and with all animals and everything in nature" (1930:186–87).

Jump Dancing also serves to renew the plants and animals of the landscape itself. When the songs are sung and the jumping held, the spirit power, the *suumesh*, in all the Schitsu'umsh landscape (especially in such plants and animals as camas, water potato, huckleberry, deer, and elk), is revitalized. The songs are a prayer, asking for an abundant winter snowfall and bountiful spring rains to help nurture the roots and berries, and, in nurturing the plants, to nurture the deer and elk who eat of the plants. The "singing and dancing in the medicine dance helped produce favorable conditions" for the animals hunted and the roots and berries gathered (Teit 1930:187). Ultimately, in the heat and exhaustion of "jumping hard" in the Jump Dance, participants seek to maintain the spiritual life-force, the *suumesh*, throughout the Schitsu'umsh family, to give back and renew all the Peoples of the landscape.

THE MEMORIAL GIVEAWAY

In the Memorial Giveaway the First Peoples have provided a means to share and, in turn, disperse the sorrow from the death of a relative. And in so

Salmon fishing at Kettle Falls, 1930s (courtesy Northwest Museum of Arts and Culture and Eastern Washington State Historical Society, acc. no. L93-75.31)

doing, the Memorial helps to prepare the way for the journey of the deceased back to the landscape of the First Peoples, and to renew the kinship among the living, as well as among the dead, of the Schitsu'umsh family.

Before considering the Memorial Giveaway, let me briefly discuss some of the general rituals connected with the wake, funeral, and burial. Of all the ceremonial expressions practiced today by the Schitsu'umsh, the ritual complex surrounding death, involving the wake, the funeral, the procession to the graveyard, the burial, and the Memorial Giveaway, is of central importance. Virtually all Schitsu'umsh families will become participants in these rituals at some point during a year's time, whether because of the death of an immediate relative or of someone else from the Schitsu'umsh family. The full ritual elaboration of this ceremonial complex does vary, depending on the number of lives the deceased touched and the extent to which the deceased and his or her family are practicing Catholics.[16]

With the death of a respected elder, an extended period of viewing the casket and offering condolences usually occurs. Some Schitsu'umsh can remember a two- or even a three-day wake period held for particularly prominent and well-known elders, with several hundred individuals attending both the wake and the burial. An extended wake allows those who must travel a great distance to arrive on time. On the other hand, while certainly mourned just as much by his or her family, the death of a younger person might not receive such an elaborate funeral. Today, it is typical for the rosary and wake to begin in the evening and continue throughout the night until the mass and burial are held the following day.

Remarkably, many of the traditional practices first noted by James Teit in 1904 (Teit 1930:173–76), involving "burial of the dead," have continued into the present.[17] While certainly varying among families, such continued practices have included use of the rosebush, orphaned children carried over the grave site, roots or berries given to the deceased, use of sweat grass, a meal provided by "good-hearted neighbors," a giveaway of the deceased's belongings, and a period of extended mourning and reduced public activity by the family members of the deceased. The following discussion offers a generalized outline of the wake and burial, with particular reference to many of these continued practices and to the use of specific items found in the Schitsu'umsh landscape.

When a person dies, the immediate family remains awake "twenty-four hours a day" until the deceased is buried. Often held in the community center (the gym and kitchen of the old Tribal School) just north of the Sacred Heart Mission at DeSmet, the "wake" involves prayer, the singing of hymns and traditional songs, the sharing of stories and remembrances of the deceased, and meals. As people enter the community center, they first sign the guest book and then "pay respects" to the deceased. Standing before the deceased, a moment of reflection, prayer, or thanks might be offered. For some, grief is more overtly expressed, as they weep openly, supported by the arm of a family member.

The open casket might be adorned with a Pendleton blanket, a braid of sweat grass, or perhaps a picture of the deceased, and flanked by many bouquets of flowers. If the deceased was a veteran of the U.S. military, he or she would also have an American flag draped over the casket. After paying respects, individuals then "greet" the family members of the deceased, as well as all others present, with a handshake or a warm hug, many with tears in their eyes. The pleasant aroma of sweat grass or sage fills the room, as these plants are periodically burnt and then fanned with an eagle feather over those assembled during the wake. This "smudging" provides a cleansing.

Throughout the evening and early-morning hours of the wake, individuals are either asked by a family member of the deceased or voluntarily come forward to offer "a few words." Besides close relatives and friends of the deceased, designated representatives from neighboring tribes, often elected council members, might be among those speaking. The words shared with all those assembled take the form of stories about the deceased, emphasizing how the speaker remembered the deceased and conveying some dominant character quality, such as kindness and generosity, or love of hunting. Speakers might speak of what the loss will mean for the living relatives, "what will be missed most." A specific event or situation that the speaker had experienced with the deceased might be referred to. Among those listening to these accounts, women and men, tears can be expressed openly. "Sometimes people tell funny things that that person did and make everybody feel good." In such cases laughter is heard. Whether serious or funny, all accounts seek to comfort the grieving family members and assist the deceased on his or her journey.

Also attending the wakes regularly are individuals known as "prayer leaders." These are men who "have been brought up in the traditional teachings" and whom the "people in the community look up to and listen to." Their words and prayers, "so respectful of Indian traditions" and spoken with deliberation and heart, bring particular "comfort to the people."

Along with Catholic hymns, "special songs" might also be sung. Certain individuals are noted for the "comfort their songs bring," and are often invited to the wakes. One woman's songs "relieve a certain feeling that a person might have," giving solace to the family. These are songs that are "in my family, my family songs." In addition, traditional honor or warrior songs might be heard periodically during the wake and funeral, sung by the members of the deceased's family, other relatives, or visitors as they stand around a bass drum. An honor or warrior song might also be sung during the burial ritual.

For the children, "the best time to be awake was the wee hours of the morning, when they'd start telling ghost stories." The stories might include "telling about man-eating bears and things that happened a long time ago. That was the best time to be awake, the small hours of the morning, telling stories or reminiscing, to keep awake."

Food is always available, "three meals during the day," with a "midnight supper." The meals are provided by "good-hearted neighbors." Following the death, a certain community member is selected by the family as the "designated cook." Her selection might be based upon her being close to the deceased, or she might be someone "whose cooking the deceased liked." The designated cook, in turn, immediately organizes others to assist her and to begin the food preparation. She contacts a designated hunter to go out and bring in some fresh deer or elk meat, which is smoked, dried, and served during the meals. The women gather all the supplies needed to prepare the meals, and then serve the food to all in attendance. In addition to serving such traditional foods as camas and bitterroot during these meals, camas and bitterroot might also be placed in a pouch that accompanies the deceased, "to feed them on their journey when they cross the creek." The eating of the "old foods" allows contact with the ancestors, and the singing of the "death songs" helps "comfort the family members and return the deceased to the Creator." For those who were given an "Indian name" earlier in life, to help them among the living, this name later helps to protect the deceased during the final journey.

There exists the general understanding that the deceased faces either a short or a long journey, depending on the good he or she exhibited in life. As one elder said, "The basis of Indian spirituality was to believe in life or spirit of all things, and the way you treated all those things in life determined your afterlife. . . . They treated everything with respect because of the belief that how you treated things [that] was living or inanimate determined your afterlife. They did believe in afterlife."

During the wake, the immediate family might bring forth and show the deceased's clothing and some of his or her personal effects, perhaps "the clothing they were wearing when they died." A large bundle of items is placed in the middle of the floor, for all to view. A family member then speaks about these items, the specific clothes that were worn, "and people would cry." These items of clothing and personal belongings will be among those gifts distributed to others during the Memorial Giveaway. In addition, other items honoring the memory of the deceased, such as photographs of the deceased at various ages of his or her life or pieces of craft or art work done by the deceased, might be located in a corner of the community center on a table or two.

To Grieve

The idea of that was to grieve openly and get it out of your system. . . . You get the grief out in the open, get it out, because if you grieve too much after the person is gone, it's like you're tying them to the earth. You have to let them go to the next life. It's like people are encouraged to cry and get their grief out, rather than hold it in. (From an interview conducted on September 9, 1996.)

On the morning or early afternoon following the wake, a mass is held, either in the community center, to accommodate a large turnout, or in the Sacred Heart Mission facilities. After the mass, the procession to the cemetery takes place. Led by the hearse carrying the deceased, those wishing to participate in the burial ritual drive their cars and pickups to the DeSmet cemetery. The cemetery is located not more than a mile north of the Mission.

As during the wake, during the mass and burial services, rosebushes and sweat grass might be used. The smudging from burning sweat grass serves to cleanse and keep away "bad influences," as does the hanging of rosebush branches. The body might also be washed in rose tea, made from the boiling of the bark of the rosebush. The grave site might be blessed by an elder brushing it with a rosebush or smudging it with burning sweat grass or sage.

At noted by Teit and mentioned by elders, children or "orphans" (1930:175) either jump or are carried by an adult over the grave site. A baby would be handed to someone standing on the other side of the grave. Everyone understands that the deceased is now "lonesome" and, because of his love for his relatives, will "try to take another relative with" him. Passing children over the grave in this manner helps protect them. Children attending the grave site, along with pallbearers, grave diggers, and all who help to cover the grave, might also wash in the "rose tea to protect themselves, . . . because the grave site is very sacred and is very powerful."

Those attending, family and friends, then file by the grave site and take turns shoveling earth until the grave is completely filled. If the deceased is a veteran, the burial also includes an honor guard made up of members of the local VFW (Veterans of Foreign Wars) posts, a rifle salute, and a display of the colors, including both the American flag and the Indian flag.

Following the burial, up to a full year of extended mourning and reduced public activity are observed by the immediate family. Members might avoid Powwows and other social gatherings, and limit travel off the reservation. The conclusion of this period of mourning is generally marked by the Memorial Giveaway.

Memorial Giveaway

After the evening meal had been served to all at the encampment, some 150 in all, a Memorial Giveaway was held. An elder stepped forward and, with a clear voice, all listened. A young man of only twenty-seven years of age had been tragically killed in a car accident one year ago. And now his mother and family sought to honor him and his memory by sharing part of him and themselves with others. It was also a time to "share in the sorrow." Tremendous grief was felt by the mother and the family. They would now share it with those assembled, so they could "carry it away," as the Bird People first did long ago. Gifts would be given to those who were present, to members of other families, to friends, and even to the strangers who knew nothing of this young man. The elder asked that all those who would receive gifts to keep this young man close at heart, and that each time you use these items, to remember this young man, remember him well, and to remember the sorrow of this family, take it away. Over a hundred individuals received gifts that evening.

The mother had known since last January that she wanted to hold a memorial for her son during the *Hngwsumn* Memorial Ride. But at about that same time she lost her job and troubles began mounting. She worried that she would not be able to gather the necessary items she wanted to give, to be able to give from her heart. She had little money. But soon after losing her job, her former employer told her that he would "donate two hams and a pop dispenser," and her sisters and cousins all came forward and provided many of the other items needed. Nevertheless, she had a heavy task before her. She "prepared for the giveaway all year—gathering the cloth and sewing." Today she was busy coordinating and, with the help of her sisters, preparing the food for all the meals served over this weekend of memorial. "It just all came together; I didn't have to do anything, just cook the salmon last night," she said. And then she would take personal responsibility in the distribution of the gifts.

Among the gifts given were hand towels and dish towels, jars of homemade jam, candy for the kids, along with flashlights and small brooms for them as well, dishes, bowls, a wind chime, baskets, nail polish and perfume, and fine blankets went to all the riders, some fifty in all. It is not unusual to have personal items of the deceased given away, directly passing on the very presences of that person. (From participant observations made during the *Hngwsumn* Memorial Ride on May 25, 1996.)

RETURNING TO THE MOUNTAIN

A Memorial Giveaway is held following the death of a family member. In the past it was conducted immediately after the burial. Today it may be held at any time up to a year following the passing of a relative, and it can be repeated, continued each year after that, if the family so decides. All the family and friends of the deceased are invited to attend. As with the wake, the Memorial can be held in the community center adjacent to the Sacred Heart Mission at DeSmet. As noted above, the Memorial might also be held in conjunction with some other large gathering, such as the *Hngwsumn* Memorial Ride. As with the wake, the Memorial Giveaway involves the sharing of a meal and and stories about the deceased. It also involves the sharing of the deceased's "gifts."

The meal is prepared by a designated cook and her helpers, with the venison or elk meat provided by a designated hunter. In addition to smoked meat, salmon and berry pies are also likely to be included in the meal. In consuming the meat of the elk and deer, the huckleberries, and the salmon, the connection and kinship with the landscape and the Ancestors who inhabit the landscape are reiterated.

Typically, many of the personal belongings of the deceased, such as clothing, jewelry, framed pictures and photos, and kitchen or hunting items, along with other items, such as blankets recently purchased especially for the event, are gathered and brought to the hall. Other items purchased for the giveaway might include towels, washcloths, pot holders, tablecloths, handkerchiefs, scarves, and quilts. Sometimes relatives of the deceased take nearly every possession of the deceased, including all the furniture, and distribute these items during the giveaway. Individuals sometimes spend a lifetime collecting particularly cherished items, such as a pair of beaded moccasins, a beaded bag, a colorful fringed shawl, or a favorite rifle, with the explicit intention that at his or her own Memorial Giveaway these items will be given to certain relatives or close friends.

Following the meal the giveaway commences. The family of the deceased will have chosen "the talker," who initiates the proceedings by "holding up the clothes the deceased was last wearing and tell of the person." In turn, as other individual family members and friends come forward to accept the giveaway gifts, they too speak of the significance the deceased had in their own lives. In so doing, as the stories are told, an entire life history is unveiled and compiled, to be remembered. The stories speak of relationships, of the grandparents and parents, the siblings and cousins, and the children and grandchildren of the deceased. Upon hearing these accounts, tears are shed and laughter heard from those in attendance. And in hearing the stories, the specific kinship ties between the living and dead are reiterated.

As the giveaway proceeds, the individuals in attendance, selected by the family of the deceased, are then called out and given some belonging of the deceased. The items first given might be presented to "close friends, then others who have traveled a great distance, and then everyone else." Often children and young people of the family carry these items to the recipients. As Bird, one of the First Peoples, originally established, the belongings of the deceased should be taken away, "sharing the sorrow with all the people, lifting the burden, and then letting it go away." "And as the feathers went to the winds, so too will the deceased fly forever. Death and sorrow are to be felt by all the Peoples. When one dies, we all die. When one lives, we all live."

In dispersing the worldly belongings of the deceased, he or she is freed to journey on "across the waters." The spirit of the deceased is released. In sharing the gifts of the deceased, the tremendous sorrow associated with an individual death is widely diffused among the many, and not left to be shouldered by a few. And in the sharing of gifts, the kinship ties between the living and dead are remembered and vitalized. Each time a particular piece of clothing is worn, rifle held, or kitchen item used, or when that favorite picture of the deceased, hung from a living-room wall, is glanced upon, something special about the deceased is recalled. His or her memory lives on among the living. Gifts are often distributed to individuals who were not necessarily closely related to the deceased, such as friends, or even acquaintances, and "those who have traveled a great distance to help honor the deceased." The circle of family is thus expanded.

At one Memorial Giveaway I attended, the importance of meat and the role hunters play within the family was emphasized. Knowing that the deceased had loved dried meat, the family asked their designated hunters to conduct an elk hunt. The 385 pounds of meat obtained from the hunt was smoked just before the Memorial. An abundance of dried meat was then distributed to all in attendance, well over 250 men, women, and children. I was given more than a dozen four-to-six-inch strips of meat myself.

During the early part of the Memorial, speakers came forward and shared what the deceased had meant to them. The comments were often serious, but just as often humorous. Then four young men came forward, all members of the deceased's family and all designated hunters. As the deceased had been a primary teacher to these young men, each spoke and conveyed a meaningful hunting story about the deceased. And when the actual giveaway occurred, all the hunters from the various families in attendance were asked to come forward and receive the bone from a buffalo horn. I estimate that more than twenty men came forward. They were told to take "the horn to the Sweat House" and use it to pray for a successful hunt, so that their own families could be fed.

The Memorial Giveaway might conclude with Powwow dancing and singing, and include an honor song for the deceased. Led by veterans holding the Indian flag and the American flag, and followed by the elders, the people are told to "dance for the deceased" and to "think of the children."

PREPARING THE CAMP

At least two families explicitly articulated the understanding that deceased persons journey to an after place, a "camp," and, once there, they prepare that camp for the eventual arrival of the remaining members of their family.[18] The camp is located "across the waters," "on the Mountain." It is "a place beside the waters of the creeks," rivers, and lakes. In another variation, one elder spoke of "death as going upriver to spawn; the bodies die but the spirit lives on with the Ancestors."

As one elder said to me, the deceased "cross over to the other side of the creek," and go on ahead of us to "have a big tipi camp ready for us, and to find the best berry patches, to find the best horses, the best camping spots, the best hunting places. He'll be there waiting for us." In this instance, the area referred to includes sites this family continues to visit each year. "When we go back to our berrying areas in the mountains, the first thing Grandpa would do is pray and sing his songs, and let our people [the deceased] know we were back in camp again." Reiterating his point, the elder continued by saying, the deceased "cross the river to the other side." Pointing to the mountains, he said the "other side is the mountains," that "is where my father is."

Look to the Mountains

If something bothers me in some way, something is too troubling to me, then I know I can look out this window and I see the mountains there and I can communicate with my people because that's where they're at. . . . That's where my father, my grandfather, my grandmother, my mother, that's where they're at, that's where they're waiting for me. . . . When it's my turn to go, then that's where I'm going. My children can look to the mountains because that's where I will be. . . . And my turn will be to go to that mountain and prepare a place for my children. (From an interview conducted on June 14, 1996.)

The parents, grandparents, and great-grandparents, the Ancestors, who have "gone on before" and "crossed over the creek to the mountains," are preparing the camp for their children, to give to them, as in a giveaway. In so doing, those who have crossed over the river repeat that which the First Peoples did when they "prepared the world for the coming of the Human Peoples," the original giveaway. Just as the Human Peoples were first brought forth from the earth and created by the First Peoples, and then nurtured by the various gifts from the landscape, upon death, they return to that landscape—to the mountains and rivers from which they originally came.

Taking Care of People

My father was very strict about having good, clean berries when we share them and we give them to people, or we take them to such-and-such a family, because they can't go pick berries. And I often wondered about that. I wondered, because they had a car, they had boys. . . . It seemed to me that they could go out and pick. But I guess, when I look back in retrospect now, my dad was providing those kinds of things from the mountains that the others [who] couldn't do it anymore, or just didn't have the strength to do it anymore, meaning spiritual strength or physical strength. And he would deliver berries to these people. It was hard work, and yet, he would bring them to them. Sometimes, the people wouldn't even say thanks. They would just take them, nod, and take them in the house.

I never questioned my father about that, and in later years, later, later years, two or three years before he died, I had one chance to talk to him about that, and he told me that there was no need for thanks. He didn't do it for a thanks. He didn't do it to be praised or patted on the back or patted on the head. He shared what was in the mountains with the Indian people, because that's what the Creator had given it to us for, was to share that. And if his hands and his children's hands was able to do that, then that blessed us, and that gave us a blessing. And that's why he did it. So even his generosity had a spiritual and a reasoning behind it. I was always learning, all the time, about goodness of your heart and generosity and taking care of the people. That's what we did. (From an interview on June 4, 1996.)

GIVE IT TO THEM

As the gifts have been shared by the First Peoples with the Human Peoples, the Human Peoples, in turn, unselfishly share the gifts with those among them in need. While fishing on the lake, berrying in the mountains, or digging roots on the prairies, it is always clearly understood that part of what you obtain (is given to you) should be freely shared with those in need, the children and elders. The sharing patterns exhibited in these hunting and gathering activities are, in turn, extended and instrumental in virtually all aspects of the Schitsu'umsh family, whether household, community, or tribe.

In the years during which I have been working closely with the Schitsu'-umsh, seldom was an interview conducted or an observation made without some overt mention or act of someone helping another. As related to me in an interview, "If somebody just out of the blue says I really like that, then you give it to them, because it's just a material thing, and they really like it, so you give it to them." Once, as I was seated, visiting with a young man in his late thirties, we both observed an elderly woman coming out from the adjacent building. He immediately interrupted our conversation in midsentence, got up, and took from the woman the rather large bag she had been carrying. He carried the bag for her as he guided the woman the short distance to her car. The prevailing attitude is summarized in the rather precise statement offered in another interview: "We give not to receive praise from others, but to take care of others." There is no expectation that a gift given must be reciprocated in kind. "If you give, why would you expect to get paid?" As reiterated by Henry SiJohn, "We avoid hoarding and gluttony. . . . Mosquito was a glutton, . . . and he bled all down the river."

As I have observed, and as several others have commented to me, it is typical for family members to share evening meals with each other throughout the week, rotating from one member's house to another on different evenings. In fact, much of the day-to-day routine sharing is conducted along sibling-based family lines, with assistance given to each other, and to the elders and children of that family. During the *Hngwsumn* Memorial Ride, a box of freshly smoked deer meat was always available for anyone to come by and take a piece or two. One individual typically keeps a box of dried meat at her work desk during hunting season just to give out to her clients.

Meat is also essential for the hundreds of family members and guests attending Powwows, celebrations, and funerals throughout the year. And once a Powwow or celebration meal is completed, plates and plastic bags of extra food (there is always more food prepared than is needed for the meal itself) are passed out to "those who have traveled far" and to all the elders in attendance. In the sharing of the meat by the designated hunters, there was absolutely no consideration of repayment or reciprocity.

Sharing is most explicit during a Naming ceremony or a Memorial Giveaway, drawing nonfamily members into the sharing network. As a child is ritually given his or her "Indian name," a name that will protect and nurture, the parents of that child distribute an abundance of gifts to members of other families and guests in attendance. No one leaves without first receiving a gift. The gifts represent the hope that when the item is used, "good thoughts [will] be given the child." In like fashion, when a family holds a Memorial Giveaway, they desire that those receiving gifts will "take the burden, the sorry, and carry it away," and that they will also honor and keep "fond memories" of the deceased. The sharing is done in abundance. Relatives of a deceased person sometimes go to that person's home and "clean it out," taking everything the person had owned, and then distributing it all to others at the giveaway, generally held one year after the passing of the person.

In times of trouble—emergencies related to health, child care, home, employment—the family and community offer immediate support. For example, the father in a white family, newly arrived in the Schitsu'umsh community, was injured and had to be hospitalized. Immediately after hearing of the troubles, Indian families from the community, none of whom had kinship relations with the family, gave assistance. One Schitsu'umsh family offered to "keep the kids." Upon arriving back from the hospital the next morning, the wife found that "there was firewood stacked on our porch and there was a meat loaf." That afternoon "some young boys came down and helped me finish up the . . . well house, and there were some trees that had blown across the house before we moved in, . . . and they finished cutting them up and stacking them for firewood." Several other boys showed up and, in the days ahead, offered to "watch the girls." "Every time I'd come home from the hospital, there was food, and the girls were taken care of." And that winter, with her husband unable to go hunting for deer, they "brought us meat. They just kind of took care of us, like we were part of the family. It was just super."

Unlocked Doors

In my home, . . . I don't lock my door. The people I know, my brothers, my sisters, my friends, I don't lock my house, because that's not my house. It's there for these people. If my brother comes down here, he lives over in Cusick [Washington], if he comes down here, he knows he can go to my house and that's his. He can go in there. He can sit down and make himself at home and feel comfortable. He's got a place to stay. He's got a place to lay down and sleep. He's got food in the cupboard and the refrig if he's hungry and needs something to eat. My brother from Nespelem [Colville Reservation] knows that my house is not locked. My family that live up in Montana knows that my house is open. . . . And that's the life-style that I lead. . . . If somebody needs something in my house, it's there for them.

And all I ask is don't abuse that. If you come in, and you sleep, that's fine. Leave the bed there and ready for the next person that comes in. If you come into my house and you eat, then take care of what you've done in my house. Don't leave a sink load of dirty dishes or a messy house. That's all I'm going to ask.

But it's there to utilize it. And that's the way I grew up. That's what my grandmother and my grandfather gave to me, of our past relatives, is there was no locked doors on tipis. You knew who that home belonged to. And that person was there to provide these things. And this was theirs, and you didn't go to them and take whatever they had, and not leave something in return. You didn't go out and didn't take from Mother Earth and Mother

Nature without giving something in return. That is the saying that the old people tried to tell us, and tried to give us, and it changed when things became mine.

I've got a vehicle out here that is my truck. But, if my brother says I need to go here, and in order for me to get here, I need to take all these things with me, can I use your truck? Here. I give it to him with gas in the tank. Use it. Take what you need. But, when you bring it back to me, don't bring it back with an empty tank in it, but it's there. It's there for the family. I'm providing that for them if they need it. My house is there if they need it. (From an interview conducted on June 10, 1996.)

At the community and tribal levels of the Schitsu'umsh family, we see the same sharing of resources. Sharing and hospitality are noted characteristics of all Schitsu'umsh Powwows and celebrations, as everyone in attendance is encouraged to partake in the meal prior to the Grand Entry and then to dance as part of the Schitsu'umsh family during any of the many Intertribal Dances. The same philosophy is exemplified in the policies of the Benewah Medical Center (run by the tribe in partnership with the local community), the Coeur d'Alene Tribal School, and the DeSmet Higher Education Program (operated in partnership with Lewis-Clark State College and North Idaho College). In each instance, services and resources are shared equally among Schitsu'umsh and white patients and students. All those who are in need, regardless of tribal or ethnic affiliation, are welcomed.

To Benefit Our People over Time

We have to prioritize the profits and earnings from this [casino] operation in a way that goes back into the community, makes us healthy, well, and creates opportunity, provides for the truly needy and maybe invest in new opportunity for young people. That's what they did.

They held all-day Council Tribal Membership meetings to talk about what our priorities were and flush them all out. They came up with a list. It included buying back the land as the number-one priority. We feel like we can care for the land better than anybody. Time immemorial to today, we have never damaged any property. We've never polluted anything and hopefully never will. To the contrary, we try to stand for cleaning up where it has been polluted. We feel if we can get our land back and we can care for it, to us the land has been reserved to us by a higher power than this government. It's nice this government recognized that reservation of our land through treaty and agreement, but to us, it's a monument. It's a great gift, a great loan from a higher power. Therefore, when it's under our ownership, it's under our guardianship and care. We feel like we can take care of it better than anybody.

We wouldn't buy it back and then build, subdivide, and profit and make all kinds of money off of it, storing hazardous waste or whatever. We would just take care of it. It would be our home like it always has been from time immemorial.

The other priorities were, youth and education, care for the elderly, including health and housing. We're already talking about buying a bus to get them around better and to get their meals to them and get them to the clinic when they need to get there. Then create a fund for donations which includes burial and funeral expenses, cultural and language preservation. All those kinds of things. I probably left out one or two, maybe three things, but that's what all the money is going for.

At the very bottom, we had a small percentage identified to go out on per-capita payment. They felt they didn't need the whole thing. They didn't want to become greedy. But they thought something would be nice, especially something for the very, very poor families. Right about Christmastime, first week of December, mail it out. That way, for a lot of the poor, young families, maybe for the first time, they would have a Christmas.

Even in thinking about sharing the money, they're thinking about how can it best serve our people. Kind of in a nutshell, it's a big nutshell, that was our thinking. Getting it going and then creating the design to benefit our people over time. (From an interview conducted on May 24, 1996.)

At a General Council meeting in 1994, attended by all enrolled tribal members, a decision was made on the disposition of "gaming monies" from the newly established Bingo/Casino Hall. As with other tribal initiatives, this action reflected the general sharing patterns so characteristic of Schitsu'-umsh endeavors. Along with land acquisition and programs for youth and the elders, major portions of the annual profits are to be directed to both the public and tribal schools on the reservation—to Indian and white students alike.

What's Mine Is Yours

In other words, my home is the same as my ten brothers' and sisters'. And what's mine is theirs and what's theirs is mine. . . . So there is no division.

Yes, I live in my house. [One brother] lives in his house, [another brother] lives in his house, [And still another brother] lives in his house. But if I would go there, to their house, what's in their house is mine. They come to my house, if they want something, and it's there, they would say I'm going to take this. Fine. If you need it more than me, take it. . . . It's kind of like everybody's the same. We're all the same. And what we have belongs to everybody. My dad used to always say whatever you have is not yours. Yes, it's in your house, it has your name on it, and this kind of thing. But if somebody wants it bad enough, let them have it. . . . And that's kind of like the thing with the white people saying that he would give you the shirt off his back. That was my dad. . . . So my dad used to always say what you have is not yours. If somebody needs it, give it to them. If somebody wants it, give it to them. If my brothers and sisters want something, give it to them. (From an interview conducted on May 1, 1996.)

It's Home: Conclusion

Our Soul

I took my son early in life up to Grassy [Mountain]. . . . And there's a ledge that comes off the mountain cliff. It's about fifty, sixty feet high, and at the bottom of the ledge is a little meadow. So you can lie in the meadow and all around you, you can see the ridge good across, even St. Joe Baldy, or look down at the Lake, or into the valley towards Cataldo. You can lie there on your back and look at the Lake and watch the hawks soaring over, down into the valleys or across meadows, and visualize where your tribe came from, where you came from. I guess maybe the soul of our tribe is those mountains and those waters. (From an interview conducted on February 19, 1997.)

HOME

In the landscape, transformed and prepared by the First Peoples, is found a "home" for the Schitsu'umsh, a place of intense "comfort and awe," the place where the people were found. Home is in the waters of the lake and rivers, on the expanse of camas prairie, and high up on the ridges and peaks of the surrounding mountains. Besides the term *chatq'ele*, another expression for "lake" is *ssaqa'qn*, meaning, literally, "water at the head" (with "head" referring to mountain; Nicodemus 1975[2]:247), suggesting the inclusiveness of lakes, rivers, prairies, and mountains. Felix Aripa spoke of Lake Coeur d'Alene as the place where he "loved to go," where he would hear the sounds of the "bullfrogs and the whistle of the trees. That was the Indian orchestra!" Felix told of how the Lake and its Animal People helped feed the Schisu'umsh. Just as the Muskrat would point the way to the water potato, the Eagle would circle the camps along the Lake's shore, and with a fish in its talons, show the people where to fish. He went on to say that when "we are troubled, . . . we go to the Lake and it would comfort us." In the 1920s, this elder related how people also went to the Lake after they got married, for it was the place in which to "begin their new life together." He also spoke of the waters as "always sacred," because the "animals depend on it and it attracts them." Lake Coeur d'Alene is "always in the heart." When the G.I.s returned from World War II, one of their first acts was to have a "reunion at the lake, where our heart is at." For the Schitsu'umsh, Lake Coeur d'Alene means, simply and unequivocally, family, and much more.[1]

The Lake Means . . .

We're supposed to be on the water. When we didn't have that anymore, I think something happened to us. It's part of our being, part of our deep identity. Not just like part of our history. It's hard to walk a mile in somebody else's moccasins because people always want to assume what it will be like from what they know, based on who they are today. So anybody today, of today's modern world, might say, "Well, Coeur d'Alenes were there, now they're not. Here's how I'd feel—I'd just go on with my life somewhere else."

Well, if a part of our creation originated here and higher powers had been communicated with, and deep religious ties were made and based upon these great elements of nature that are here, of our homeland, traditional homeland, that was fought for and protected, no different than World War II veterans went and fought Hitler for, then it's got a different kind of a meaning and much, much deeper appreciation.

So, the Lake to us, I think, means identity. It means religion. It means spirituality. It means our food. Some of our transportation was upon the water. All of our villages, there might have been one at Cataldo and Coeur d'Alene and down by the mouth of St. Joe, [were located near the water]. We transported upon it. I even read in some old book that some explorer, or trappers that came around, along the lakeshore, [there] were all kinds of jewelries and beadworks and quill works from our people leaving offerings to the Water Spirits. And maybe they would do that before they crossed, before the children could go swim, before they go out and try to get some fish. These native fish around here, they're a great part of our original diet.

So all that was taken away from us. And how would that feel? I guess somebody would have to imagine they'd have their home today—they worked for it, they developed it, they sacrificed for it, they went without so they could keep it. Somebody just came walking in and told them, "Get out, I'm taking everything you have and everything you own, plus your career, job, and identity." Before they could really understand how we would feel about it, it was to that degree that our people felt hurt, to be taken away from. (From an interview conducted on June 12, 1996.)

One elder related how his father, upon arriving in the Mountains to hunt or gather berries, first built a Sweat House, and then sang his sweat songs and prayed. For him, the items obtained from the Mountains were "gifts from the Mother Earth." Another man was once told, while in the Mountains at the family's huckleberry camp, to "listen to the Trees." They are the "link to your grandmothers and grandfathers." For another elder, both Lake Coeur d'Alene and Grassy Mountain are considered as part of his family. When he travels to his family's berry territory, to the Mountains, "it's like coming home." The Cataldo area was a revered place long before the Jesuits arrived. It is where the "grandmothers are buried," and where, from a nearby hill, medicine people, the Skitswish, prayed. Some families understand that, when a relative dies, he or she crosses the waters and goes over to the other side, goes to the Mountains. "That's where my father, my grandfather, my grandmother, my mother, that's where they're at, that's where they're waiting for me. . . . When it's my turn to go, then that's where I'm going. My children can look to the Mountains because that's where I will be. . . . And my turn will be to go to that Mountain and prepare a place for my children." "It's home."

Mountains, Water, and Trees

I love my mountains. I love my water. I love my trees. I can stay gone for a while, but then I get sick. I stayed down at Fort Hall [a reservation located in southeastern Idaho] for a while, and I got sick. It was rough on me, and I got homesick. Not for the people. Maybe for the people, too, but I got homesick for my mountains and my water and my trees. Physically sick, I felt it. I had to come home. They took me up to the mountains that they have, about an hour, two hours away from there, and it's not the same. I feel if I'm going to travel somewhere, and it's fun, and it's always nice, and the people are . . . good. And then when I start coming home, and . . . I start seeing the familiar land, and I see Steptoe, and I know I'm home. . . . This is my house, and this is where, I suppose my ancestors, the old ones, are. Just a sense of ownership. I don't mean ownership in the way of ownership like you own a house or you own a car. It may be more of a, I guess a family, a kinship . . . a home. Like an extended, an extended part of me. . . . It's the whole sense of family, the whole sense of home. I can't describe that feeling. (From an interview conducted on June 14, 1996.)

Taking my cue from the idea expressed in the previous vignette, I offer the following interpretative analogy. As a "whole sense of home" transcending the mere physicality of landscape, the home within which the Schitsu'umsh live is a multidimensional, multistoried home.

The foundation of the home—the ground floor, if you will—is the world in preparation for the coming of the Human Peoples. Here is a landscape well traveled by Crane and Coyote, and the other First Peoples, and, through their deeds and actions, a landscape transformed and readied. The teachings are firmly implanted into this landscape, orienting the design of the ground floor, and the *suumesh* is fused throughout it, animating the fibers of the home. And here, too, are the camps of those who have crossed over the rivers, the deceased preparing for the eventual coming of their children.

But as the oral traditions distinguish between the *meymiym q'esp schint* ("he/she/they are telling stories and learning about the time before the human beings") and the *meymiym łu' schint* ("he/she/they are telling stories and learning about the human beings"), home, too, bears this distinction. There is a second floor to the Schitsu'umsh home: a landscape traveled by the Human Peoples, the world prepared for them. And it is the Human Peoples who, through their deeds and actions, have been charged with maintaining and perpetuating the vitality and animation of the landscape. The designated hunters seek to feed the grandmothers and children with the Elk's meat. With the *suumesh* of the Wolf or Blue Jay, the prayers and blessings of the Jump Dancers seek to heal the wounds of a wayward adolescent, a family feud, and an ill grandfather, as well as to nourish the roots and berries, and the deer and elk, of the prairies and mountains. The words of the storytellers seek to teach and reiterate to young and old the moral truths set forth by Crane and Coyote and the other First Peoples. And here, too, is the place from which, perhaps through the windows of your office, you look to the Mountains to see the camps being prepared by those who have crossed over the creek.

Yet if the landscape is to remain a home, "the soul of our tribe," providing comfort and awe, the people must continually have access to what is on the ground floor. The stairways connecting the two floors of the

Schitsu'umsh home must be well used. And indeed, when they are well traveled, any distinctions between the floors become blurred and, at times, nonexistent, as temporal and spatial barriers disappear. The floors of the Schitsu'umsh home are separated not by steel rebar and concrete but by tule-reed mats, which can be rolled up.

In maintaining the vitality of their whole sense of home, the Human Peoples journey along their home's stairways each time the oral traditions are retold. Having their origin in a landscape traveled by the First Peoples and handed down since time immemorial, the oral traditions are imbued with qualities essential to the Schitsu'umsh. In preparing themselves to tell the stories, storytellers have had to travel the stairways and reach into the primal landscape of the First Peoples. In the act of retelling the oral traditions, the spoken words themselves have the power to help revitalize and "make the world." As the children and adults participate in the telling, they travel and "swirl around" with Crane and Coyote in the unfolding landscape of the First Peoples, and by doing so they learn and remember the teachings firsthand. The Creation is witnessed and traveled. After the telling, the story's participants carry forth those teachings as they, in turn, travel the landscape of the Human Peoples. In the retelling of the oral traditions, the landscape becomes reinvigorated with the teachings of the First Peoples.

The vitality of the whole sense of home is further maintained each time the Human Peoples quest for *suumesh* and sing the acquired songs. Upon ascending to the mountaintop and fasting from food and water within a prayer circle, or by simply listening to the Trees, a young man or woman may receive a *suumesh* song. One of the First Peoples, as an Eagle, a Wolf, or some other Animal Spirit, had "paid a visit." In the songs sung in the Sweat House, and during the Powwow and Jump Dance, the transformative powers of the *suumesh* and the First Peoples themselves are brought back up the stairs onto the floor of the Human Peoples. During the Powwow you "can feel the energy and feel the Spirits." During the Jump Dance you may witness a Human dancer "jump back into this world of the First Peoples" and become the Blue Jay or the Wolf, become his *suumesh* spirit. At that very moment comes the realization that the Animal Peoples and the First Peoples are, in fact, the same Peoples. The dancer is inexorably linked not only to the Mountains, the place from which his particular vision emanates, but also to the Creation, the perennial time from which all *suumesh* originated. And with the life-giving power at hand, a healing may be bestowed upon a sick child or grandmother, and the *suumesh* is imparted to the landscape, as the camas, deer, and other Animal Peoples are renewed. The *suumesh* is thus redistributed back into the landscape, for the benefit of all its various Peoples.

While multifloored, the Schitsu'umsh home thus thrives and flourishes when it is made whole and indivisible, when its floors are rendered indistinguishable. Whether it be Tekoa Mountain or Lake Coeur d'Alene, the Schitsu'umsh landscape is ultimately a single landscape traveled by both Rabbit and Jackrabbit and Chief Child of the Yellow Root, and by the Human Peoples. It is a single landscape: one that is *in preparation* for the coming of Human Peoples, the world of the First Peoples; and one that is a *fully prepared* landscape, the world of the Human Peoples and the Animal Peoples. The First Peoples and the Animal Peoples are thus made synonymous. It is a single landscape, animated by the *suumesh* and made meaningful by the teachings brought forth from the landscape by the First Peoples, and then through story and song, reinvigorated by the Human Peoples. At first oscillating between worlds, the participants in a story, a Powwow, or a Jump Dance, or simply those who walk on "the trails over the hills and into the distant mountains," inevitably fuse the world of the Human Peoples with that of the First Peoples and Animal Peoples, leaving all temporal and spatial dichotomies dissolved.

LANDSCAPE TRAVELED BY CRANE: THE TEACHINGS

When Little Squirrel and Chipmunk came to Crane, they were welcomed into his "lodge" and received "two quarters" of meat on each of their plates. When Crane hunted, "he never takes more than two" deer, and there would always be "plenty of deer meat hanging from his lodge." And Crane provided meat for an entire village. In his actions, Crane became the archetypical "designated hunter," and reiterated many of the quintessential values that would help define the landscape for the "people who are coming." The Schitsu'umsh landscape was thus infused with certain teachings—a spiritual origin and animation, bounded by kinship ties, and governed by an ethic of sharing and a respect for all. Crane and the other First Peoples transformed a landscape and provided a home for the Schitsu'umsh.

The phenomena of the landscape are spiritually derived and endowed. It was a landscape engendered by the First Peoples and the Creator. When digging roots, gathering berries, and hunting deer, prayers and offerings of thanks are made to the Creator. While seeking a vision and fasting in the mountains, a "*suumesh* song" may be given. A Blue Jay Jump Dancer has become *suumesh*, and brings to bear those healing properties. A small

Skip Skanen viewing the landscape near Cataldo, August 1997

pouch of camas may accompany the deceased on his or her spiritual journey to their camp across the waters. The ceremonies are held in conjunction with the gathering and hunting, as exemplified in a boy's first kill, the Water Potato Powwow, and the offering of a basket of huckleberries when the berries are first collected.

The phenomena of the landscape are defined and related to in terms of shared kinship. It is an expansive, though bounded, kinship, inclusive of Lake Coeur d'Alene, and Cataldo, St. Joe Baldy, Grassy and Moses Mountains, as well as the Deer, the Sweat House, and the Ancestors. The Creator, as the "Father," is atop the mountains—on St. Joe Baldy and Grassy, for instance—with the Mountains themselves known as "Grandmothers" and "Grandfathers." The Sweat Rocks from those Mountains are called "Grandpas," and the Sweat House, within which they live, is called "Grandmother." The Animal Peoples are understood as "brothers and sisters." To dance at the Powwow is to become the Eagle and the Porcupine, and to sing is to have listened well to the voices of the Trees and to Mother Earth. Kinship with the surrounding Mountains is made immediate for one who has "Blue Jayed." Across the mountain creek or on the mountaintop of St. Joe Baldy and Moses, on Cataldo Mountain, and at the site of the Sacred Heart Mission, are the camps of the deceased, the Ancestors. They have gone on to prepare the camps for the coming of the rest of the members of their families. In consuming the camas and dried meat, if only a small portion, one feels a deep affiliation with the Ancestors and with the landscape itself. The Lake and the Mountains are thus imbued with a sense of family.

The phenomena of the landscape, such as camas, water potato, venison, huckleberries, *qhasqhs*, and *suumesh* song, are understood as gifts from the First Peoples and the Creator to the Human Peoples. The fundamental principle of gifting, of sharing, was first established and brought forth in the primal act of the First Peoples' preparing the world for the coming of the Human Peoples. The Animal Peoples, such as Deer, reiterate that act as they offer themselves up to the Human Peoples as physical sustenance— as dried meat—or for spiritual nurturing—as a *suumesh* song. The Cedar also offers its bark and the Camas its root, each as a gift. In turn, the Human Peoples share these gifts with those in need, the children and elders. The sharing also gives back the gifts from whence they came. In the retelling of the oral traditions, in the heat of the Sweat House, and in the exhaustion of the Jump Dance, the landscape itself is reinvigorated with meaning and vitality, with *suumesh*. The Deer thus continue to offer themselves to the hunter and the water potatoes grow in abundance. And Crane and Coyote, and all the First Peoples, thus continue to travel their landscape. All the varied gifts bestowed, whether from the First Peoples or the Human Peoples, are made without obligation to reciprocate or expectation of return. The First Peoples, the Animal Peoples, have provided the prototype for all "giveaways." And in the final giveaway, that of death, the deceased crosses over the waters and prepares the camp for the eventual coming of family members, replicating the original giveaway enacted by the First Peoples as they prepared for the coming of the Human Peoples. The principle of sharing is reiterated throughout the fabric of the Schitsu'umsh family.

The gifts of the landscape—camas and venison, for example—are thus either to be shared unselfishly with kinsmen in need, especially children and the elders, or exchanged competitively with rivals to gain an advantage. The intent in both instances, however, is to strengthen the welfare of the Schitsu'umsh family. All members of the Schitsu'umsh family are bound in an ethic of sharing with those in need, and enter into a comprehensive sharing network—with Humans, Animals, Mountains, Lake, Ancestors, and the Creator.

The phenomena of the landscape, such as camas, water potato, venison, huckleberries, *qhasqhs,* and *suumesh* song, are to be respected and not abused. They are, after all, an offering of the Deer's own flesh, the Cedar's own bark, and the Camas's very root. When respected, a *suumesh* song can watch over and heal a family member. Among the ways such gifts are to be respected is by asking permission through prayer, by digging or hunting no more camas or deer than the family needs for its subsistence, and by sharing the berries or the venison or the *suumesh* song with those in need. Above all, a deeply felt thanks is to be given for all that is received—thanking the Creator and the Deer that has offered itself to the hunter. The pattern is set forth by Crane, who hunts only two deer at a time, and, in turn, has an abundance of meat hanging in his lodge. In contrast, when Coyote attempts to take too many deer, he often has little show for his efforts. A home is open for all relatives who need a place to stay, so long as they leave it the way they found it. The gifts and kinsmen of the landscape, the camas and deer, as well as the mountains and lakes, are to be respected as one's own grandmother and granddaughter are respected.

These teachings are manifested and reiterated each time the stories of Crane and Coyote are told. In the act of telling the stories of Crane and Coyote, listeners become participants and are allowed to travel with the First Peoples in the landscape they have prepared. The young and old gain an awareness of the teachings, of their own origins, and of "how to do and how not to do." The landscape itself is reinvigorated with significance and meaning; it is morally endowed. Upon viewing Tekoa Mountain or the turned-down beak of a hawk, the young and old are reminded of the camas and bitterroot brought to feed a hungry relative, or that "everyone is equal here on this earth." Thanks for the gifts received and shared are conveyed each time the ceremonies associated with the elk hunt or berry gathering are held. And in so doing all those in need are looked after. In the venison, water potato, and camas consumed at Powwows, Memorial Giveaways, or Jump Dances, the young and old, if only for a moment, are invariably linked with the landscape and reunited with the Ancestors and the Animal Peoples, with the entire Schitsu'umsh family. As expressed through the Powwow songs and the dance regalia, the Animal Peoples once again sing and dance for all to see. In the prayers said, sung, and danced during the Jump Dance and Sweat House rituals, the varied needs of those who suffer are conveyed. And the *suumesh*, acquired atop a Mountain, as a Blue Jay or as a "scared" child, is brought to bear in healing. In the exhaustion from jumping and in the heat of the sweat, something of one's own spiritual essence is given back to the landscape, helping to vitalize the animals and plants. In the Memorial Giveaway, the sorrow from the passing of a dear one is allowed to fly away, kinship is remembered, and the camp is prepared for the reuniting of the Peoples with the landscape, across the waters, on the Mountain.

It is precisely because the Schitsu'umsh teachings and their essential linkage with the landscape remain so vital that the degradation and loss of access to the landscape is so detrimental to the well-being of the Schitsu'umsh people. To be alienated from the mountains, lakes, rivers, and valleys, from the camas and deer, for whatever reasons, is to be severed from what is essential to one's identity and survival. When part of the Schitsu'umsh family is estranged from others, the health of the whole is impaired. When part of the Schitsu'umsh family is ill, so too are all of its members. Within the landscape of the Schitsu'umsh, when a lake or stream or mountain is polluted with waste materials, the resulting illness is felt as deeply as if the harm had been inflicted on one's own grandparent or child. Hence the health of the people is inseparable from the health of the camas, deer, and *qhasqhs*, and from the health of the rivers, lakes, and mountains of the Schitsu'umsh landscape.

If the Schitsu'umsh had become fully acculturated into Euro-American society, there would now be no such intense feelings of loss and illness but

Merle SiJohn holding the Indian flag, May 1996

only historical memories of such. But the Indian flag of the Schitsu'umsh people still flies strong. While the dust can no longer be seen "rising from the feet of our grandmothers as they walked the trails over the hills and into the distant mountains," the trails through the landscape of the Schitsu'umsh nevertheless remain vital and alive each time the stories are told, the dances held, the songs sung, and the gifts given.

Appendix A
Research Considerations

"Collaboration," from the Latin, *collaborare*—i.e., *com-*, "with"; and *laborare*, "to work"—can be defined as "working together, especially in an artistic, literary, and/or scientific manner." There can be no more appropriate word to characterize how and why *Landscape Traveled by Coyote and Crane: The World of the Schitsu'umsh (Coeur d'Alene Indians)* came into being. By its very nature, ethnography is never a solitary endeavor. And in this particular case the contributions of a great many voices—some artistic, some literary, and some scientific, at least one Euro-American, many, many Schitsu'umsh, and now, perhaps, you, the reader—are brought together. The following discussion will highlight the how and why of this collaboration.

The selection of a conceptual framework and the use of certain terms, such as "landscape" and "teachings," for presenting the Schitsu'umsh story was done with much deliberation. How does one attempt to describe, to an audience made up primarily of Euro-Americans, the experience of a people so unlike their own? An interpretive framework and specific constructs are needed, and these must both accurately represent the Schitsu'umsh experience and, at the same time, be understandable and accessible to the non-Schitsu'umsh. A bridge is needed. The search for appropriate terms and categories to refer to such items as "camas" and "deer," "mountain" and "lake," for example, led to the use of the more inclusive and culturally sensitive terms "gifts" and "landscape." Use of what for many would be a more readily identifiable term, such as "natural resource," to capture and communicate the meaning of "camas" would have left our bridge without a Schitsu'umsh foundation. While natural resources may be identifiable for Euro-Americans, the term is problematic for the Schitsu'umsh. To the extent that it can be interpreted to denote a commodity of monetary value, exploited from an environment for its utilitarian worth, lacking spiritual properties, and implicitly objectified and inexorably distinct from the human experience, the term not only fails to correspond to the Schitsu'umsh experience but distorts the story of the Schitsu'umsh. Thus the term gifts was consistently used to refer to specific phenomena. It more effectively conveys the understanding that camas, deer, and water potato were created by the First Peoples in preparation for the coming of Human Peoples, who, in turn, share them unselfishly with those in need.

Let me briefly elaborate on how I have come to define and use two of the key concepts incorporated throughout this study: landscape and teachings. Landscape refers to the way a people have conceptualized the phenomena of their environment (lakes, rivers, mountains, animals, fish, and plants), investing those phenomena with cultural significance and meaning.[1] While essentially denoting and anchored in a physical geography, the significance of landscape transcends material properties and resides in the symbolic and cultural meaning it holds for a particular people. Hence a landscape can entail phenomena that are fundamentally aesthetic, affective, moral, and/or spiritual, as well as economic in nature.[2] Landscape is to be understood and felt. Comprehending the Schitsu'umsh landscape is not unlike comprehending the significance of the oral traditions. As Cliff SiJohn constantly reminded me in reference to the stories, you have to use "your heart [gently patting himself on his chest], not up here [pointing to his head]. If you tell it with your heart, you'll have clean hands" (Frey 1995:216).

As an individual grounded in Euro-American cultural sensibilities, I have always found it challenging when, as an ethnographer, I am confronted with a world lacking in something that, to me, seems so fundamental—the Cartesian duality. But this is exactly what we must wrestle with in the Schitsu'umsh world. As I venture to give definition to such a pivotal construct as landscape, the particular meanings of the teachings, especially the second teaching, which speaks to the notion of "kinship inclusivity," adds new dimension to the construct. Implicit in my usage of landscape, as applied to the Schitsu'umsh experience, is thus the understanding that landscape does not have an existence separate from that of the human, as if viewed from afar. The Human Peoples, in kinship with the Animal Peoples, exist only to the extent that they are a part of the world, and not living apart from it.

We see this understanding expressed in the act of giving voice to a story, in the rhythmic movements of the Jump Dancers, and in the song sung in the heat of the Sweat House. In each instance, the human assumes an active and essential role in continuing to bring forth the world, and, by so doing, places himself firmly within it. Consequently, as the Schitsu'umsh experience is multidimensional, inclusive of aesthetic, affective, moral, spiritual, and economic significances—something understood, something felt—landscape *and* its many Peoples are necessarily and indivisibly so endowed. Landscape has neither solitary nor objectified qualities.

A second key construct is teachings. Expressed in the Schitsu'umsh term *miyp*, meaning, literally, "teachings from all things" (Frey 1995:42), teachings refer to the knowledge—practical, ceremonial, social, and moral—that has been handed down from the First Peoples and that is indispensable to life as a Schitsu'umsh.

The concept has affinity with Clifford Geertz's notion of "religion" as a "model of" and "model for" the world (1973:123). The teachings not only reflect the way the world is perceived, passively describing it (a model of the world) but, most critically, contribute to the conceiving of the world, actively helping to bring it about (a model for the world). Through the teachings, the Schitsu'umsh come to learn about their world (i.e, the teachings serve as a model of it) and, at the same time, contribute to the making of it (i.e., the teachings act as a model for the world).

In the instance of "teachings," it is itself a concept used by many of my Schitsu'umsh consultants. In my application of the term and in how I approached my research, I have attempted to parallel this usage. As the First Peoples, such as Coyote and Crane, taught the people how to behave and conveyed that knowledge through the oral traditions, I first studied the oral traditions to identify the teachings. In turn, since the ceremonial expressions "bring to life" that which was taught by the First Peoples, I then looked at the Jump Dance and the Memorial Giveaways, for example, to see how the teachings are manifested. From the teachings the world is made and the Schitsu'umsh understood. My usage of teachings became the cue for another consideration.

The organizational presentation of the ethnographic materials in this book— e.g., "Preparing the World," "Receiving the Gifts," and "Sharing the Gifts"—may seem somewhat unconventional. By way of this approach however, I believe we are better able to approximate how the Schitsu'umsh approach the nature and the knowing of their world, better able to approximate a Schitsu'umsh ontology and epistemology. As so many elders reminded me, the place to begin is with the oral traditions. It is from the First Peoples that the world was first created and all that would be needed for Human Peoples to thrive was brought forth. From the First Peoples the various ways to relate to the Spirit, Animal, and Human Peoples were instituted, in prayer and song, and through the Sweat House and the Memorial Giveaway, for example. In continuing to tell of the First Peoples, these ways of relating and the world of the Schitsu'umsh itself are perpetuated. In turn, it is with the oral traditions that an elder would seek to teach and pass on to a grandchild that which is most vital to the Schitsu'umsh, or even attempt to educate a stranger to the Schitsu'umsh ways. It is for this reason that I did not select a more customary ethnographic structure, whose chapter headings might have been "Subsistence and Economics," "Social Organization," "Religion," and "Mythology," for example.

In incorporating a Schitsu'umsh perspective in the organization of this book we have not, however, neglected consideration of many of the critical and diverse topics that characterize Schitsu'umsh ethnography or, for that matter, Plateau ethnological research in general. Such items, interspersed throughout the book, include consideration of ecological and subsistence activities, the economics of redistribution, the inclusiveness of kinship and the cultural boundaries of intertribal relations, religious ceremonialism, aesthetic expression (as in the Powwow and storytelling), and the richness of the creation-mythic accounts. In addition, key historical and Indian-white contact issues, such as the influence of the Jesuits and the U.S. government on Schitsu'umsh society, are considered. As an unconventional framework for presenting the Schitsu'umsh story, one that I have not previously seen in the literature of Plateau peoples, the book's structure will, I hope, spawn further ethnographic discussion, finding application and contributing to a better overall conceptualization and understanding of Plateau peoples.

RESEARCH METHODS AND ETHNOGRAPHIC SOURCES

Research for this project was based extensively upon three types of ethnographic methods and, in turn, sources of information—participant observations, published and unpublished materials, and consultant interviews. For each source I have focused particular attention on the oral-literature texts, the subsistence and ceremonial activities, and the exchange relationships revealed within those texts and that transpire during those activities. The order of the following discussion does not reflect the respective ethnographic importance of each method and type of information. Each was essential and complemented the others.

The first source of ethnographic information came from my observations of and participation in the lives of the Schitsu'umsh. The time frame and bases for this field research began in 1991 and continued through March of 1998. During this period, I observed and participated in such activities as digging and gathering camas and water potato, evenings of storytelling, a Mother's Day quilting bee, horse races (as a spectator), Tribal Council meetings, Powwows, wakes and funerals, Memorial Giveaways, Sweat House rituals, and Jump Dances. I attended the *Hngwsumn* (Steptoe) Memorial Ride (from the Agency near Plummer, Idaho, to a site near Rosalia, Washington) in May of 1996, and the annual Pilgrimage to the Cataldo Mission and the Feast of the Assumption in August of 1996 and 1997.

As I participated in these events, many of which expressed intense family and religious sentiments, the significance of what had been described to me in interviews was in many instances brought to life, and made more accessible and understandable. This was certainly true when I experienced the exertion of digging water potatoes in knee-deep mud and observed the reaction of the elders who received the gift of the water potatoes. In so doing, I began to better understand the "ethic of sharing." Minute and seemingly insignificant aspects of family relations or ritual procedures may simply be taken for granted by an interviewee, only to be enunciated by an ethnographer's observations. In addition, by participating in these aspects of Schitsu'umsh life, insights and significances are revealed that even the words of an elder might have difficulty capturing. Until you have undergone a sweat for yourself, no amount of interview discussion can possibly convey the "life" found in those Sweat House rocks. A consultant can speak of the meaning of the wake and, in turn, those words can help guide you through the unfolding of an evening's events. But those same words alone cannot prepare you for the grievous cries of a mournful grandmother as she stands beside an open casket, supported by a granddaughter. And I learned something more about what it means to "arise from the womb" and to "get the grief out in the open." Participant observation can disclose meanings inherent in an event but that have heretofore found only awkward verbal articulation, or perhaps no words all, by their Schịtsu'umsh participants. The rich details as well as the overarching gestalts are made more accessible for a stranger.

The second source of ethnographic information derived from an examination of previously published materials and unpublished documents—e.g., the observations of Joset (1838–77), Teit (1930), and Reichard (1947). It is primarily on the basis of the Gladys Reichard and James Teit materials, along with the Joseph Joset (1838–77), Nicolas Point (1967), Verne Ray (1942), and Joseph Seltice (Kowrach and Connolly 1990) materials, that the historical time frame for the Schịtsu'umsh can be extended back to the mid-1800s. A bibliography of all sources used is provided.

It is important to note that James Teit (1917, 1930) did his field research among the Schịtsu'umsh people in 1904, working with elders who were most likely middle-aged, if not older. One of Teit's primary consultants was Croutous (Cyprian) Nicodemus, the husband of Dorothy (Dorothea) Nicodemus and one of the signers of the Agreement of 1889. His Schịtsu'umsh name was *Kwaruutụ* (Teit spelled it "Qwaro'tus"), referring to "something yellow or gold, apparently on the face" (Palmer, Nicodemus, and Connolly 1987: 32). In turn, Croutous and Dorothy Nicodemus were the paternal grandparents of Lawrence Nicodemus, one of my consultants.[3] Lawrence's maternal grandparents were Louis (baptized Xwipep and often known as "Walking Antelope") and Susan Antelope.

Verne Ray did his fieldwork on the Coeur d'Alene Reservation in 1937, working exclusively with Morris (Moris or Maurice) Antelope, who "was born about 1870 near the south end of Lake Coeur d'Alene" (1942:103).[4] His Schịtsu'umsh name was *Ats'qhụ'lumkhw*, which means "Looking at the Earth," and implies watching over and guarding the earth (Palmer, Nicodemus, and Connolly 1987:10). Morris Antelope (see his letter to the Indian superintendent on pp. 71–72) was the stepson of Susan Antelope, who was cited by Reichard for her "reputation" in camas baking (see pp. 160–61), and the stepbrother of Julia Antelope Nicodemus, the mother of Lawrence Nicodemus and daughter-in-law of Dorothy Nicodemus. Morris was born to Louis Antelope and his first wife, Mary Catherine.

Gladys Reichard did her field research in 1927 and 1929; her primary consultant was Dorothy Nicodemus (then "over seventy"), Croutous Nicodemus's wife (1947:33). Her Schịtsu'umsh name was *Qwntạ'l*, likely meaning "Blue Clothes" (Palmer, Nicodemus, and Connolly 1987:57). Reichard's other consultant was Tom

Lawrence Nicodemus, September 2000 (photograph by Rosie Peone)

Miyal. Julia Antelope Nicodemus assisted Reichard in her English translation of Dorothy's Schi̱tsu'umsh narratives (1946, 1947). In Reichard we can view Schi̱tsu'umsh oral literature from the last half of the nineteenth century into the first quarter of the twentieth. I relied exclusively upon Gladys Reichard's materials—her "Coeur d'Alene Texts" (1946), in conjunction with her "An Analysis of Coeur d'Alene Indian Myths" (1947)—for four of the narrative accounts included in this work: "Crane and Coyote," "Coyote and the Salmon," "Coyote and Woodtick," and "Chief Child of the Yellow Root"; the "Chipmunk and Snake" story is based solely on Reichard's 1947 work, and the "Little Muskrat and Otter" narrative is based on Reichard's 1938 linguistic study supplemented by her 1947 work. The "Rabbit and Jackrabbit" narrative is based on the Julia Antelope Nicodemus manuscript (undated) and the Dorothy Nicodemus text in Reichard (1947).

It is worth reiterating: The research of James Teit, Gladys Reichard, and Verne Ray, working closely with Croutous and Dorothy Nicodemus and with Morris Antelope, has provided the essential foundation for much of our early ethnographic understanding of the Schi̱tsu'umsh.

Research on the contemporary expression of Schi̱tsu'umsh oral traditions was based significantly upon my association with Lawrence Aripa, the great-grand-son of Rufinus Shi'itsin.[5] Beginning in 1991, I had opportunities to observe Lawrence present the stories of Coyote and the traditions of his own family to a variety of audiences. Throughout our seven-year association, I interviewed Lawrence extensively, and on numerous occasions I informally discussed with him the role and significance of the stories. The culmination of this oral-litera-ture collaboration is presented in Frey (1995, 1998) and here. The "Hawk and Turtle" and the "Coyote Devours His Children" narratives were provided by Cliff SiJohn. They were first told to Cliff by the elders of his family, and he, in turn, continues to share them, along with other oral traditions, with family members and others. Albeit a limited collection, these sources record a sampling of the Schitsu'umsh oral literature as told at the end of the twentieth century.

The third ethnographic source involved working directly with twenty-four Schitsu'umsh consultants. More than fifty scheduled interview sessions were con-ducted with these individuals, and these tape-recorded interviews typically lasted from two to three hours each. In the process of reviewing an earlier draft of the book, an additional twelve follow-up interview sessions were held. Complementing these more formal sessions were scores of ad hoc interviews conducted with the key consultants throughout the project. Initiated in April 1996, the scheduled inter-views were completed during March of 1998; the last ad hoc interview took place in December of 1999. Fourteen consultants were men and ten were women; they ranged in age (at the time of the interviews) from twenty-four to eighty-nine. In all, the consultants represented thirteen different Schitsu'umsh families. A list of the names of these consultants and their associated Schitsu'umsh families is pro-vided below.

With the exception of one interviewee, who declined to have his interview tape-recorded, I found all the interviewees cooperative and enthusiastic about the pro-ject's intent, and willing to give up considerable time to be interviewed. Virtually all interviews were conducted in a setting familiar to the consultants, usually in their homes or workplaces. Many of the ad hoc interviews took place during fam-ily or tribally sponsored events, whereas others were in the form of follow-up questions asked while I was working on some section of the manuscript. More than one of these follow-up interviews was actually conducted over the telephone. With the exception of a few key consultants whom I first met during the course of this project, I had already established, from my involvement in other projects, a good working relationship with the key consultants before conducting the inter-views. The nature of this earlier involvement will be discussed below.

While an extensive questionnaire was designed, made up of a series of gener-alized as well as consultant-specific, open-ended questions, the questionnaire for-mat only set the stage, in broad outlines, for the scheduled interviews. Among other uses, the standardized questionnaire allowed me to compare and corrob-orate specific ethnographic points. But the questions formulated in such a tool,

Felix Aripa, September 2000 (photograph by Rosie Peone)

often composed prior to fully engaging the specific Schįtsu'umsh activities under consideration, can falsely presuppose that which they seek to reveal. So in practice I engaged each consultant in what was more akin to a semistructured interview, and, for a couple of elders, an unstructured interview. Having offered a question from the questionnaire, I would typically pose a series of follow-up questions based upon the information initially shared by the consultant. As a result, the interviewees ultimately set the course of the unfolding conversation. Only following completion of a specific topic, which was not always easy to delineate, would I then pose the next designated question from the questionnaire. Conversations often, and thankfully, strayed far from the intended course sought by the questionnaire, thus revealing what could not possibly be anticipated by a predetermined set of rigidly adhered-to questions.

With regard to the selection of consultants, two considerations helped define my sampling criteria. First, I sought individuals who were generally recognized by other Schįtsu'umsh as the most knowledgeable on such subjects as the oral and ceremonial traditions and subsistence activities. Throughout any given interview, and as we completed consideration of a specific topic, I would ask, "Who today among the Coeur d'Alene people is the most informed on and able to discuss this subject?" The responses were cross-referenced, and helped assure that individuals consistently referred to were among those I interviewed. Second, I wanted to make sure that I interviewed individuals who continue to be active participants in the events under consideration. Those referred to in the interviews were then compared with the individuals whom I personally observed participating in the storytelling, camas digging, Powwow singing, or Sweat House prayer, for example. This further refined the selection of potential interviewees.

Thus the most informed elders, while perhaps less active today as participants in certain activities, were nonetheless interviewed.[6] Such interviewees offered tremendous breadth of knowledge, historical perspective, and, most important, wisdom, or what Cliff SiJohn calls "heart knowledge." But I also gained access to individuals who could typically provide more technical, detailed knowledge on contemporary expressions of the activities under consideration. This selection technique is known in the research literature as "snowball sampling." Those selected for interviews were determined according to criteria generated by the host people themselves, triangulating a series of interview responses with each other and against field observations. Through a progressive expansion, focusing on the "informed" interviewees, I was eventually able to define the sampling parameters and my key consultants.

While I sought out the "most informed," it is important to acknowledge that the selection and complete interviewing of interviewees is never a fully realized process. In retrospect, I can point to an elder with whom I wish I had conducted an additional follow-up interview, and, in at least one instance, I lament not having put greater effort into contacting a potential interviewee in the first place. But such is the researcher's burden.

As the focus of this project was on researching the level of continuity and contemporary expression of the Schitsu'umsh teachings, it was among the same individuals I interviewed that I witnessed, during the eight-year period from 1991 through March of 1998, sponsoring, organizing, and/or actively involved in the Schitsu'umsh ceremonial and subsistence life. For example, members of two Schitsu'umsh drums (Pierced Heart Singers of the SiJohn family and the White Horse Drum of the Nomee family), who provide song for and the man who often emcees at the various Schitsu'umsh Powwows, were among those interviewed for this work. In addition, the individual most often responsible for organizing and cooking the Powwow dinners as well as for smoking the venison distributed at such events, was among those interviewed. Wakes and funerals are routinely assisted by individuals interviewed for this project. Such assistance may come in the form of a song sung to help comfort the family of the deceased, participation in a veterans honor guard that helps officiate the event, or contributions of food and cooking expertise to the meals served.

The interviewees are individuals whose families continue to hold elaborate Memorial Giveaways and dinners one year after the passing of a relative. It is among these individuals that the stories of Coyote and the other First Peoples continue to be told and revered as "true." It is among these individuals that families continue to sponsor and attend the Jump Dances, and throughout the year conduct the Sweat House rituals. These individuals continue to dig for camas in June and water potato in October, and distribute the gathered gifts to those in need. And these individuals are members of families whose designated hunters continue to hunt deer and elk, and who address deer and elk as "brothers" and give prayer offerings when the hunting is successful. The venison and elk meat thus provided may become the primary source of meat for their families, and will be freely donated and served at Powwows, wakes, Memorial dinners, and other celebrations.

To the extent that Schitsu'umsh oral literature, subsistence activities, and ceremonial life continue to be expressed with vitality, they are expressed in the words and actions of those I have interviewed and observed. All generalizations made about the contemporary oral and ceremonial traditions and subsistence activities of the Schitsu'umsh are in reference to the views held and actions carried forth by this core of participants and their families.

While those I interviewed are among the key individuals who continue to sponsor and organize Schitsu'umsh religious and cultural activities, they are not the only Schitsu'umsh people involved in such activities. Attendance at Powwow meals and dances held on the reservation and at Cataldo ranges from 50 (for individual family celebrations) to an estimated 1,500 individuals (for the Powwow held during the Feast of the Assumption), with 300–400 typical for the Powwows held in the fall. With white friends and guests of the tribe generally comprising up to a quarter of those in attendance at these Powwows, an average of 225–300 Schitsu'umsh regularly share in the dried meat brought in by the designated hunters, enjoy and dance to the song provided by the two Schitsu'umsh drums, and stand to honor the elders, children, and veterans as they are recognized during the Powwows. Many of these Schits'umsh also contribute food, such as ham, pies, or potato salad, for the meal served to all in attendance. With the initiation of the very successful *Julyamsh* in 1998, the Schitsu'umsh now sponsor one of the largest Powwows in the country, drawing in tens of thousands dancers, drum groups, and spectators from throughout the United States and Canada. While few Schitsu'umsh compete in the various judged dances, such as the Fancy or Grass Dance, they do enjoy and regularly participate in the social and noncompetitive Intertribal Dances, as well as the Owl, Rabbit, and Round Dances, for instance. The competitive dances held at a Schitsu'umsh Powwow typically attract dancers from area reservations, such as the Spokane, Nez Perce, and Yakama. I know of at least three different families who regularly sponsor the Jump Dances. At each of these Jump Dances, members of families other than the sponsor's also "jump," with total attendance of men, women, and children amounting to an estimated 45–70 participants. The stories of Coyote continue to be heard by all the youth of the Schi̱tsu'umsh, as they attend summer youth camps and the elementary schools, both public and tribally operated. And the elaborate wakes and Memorials held throughout the year affect virtually every Schi̱tsu'umsh household at some time, whether through an immediate or distant relative that is directly involved.

Based upon these observations, I estimate that at least a third of the Schi̱tsu'umsh people regularly plan their lives around ceremonial activities expressive of the Schi̱tsu'umsh teachings, and virtually all Schi̱tsu'umsh people have participated in such activities at some point in their lives (for example, as a child listening to Coyote stories or dancing at a Powwow, and certainly as an adult attending a wake).

CONSULTANTS

As a collaborative project, many voices have contributed to this book. Individuals I have interviewed are listed here by family affiliation, including his or her date of birth and, if applicable, death. Antelope Family: Dixie Stensgar (7/1/62) and Lawrence Nicodemus (7/21/09). Aripa Family: Felix Aripa (9/9/23), Lawrence Aripa (3/26/26 to 10/11/98), and Hillary "Skip" Skanen (3/6/37). Campbell Family: David Matheson (11/5/51) and Marjorie Zarate (12/14/52). Massaslaw Family: Alfred Nomee (9/12/46) and Mariane Hurley (9/20/42). What-kan (Daniels) Family: Lucy Finley (10/2/12 to 12/16/00). Finley Family: Jeannette Whitford (10/18/28). Garrick Family: Roberta Juneau (10/2/40) and Joe Chapman (11/23/63). Joseph Family (descendants of Circling Raven): Ernie Stensgar (5/29/45), John Abraham (6/10/51), and Vicki Abraham (6/20/54). Matt Family: Bob Matt (8/17/73). Peone Family: Ann Peone McAlister (10/31/40). Seltice Family: Marceline Kevis (3/31/14). SiJohn Family: Henry SiJohn (8/6/17 to 2/9/99), Cliff SiJohn (5/24/45), and Frenchy SiJohn (6/8/67). Zachariah Family: Richard Mullen (7/10/57). Others (non-Coeur d'Alene): Thomas Connolly, Jesuit priest (4/27/29) and Jannette Taylor (12/20/51).

VIGNETTES

In attempting to better represent the voice of the Schi̱tsu'umsh, I have included in this book a series of what I call "vignettes." They are composed of texts from interviews I conducted with consultants, field observations I made, and oral narratives from previously published and unpublished sources that I have reformatted for this project.

In deciding which interview segments to include as vignettes, I focused on such criteria as insightfulness, cultural representativeness, and clarity of articulation. But as verbatim transcriptions of the audio-recorded conversations, I realize that they, like the oral-tradition texts, may not make for easy reading. There were no alterations made in the actual language used by an interviewee; the grammar was not "cleaned up." As a result, the vignettes convey not only the sentiments and ideas of the interviewee but also elements of "Indian English" and qualities of the speaker's voice. Within any given text, as noted by the series of dot ellipses, I did, however, delete discussion that strayed from the direct subject under consideration or phrases that were incompletely developed. In one instance, "They Blue Jayed" (p. 234), the order of the interview text was rearranged to better present the chronological sequence of events as discussed by the interviewee. As the actual interview unfolded, the interviewee jumped around considerably as she proceeded to recall events, continually going back to previously mentioned references to elaborate and more fully discuss them.

I have also presented a number of observational vignettes throughout the text of this book. Each presents a first-person description of a cultural scene, such as camas digging or a Sweat House ritual. The first-person account is, of course, from myself, a participant in the event. In each instance I attempted to capture some of the detail as well as the sequencing of events, and then present my experience in such a manner as to invite the reader to imagine himself or herself as an eyewitness observer. In so doing the reader may gain additional insights into the lives of the Schitsu'umsh.

With regard to the oral-narrative vignettes, I should remark upon how I presented the Dorothy Nicodemus narratives (Reichard 1938, 1946, 1947). As we have already considered, *how* the stories are told aloud is as vital as *what* is said. In the conveyance of oral tradition, the "voice" of the storytellers is critical to the understanding of the story texts. Various techniques of storytelling used by the raconteur and specific linguistic structures and features within the narrative text itself all contribute to the conveyed meaning of the narratives. With this in mind, it is essential that as much of the original and contextual storytelling and linguistic nuance as possible be represented in the literacy-formatted narratives of this book. This concern is reflected in my use of a poetic style, and in my demarcating of intonation and pause patterns in formatting the stories of Lawrence Aripa.

Relying upon the interlinear translations of Dorothy Nicodemus's stories (Reichard 1938, 1946), which we are so fortunate to have, I was able to include such linguistic features as deictics (e.g., "here" and "there") which help anchor the story in a spatial immediacy, repetition of key words and phrases, and the insightful narrative ending "then, the end of the trail" in the formatting of the narrative texts for this book. As with the reincorporation of the adverb "then," I have tried to format the texts consistently in the present tense in order to give the reader a greater sense of temporal immediacy. These features were typically not represented in Reichard's 1947 free-translations.

I also acknowledge that in attempting to convey something of the "how they are told," as well as to provide a relatively closer translation of the actual

Schịtsu'umsh phrases used, the story texts are not necessarily easy to read. As my students might say, "They're a little choppy." Nevertheless, the reformatting of the Reichard texts can offer the reader insights into the oral traditions not otherwise available, hopefully facilitating a greater sense of participation in the stories while still replicating the original story lines and plots. In the instance of the rather lengthy "Chief Child of the Yellow Root" narrative, I did slightly abbreviate the text while trying not to compromise the story's integrity.

Let me illustrate the reformatting process by sharing a short sample. The following two text segments are from the "Crane and Coyote" narrative, comparing (a) Reichard's original literal translation, interlinear transcription, and orthography (1946) with (b) her free-translation (1947:100) and with (c) my reformatted text. Note the reinclusion of the deictics *hɔi* ("then") and *hu·ʾu* ("there"). While this example is anchored rather closely in Reichard's interlinear transcription, in order to avoid the story texts becoming overly choppy, much of my reformatting of the Dorothy Nicodemus narratives does take into consideration Reichard's free-translations as well.

(a) *hɔi   xʷist   ła skʷa'rcɛn,   xʷist   lut uwi'hu'   äkʷn*
   then   he went Crane   he went not very far he said
   hɔi naʾa tetaptqʷi'ĺkup....
   we'll stop to make fire...."

(b) They had not gone far when Crane said, "Let us stop here and make a fire. . . .

(c) Then Crane and the others go off. Having gone not too far, he says, "Now, we'll stop to make a fire. . . ."

(a) *xʷiỷä   sm:yi'w ł   tcta'ĺqalqʷ,   lutäsgwä'lps,*
   this   Coyote that's when he kicked the tree it did not burn
   tätc hu·ʾu   tä'k' uk'
   toward there   he fell

(b) Coyote went to another tree and kicked it, but it did not burn. The impact made him fall

(c) This Coyote goes to that tree, but when he kicks it, it doesn't burn, and he falls on his

(a) *tsaqtsaqli'päp,   äkʷn   uʾuna's,*
   on his back   he said it is wet

(b) over backwards. "Oh! That one must be wet," he said,

(c) back over there. He says, "It's wet!"

USE OF THE VIGNETTES

Let me explain briefly my intended use of the vignettes throughout this book. Whether based upon observations, interviews, or the oral-narrative texts themselves, the vignettes allow the reader access to a more authentic voice and image of the Schitsu'umsh people. But there is another important rationale as well. While teaching at a small liberal-arts college in Montana in 1983, I was involved in sponsorship of a conference on storytelling from around the state. A "cowboy" storyteller had just completed his session at the conference, and, with a booming voice, had delivered his stories squarely into the laps of the audience. Agnes Vanderburg, a Bitterroot Salish elder from the Flathead Reservation, was next to speak, and she came forward.

With neither the physical frame nor self-amplified voice of the previous teller, Agnes Vanderburg began her stories. Soon all in the audience were moving their chairs a little closer, and closer still, to catch every one of Agnes's deliberately spoken words. In no time, the members of the audience seemed completely engaged, eyes moving this way and that as Agnes pointed here, then looked there, leading the way through an unveiling of her stories. Upon finishing, and unlike the previous teller, she simply returned to her seat, offering neither commentary, explanation, nor Aesop-like moral lessons.

You had to work for Agnes's stories. They would not be delivered to you, unwrapped and ready for use. Yet her stories spoke as easily to the six-year-old child who sat in the front row as they did to the thirty-six-year-old Salish man standing to the side as they did to the sixty-year-old scholar of religious studies seated in the back row. For there was something that awaited discovery for anyone who was willing to travel the territory of Agnes's stories. As a masterful storyteller, this was, indeed, part of her magic.

Taking my cue from Agnes—a cue consistently reiterated to me by Schitsu'umsh elders such as Lawrence Aripa and Lucy Finley—I have concluded that there is something essential in the "discovery process." While I have wrapped each of the vignettes with considerable contextual information, both historical and cultural, and their particular placement throughout the book was done with deliberation, I have typically not provided specific interpretive anchoring. No individual analysis of the stories is provided, no moral lessons offered. As suggested by Agnes, given the multiple and varied levels of meanings that inundate any given story, and recognizing the different orientations and levels of maturation of listeners, to offer a particular moral lesson would obscure a story's full richness and potential. Agnes required everyone in her audience to engage in the stories fully and discover for himself or herself what was meaningful. And upon reengaging in the same story at some future point, a listener's greater maturation might cause some new discovery. Agnes required participation in her stories. Accordingly, I invite and challenge readers to engage thoroughly and explore the territory of each of the vignettes, and thereby to discover their meanings and connections. What are the linkages, for example, between the "Crane and Coyote" and "The Water Potato" vignettes in the introductory chapter? This is a pedagogy much more in keeping with that followed by the elders themselves.[7]

VIGNETTE ANONYMITY

I should explain why authorship of vignettes quoted directly from consultants is not attributed. As discussed in "Continuity and Variation," in the introductory chapter, while the texts can and do reflect elements and aspects of individual family traditions (and thus minor distinctions among and between various family traditions), the Schitsu'umsh elders see this entire body of knowledge as more generally representing them as a single people and, most important, as ultimately derived from a single source. In this sense it is knowledge that cannot be claimed individually or "owned" at all. Rather, it is communal knowledge that is to be shared freely with "those in need."

What I have now come to realize is that the elders, in sharing their teachings with me, the public, and future generations, demonstrated exactly what they were attempting to convey in words and deeds about their teachings. The teachings are gifts to be shared freely with those in need, not something to be owned. When huckleberries are shared, the giver never seeks acknowledgment from the recipients for what was, in turn, shared with him by the Creator. In keeping with the Schitsu'umsh perspective, if attribution is to be made, it is the First Peoples who are the authors of these texts. It should also be pointed out that "final approval" of the various elders' groups and the Tribal Council to publicly present this information was based on keeping the individual vignettes anonymous, while at the same time acknowledging the specific elders who contributed to the project as a whole.

THE TEXT AS A MAP

One of the elders, Mariane Hurley, was at first rather reluctant to participate in this project. She did not want her words "written down," because she felt that "the words can be interpreted any which way," losing their meaning, as she "wouldn't be there to correct someone." Most important, "the words were dead." For Mariane, it is only through the spoken words of "our fathers and grandfathers, mothers and grandmothers," by being in their very presence, that you can come to learn the teachings. She eventually changed her mind and, in fact, became one of my most indispensable and beloved teachers. But her reluctance does highlight an important point about the nature of the texts included in this book.

In conversation with Mariane, I concurred that something vital was indeed lost when the spoken word was rendered into printed text. I tried to acknowledge to her my understanding that what is lost in this orality-to-literacy transformation—that which is associated with oral nuance—is often essential to the meaning of the text (Frey 1995:141–77). This is particularly apparent in connection with the oral traditions of Crane and Coyote and the other First Peoples.

Further, I agreed that only in the direct presence of the elders can the teachings truly be taught. I recall special moments I experienced with an elder, when a tear was shed, followed by a deafening silence, and then perhaps a laugh. Did I truly understand what he had just attempted to share with me? Ethnographers shoulder a heavy burden in attempting to comprehend and then convey to others what is so integral to and revered by someone else. And I ask myself, Did I listen well enough? Finally, there can be something about the nature of a book that so formalizes and intellectualizes a people that what they most cherish—as, in this instance, "heart knowledge,"—can be absent from the pages. And further, in using a book as the medium of communication, one can run the risk of compromising the goal sought and "objectify" a non-Cartesian ontology (Frey 1995:141–47). And I ask myself, How do I write down that cry, that silence, that laugh? How do I convey the dynamic of a human who "Blue Jays" or who has gone "inside and become the Coyote"? Did I come close to getting it right? And in turn, when engaging the pages of this book, will strangers have an opportunity to come close to getting it right?

As we continued our conversation, I reiterated to Mariane that I sought to convey the actual voices and deeds of the elders through the many vignettes in the book. As context can be so important in understanding a people, I spoke of placing the Schitsu'umsh within their unique historical and cultural setting. I assured Mariane that I sought to represent the world of the Schitsu'umsh from the perspective of the people themselves. And to amplify that goal, I referred to the extensive review process, stressing that nothing would be publicly shared that the elders thought should not be.

Ultimately, recognizing its shortcomings and in all humility, I conceded to Mariane that *Landscape Traveled by Coyote and Crane* might best be understood as a "secondary source." It will, I hope, inspire Schitsu'umsh youth to seek out their elders, and it can be used as a kind of "road map" by Indians, as well as by whites, to travel the landscape of the Schitsu'umsh. (Given the understanding that "the story is like traveling a trail," use of the "map" metaphor seems most appropriate.) But as a map, this book is most assuredly not the landscape itself. It cannot, for example, replicate the experience of being in the presence of Lawrence Aripa as he tells of Coyote, or that of looking down at Lake Coeur d'Alene from atop Grassy Mountain with your son at your side and feeling the soul of your tribe.

Ours is a very special sort of road map. When Lawrence Aripa or Agnes Vanderburg would tell of Coyote, the story would come alive and be meaningful to the extent that it was participated in by the listeners. In attempting to approximate an Indian epistemology and pedagogy, the text of *Landscape Traveled by Coyote and Crane* will similarly become meaningful at that moment when the reader actively engages its many voices. You must attempt to travel the trails of the stories and "swirl around" with Crane and Coyote, and then explore the story's linkages with the gathering and distribution of the water potato. Upon first encountering these stories, try having someone else read them aloud to you, paying attention to the deictics and to the pauses and intonations in Lawrence's voice. Imagine yourself bent over, with a *pitse'* in hand, digging the bitterroots or camas with your grandmother. Feel the intense heat of the Sweat House as a young boy shares his tears and heart with his elders. You are asked to participate in this text, not observe it and its stories from afar. By engaging the text, the distance between the map and landscape may be narrowed.

If this particular map is to be of value for a wide audience, this book must not only seek to chart the landscape traveled by Crane and Coyote but also accommodate the landscape's many and diverse non-Schitsu'umsh travelers. As suggested at the beginning of this appendix, an interpretative framework is needed to bridge the Euro-American and the Schitsu'umsh experiences. While I seek to identify the same trails traveled by Coyote and Crane that would appear in an exclusively Schitsu'umsh-traveled map, the trails enunciated here must also acclimate travelers, wholly accustomed to a distant landscape, to a landscape that defies many basic Euro-American philosophical, economic, and religious sensibilities. Extra, well-marked signposts and even a few rest areas must line the way: a historical context outlined, a scientific-based botanical taxonomy provided, pivotal constructs deliberated and used, an interpretative analogy offered, and then all told in the English language and disseminated in a printed format. Our map is a translated map, with an expanded legend.

By encouraging participation in them, the stories of Lawrence can, in some sense, come alive and be appreciated; the words can be made not quite so dead. By encouraging a participation that accommodates many and diverse travelers, strangers can begin to appreciate a Schitsu'umsh perspective and chart a distant landscape traveled by Crane and Coyote. But in succeeding to do that, the text necessarily becomes a map distinct from one experienced exclusively by Schitsu'-umsh travelers. Extra signposts have lined the way for the participation of strangers who bring to the story their own experiences. Involvement by non-Schitsu'umsh, in itself, does not render something any less Schitsu'umsh, as whites routinely partake in the stories, dances, songs, prayers, and gifts of the Schitsu'umsh. But this text, no matter how aptly it may map a landscape, remains a *translated map of a landscape*, and when engaged by non-Schitsu'umsh, it is animated solely by the participation of those who are likely *strangers*. Regardless of the level of engagement, these travelers wear an assortment of clothing styles—an array of upbringings and maturations, attitudes and expectations, each engendering experiences distinct from the Schitsu'umsh host.

Consequently, this engaged text must inevitably encompass a diversity of experiences, all of which are themselves ever so different from Mariane Hurley's own unmediated experience of her landscape. Hence her reluctance. But within the engaged text itself, Agnes Vanderburg would anticipate nothing less than diversity. From the mix of experiences, (each traveler in interaction with the trails of this text), the reader can uniquely discover those meanings held within the stories befitting his or her particular wardrobe. Paradoxically, but appropriately so, while the text of *Landscape Traveled by Coyote and Crane* may in the hands of the reader culminate in a portrayal of a landscape distinct from that which it seeks to represent and is experienced by Mariane, the text may also approximate some of the epistemological and ontological premises of the world within which that landscape is conceived and Mariane experiences. It is a world precipitated by the participation of its travelers, guided by the teachings of Crane and Coyote.

These realizations need not deter us from the primary goal of this project—that of articulating a Schitsu'umsh view of their landscape—but rather can expand our appreciation of the challenges in attempting to do so and can reiterate our awareness that the map is not the landscape itself.

REVIEW PROCESS

As accomplished storytellers, Agnes Vanderburg's and Lawrence Aripa's "magic" was not only in transforming the listeners into participants within the stories but also in "staying on course." While succeeding in so completely engaging their audiences that listeners became travelers (thus accommodating the idiosyncratic experiences of the stories' participants), Agnes and Lawrence never allowed their travelers to wander from the trails of those stories. It was their utmost responsibility to identify the trails originally and continually traveled by Crane and Coyote, and then to lead travelers over those trails vigilantly.

As first asked with some trepidation in the introduction to this book, "Could I truly convey to my readers a Schitsu'umsh perspective?" Given our previous discussion, how close could the resulting translated map, engaged by its many diverse travelers, come to identifying the actual trails traveled by Crane and Coyote? Would the book "stay on course"? Were all the "bones" included? Would this bridge of reinforced girders be firmly anchored in the landscape of the Schitsu'-umsh? In order to help answer these questions, a thorough review process was initiated and completed. While not presuming that such a process would result in some sort of guarantee, I believed it would contribute significantly to the ethnographic accuracy, authenticity, and appropriateness of the book.

The review process would also help address the important ethical issues associated with a public presentation of another people's culture. Would I have the permission of the Schitsu'umsh to share with strangers that which they consider most cherished? Would the strangers become invited guests?

During October of 1997, a draft copy titled "The World of the Coeur d'Alene" was distributed for review and comment to each of the several elders and interviewees who had been working closely with me on the project, as well as to all the members of the Tribal Council. Follow-up interviews were then made over the next five months with my consultants. They included John Abraham,

Lawrence Aripa, Mariane Hurley, Alfred Nomee, Henry SiJohn, Cliff SiJohn, Frenchy SiJohn, Dixie Stensgar, Ernie Stensgar, and Marjorie Zarate. Felix Aripa was given a copy in January of 1998, with a follow-up interview held in March; Lucy Finley received a copy in March of 1998. In addition, oral presentations discussing the methodology, subject content, and conclusions of the project were made to key Schitsu'umsh elders (Lucy Finley on February 11, 1998, and Jeannette Whitford on February 2, 1998), along with the dozen or so other Schitsu'umsh elders who regularly attended the Seniors Luncheons sponsored by the tribe (on February 9, 1998, and March 2, 1998), and to key elders of the Spokane Tribe (Robert Sherwood, Hank Wynne, Alice "Vi" Cornelius Seymour, and Pauline Flett, on March 27, 1998). The Spokane elders were consulted in light of their critical involvement in many Schitsu'umsh activities (e.g., Powwows, funerals and wakes, and Memorial Giveaways), and because they are "respected for their opinions" by the Schitsu'umsh. The manuscript was also reviewed by the tribal attorney for any possible impact on ongoing tribal litigation. None was found.

As a result of the comments and suggestions made by these elders and interviewees, I made numerous additions, clarified many unclear aspects, and reorganized major sections of the manuscript. No one asked that any of the materials be deleted. During the course of interviewing, several specific "prayer circles" and other sacred sites were identified by consultants. I elected not to include reference to these locations out of concern for improper visitation by "pot-hunters" and the curious. Having been with elders when we came upon the consequences of pot-hunter activity, I can vividly remember on their faces how this terribly senseless and irreverent act ripped at their hearts.

Without exception, all those I had contacted as part of the review process agreed that the Schitsu'umsh teachings were appropriately identified, that these teachings were best anchored in and identified through the oral traditions of the Schitsu'umsh people, and that these materials should be disseminated for their educational value.

On April 16, 1998, the Tribal Council, acting on "CDA Resolution 116-A (98)," voted unanimously to approve "The World of the Coeur d'Alene Indians: Landscape Traveled by Crane and Coyote" (as the manuscript was then titled) for use in the tribe's Natural Resource Damage Assessment (NRDA), and, along with the photos and interviews I conducted as part of the project, for use in "nonprofit, educational purposes" and for publication consideration.

At a time when anthropological inquiry is maligned by some in the Indian community (in many instances, rightfully so), I have been gratified to be involved in a project resulting in a document that the Schitsu'umsh themselves feel accurately represents their perspective, and that they, in turn, desire to have publicly disseminated and published. I believe this enthusiastic support is a direct by-product of the collaborative nature of the entire project.

Through August of 2000 I continued "fine-tuning" and editing the entire manuscript, expanding the "Since Time Immemorial" and "Winds of Change" chapters, including several vignettes based upon the interviews conducted for the NRDA, and adding the three Lawrence Aripa Coyote stories, which had originally appeared in *Me-y-mi-ym: Oral Literature of the Coeur d'Alene People* (Frey 1994). Some of the fine-tuning was initiated by the invaluable comments and suggestions of Robert McCarl of Boise State University and Gary Palmer of the University of Nevada, Las Vegas, who reviewed earlier drafts of the manuscript.

The anchoring of the bridge had been inspected and certification granted. It was now ready to welcome its travelers, Schitsu'umsh and non-Schitsu'umsh alike. Only in time, and with the subsequent participation of those who use it, can it be said whether the bridge has offered an accurate, authentic, and appropriate mapping of the landscape traveled by Crane and Coyote.

FREY'S VOICE

Landscape Traveled by Coyote and Crane is truly the culmination of the efforts of many. As a collaborative project, this book presupposes a conversation among distinct voices, each in partnership, and hopefully harmonious, with the others. While my goal throughout this endeavor has been to convey the voice of the Schitsu'umsh people accurately and authentically, I also acknowledge that something of my own voice is embedded within the text. To help the reader sort through the conversation and better understand the collaborative nature of the book, let me share a little about my history of involvement with the Schitsu'umsh people and what I may have contributed to the conversation.

Several years ago some words were spoken to me that have resonated ever since. Vic Charlo, a Bitterroot Salish poet and playwright, was responsible for the first of those words. He told me, "The stories define us. When the story ended, the elder would say, 'And this is true,' pointing to that hill where the heart of the Monster is. And you look and see, see the story; we are linked. It's a matter of just claiming that linkage" (Frey 1995:39). A short time later, Tom Yellowtail, a Crow elder, also spoke of stories.[8] "Grandpa" had just finished retelling a series of his favorite oral traditions when he turned to me and said, "If all these great stories were told, great stories will come" (Frey 1995:177). Stories first brought me to the Schitsu'umsh people.

In the fall of 1991, I was asked by the Coeur d'Alene School District (the city of Coeur d'Alene is a predominantly white community, some twenty miles to the north of the reservation) to serve on its Language Arts Curriculum Committee. As we were in a K–6-grade curriculum-adoption phase, and as there was little mention of the history and culture of the people whose name the community had taken, I contacted elders of the Schitsu'umsh tribe to inquire if they would be interested in helping with a project. They were. Soon I was working closely with Lawrence Aripa, Cliff SiJohn, Bingo SiJohn, and Mariane Hurley, among many other elders.

Over the course of the next few months, and with funding from the Idaho Humanities Council, we developed a videotape of several Schitsu'umsh oral traditions, an anthology of stories was collected, a teachers guide written, and a teachers workshop held. In April of 1993, the school board formally adopted the fourth-grade Coeur d'Alene Indian language-arts curriculum, "Me-Y-Mi-Ym: Oral Literature of the Coeur d'Alene Indian People." After additional discussion with the elders and a rewrite of the text for the teachers guide, *Stories That Make the World: Oral Literature of the Indian Peoples of the Inland Northwest As Told by Lawrence Aripa, Tom Yellowtail, and Other Elders* was published in 1995. The greatest gratification the project has brought me was in hearing from those who knew Lawrence Aripa or Tom Yellowtail that "we can hear his voice when we read this book."

Beginning in the 1992–93 academic school year, I found myself involved with the Schitsu'umsh in a new project. At the time, I was serving as Director of Lewis-Clark State College's North Idaho Programs. Working in consort with Cliff SiJohn and later Dianne Allen, succeeding Directors of the tribe's Department of Education, we built a partnership between the Coeur d'Alene Tribe and Lewis-Clark State College.[9] We invited anyone from the reservation community, Schitsu'umsh or white, who sought a bachelors degree in Business Management to join a "learning community." Students could complete a four-year degree, in four years, from their home community, and they could do so while maintaining their jobs and family ties.

In the fall semester of 1993, the DeSmet Higher Education Program began offering courses, all of which were taught in DeSmet. Over the next four years, using some rather creative scheduling, I coordinated the delivery of the entire curriculum to DeSmet, served as the students' academic advisor, even taught a couple of the courses, and helped to facilitate the approval of a yearlong "Coeur d'Alene language" course for satisfaction of the LCSC General Education Core Language requirement. In the arena of college academics, it was gratifying to be able elevate the Schitsu'umsh language to the same status as that of Spanish or French. The DeSmet Higher Education experience was a unique situation for me, with many of my college students also among my most important Schitsu'umsh cultural teachers, as we reversed our roles in and out of the classroom! In May of 1997 we celebrated our first graduating class.

A word on my involvement in the Jump Dances of 1994 and 1996: The "very personal" and intensely spiritual nature of the Jump Dance can affect *all* its participants. Consequently, clarity about one's intentions during and following such involvement is both ethically and ethnographically essential. My participation in both Jump Dances came as a result of an unsolicited invitation by its sponsor. In 1994 an invitation was also extended to and accepted by one of the white physi-

Coyote's Laugh
(watercolor drawing by Lawrence Aripa, a Christmas gift to the author, 1997)

cians associated with the Benewah Medical Center. I was the only white participant at the 1996 Jump Dance. The sponsor certainly viewed me as a white educator and "anthropologist," but he also saw me in an another light.

During the dances, as I listened to the often emotionally charged "heart talk"
and then "jumped," sweat running down my brow in the company of "family,"
I too prayed and "gave" with all my sincerity. During the early morning hours
of the 1996 Jump Dance, this sponsor asked if I would "say a few words" and, in
front of all assembled, introduced me as a "Crow Sun Dance man." He knew I
had been under the guidance of Tom Yellowtail and had been Sun Dancing with
the Crows for many years, in fact, completing my seventh and eighth dances during the summers immediately following each of these two Jump Dances. As I
"jumped" I participated in the Jump Dances first and foremost as a human being,
offering prayer for those in need. I could not have participated in this most spir-

itual of endeavors for any other reason. But in who I am and how I have come to serve the Schitsu'umsh community, I also participated as an ethnographer and educator, desiring to facilitate an appreciation of the Schitsu'umsh by others.

It should be noted that it was this sponsor who had helped me write a fourth-grade language arts curriculum and had been one of my college students. And as an indispensable consultant in the NRDA project, it was also this Jump Dance sponsor who reviewed and approved the use of the ethnographic descriptions of the Jump Dance for this book.

In January of 1996, I was approached by Alfred Nomee, Director of the Coeur d'Alene Tribe's Department of Natural Resources, and Phil Cernera, Project Director for the tribe's Natural Resource Damage Assessment, and asked to assist in their Natural Resources Damage Assessment. I was soon under contract as an employee of the Coeur d'Alene Tribe, with my particular focus on a "cultural study." My study would be part of a larger team endeavor, which included many specialists, such as wildlife biologists, economists, historians, attorneys, and other anthropologists. The "cultural study" segment was thus a project sought and initiated by Schitsu'umsh, in which I was asked to organize and facilitate its completion. Among the questions I would ask were: "What does the surrounding landscape mean to the Schitsu'umsh people? and what effect does that understanding have on how they relate to the landscape and to each other?" In whatever sense the lake, rivers, and mountains continue to be of significance, hold meaning, and are related to by the Schitsu'umsh, the varied impacts of environmental degradation on those relationships and meanings could be better assessed and understood.

It was auspicious that the first two elders I interviewed would be of such significance throughout the project. For it was Lawrence Aripa and Henry SiJohn who established the orientation and set the tone for the interviews and observations to come. And throughout the project, they were among my primary advisors. Lawrence and Henry could not have been better guides. As you have read, more than fifty interviews were then conducted, archives were consulted, and a wealth of observations made while participating in the many dimensions of Schitsu'umsh life over an eight-year period.

I continue to be involved, professionally and personally, with the Schitsu'umsh people. Under the coordination of Tiffany Allgood, and beginning in April 1998, I have been assisting in the tribe's Environmental Action Plan, chairing the Quality of Life subgroup. The stated objective in developing an Environmental Action Plan (EAP) is "to identify and reduce risks to human health, ecosystems and quality of life and to assist in the overall management of human and natural environments." In the fall of 1998, many of my University of Idaho undergraduate and graduate students became involved in the project as well. To solicit additional information for the assessment phase of the plan, the students conducted interviews of reservation community members, and did so while "partnered" with and mentoring local high school students. That same October also saw many of those university students, under the guidance of Alfred Nomee, ankle-deep in the mud and among the reeds of Lake Coeur d'Alene, digging for water potatoes. Then at a senior citizens noon luncheon, the students handed what they gathered to the elders, such as Lucy Finley and Bingo SiJohn, sharing with those "who could not make it down here today, someone in need of this water potato."

On October 15, 1998, again on February 13, 1999, I stood with many other family members and friends who offered tears, as we sought to grieve, honor, thank, and remember first Lawrence Aripa and then Henry SiJohn. As we returned Lawrence and Henry to the earth, from which they came and that they so dearly loved and companioned, I know their voices will live on as long as we listen with our hearts. And the stories of Crane and Coyote continue to be told, the linkages reclaimed, and I am confident that great stories will come.

Appendix B
List of Plants and Animals

The following list identifies many of the bird, mammal, fish, and plant species used by the Schitsu'umsh. It is only a partial list of the plants and animals relied upon. The botanical names accompany the list of English terms commonly used by Schitsu'umsh.

Bitterroot (*Lewisia rediviva*)
"Black moss" (*Bryoria fremontii*; syn. *Alectoria jubata* and *A. fremontii*)
"Black root" (perhaps *Frasera montana* or *Valeriana edulis*)
Camas (*Camassia quamash*)
Chokecherry (*Prunus virginiana*)
Cous (*Lomatium cous*)
Elderberry (*Sambucus racemosa*)
Huckleberry (*Vaccinium membranaceum*)
"Indian celery" (*Heracleum lanatum*)
Jerusalem artichoke (*Helianthus tuberosus*)
Oregon grape (*Mahonia aquifolium*)
Serviceberry (*Amelanchier alnifolia*)
Soapberry (also known as "foam berry" or "Indian ice cream"; *Shepherdia canadensis*)
"Sunflower" (also known as balsamroot; *Balsamorhiza sigittata*)
Thimbleberry (*Rubus parviflorus*)
"Thornberry" (Black hawthorn; *Crataegus douglasii*)
Wild carrot (*Perideridia gairdneri*)
"Wild onion" (*Allium cernuum* or *A. geyeri*)
"Water potato" (*Sagittaria latifolia*)

HEALING PLANTS

Chokecherry bark (*Prunus virginiana*)
"Cub ears" (likely wintergreen; *Pyrola asarifolia*)
Lovage (*Ligusticum canbyi*)
Mint (*Mentha arvensis*)

Ponderosa pine (*Pinus ponderosa*)
Western red cedar (*Thuja plicata*)
Wild rosebush (*Rosa acicularis*)
"Yellow root" (Indian hellebore; *Veratrum viride*)

MAMMALS

Black bear (*Ursus americanus*)
Elk (*Cervus canadensis*)
Moose (*Alces alces*)
Mule deer (*Odocoileus hemionus*)
Porcupine (*Erethizon dorsatum*)
White-tail deer (*Odocoileus virginianus*)

BIRDS

Canada goose (*Branta canadensis*)
Cinnamon teal (*Anas cyanoptera*)
Grouse (*Bonasa umbellus*)
Mallard (*Anas pletrhynchos*)
Robin (*Turdus migratorius*)

FISH, CRUSTACEANS, AND MOLLUSKS

Chinook salmon (*Oncorhynchus tshawytscha*)
Cutthroat trout (*Oncorhynchus clarki*)
Mountain whitefish (*Prosopium williamsoni*)
Sockeye salmon (*Oncorhynchus nerka*)
Steelhead trout (*Oncorhynchus mykiss*)
Crayfish (*Astacus spp.*)
Freshwater clam (*Margaritifera spp.*)

Note: Botanical identification of many of the healing plants in this appendix was greatly assisted by Nancy Turner of the University of Victoria (personal communication, October 1999) and by the unpublished study of Palmer, Kinkade, and Turner (1996).

Notes

1. The story of Crane and Coyote was originally told by Dorothy Nicodemus, who was in her mid-seventies, and was recorded by the ethnographer Gladys Reichard, in 1927 or 1929. This narrative is a free translation based upon the text from Reichard's "Coeur d'Alene Texts" (1946:5–26), with reference to her "Analysis of Coeur d'Alene Indian Myths" (1947:99–101). The continuation of this narrative is found on page 121. Reichard noted that the character of Crane is unique to the Schitsu'umsh and not recorded by any other Plateau people (1947:105). See "Appendix A. Research Considerations" for a discussion on how this and other narratives in this book were assembled and formatted.

2. Guests are supposed to receive more food than they can eat, taking home what is not consumed.

3. Crane will periodically demonstrate his *suumesh* powers, as when he makes the meat bundles "very tiny," when he "calls in the deer" during a hunt, or in various contests with Coyote.

4. The chief's family is responsible for further distributing their portion of meat, ensuring that none go without food.

5. Unless otherwise noted, the orthography, spelling, and meaning of Schitsu'umsh terms used throughout this work correspond to Palmer, Nicodemus, and Connolly (1987); Palmer, Nicodemus, and Felsman (1987); Nicodemus (1975); and the Coeur d'Alene Language Preservation Program. Underlined vowels are stressed; ' signals a stop.

6. Plante's Ferry was named after Antoine Plante, who established a settlement and ferry along this shallow section of the Spokane River. It was traditionally used as a crossing by local tribes. Plante had served as a guide in Governor Isaac Stevens's 1853 Northern Pacific Railroad surveys.

7. "Schitsu'umsh," while generally applied to all tribal members today, may have originally referred to a specific locale and a single band living at the southern end of Lake Coeur d'Alene. However, Father Joseph Joset (1838–77; JP 41) reported that during the mid-nineteenth century "the real name" of the Coeur d'Alenes was "the Schitsus." Schitsu'umsh has also been translated as the "found people" or the "discovered people." Other historical spellings of the term include: Skeetsomish, Skitswish, Skitsuish and Skit-mish. Distinguishing the "Skitswish people" from the main body of the tribe, one elder referred to them as a special class of "powerful medicine people,

who performed their ceremonials high in the mountains above Cataldo." A mountain to the northwest of Cataldo continues to bear the name Skitwish Peak.

8. When I began my fieldwork with the Schitsu'umsh, I anticipated an exchange network based upon direct reciprocity, as I had been accustomed to seeing after years of association with the Crow of Montana (Frey 1987). But the Schitsu'umsh clearly express a different exchange pattern.

9. Rose Lake is one of many small lakes associated with the lower drainage of the Coeur d'Alene River.

10. This is not to suggest that strangers, Crows, or non-Indians in need of assistance would not be helped by a Schitsu'umsh. They certainly would. The sharing patterns, so characteristic of Schitsu'umsh family transactions, are, in fact, typically and routinely extended by the Schitsu'umsh to include all those in their community who are in need—Indian and white alike. The need may be based upon a financial hardship or sudden illness, for example. In addition, the Schitsu'umsh family has itself come to include Indians affiliated with other tribes and whites, as for example those who have married into the tribe, those who are addressed as "the fathers" (the Jesuit priests) and those who, if only temporarily, attend a Powwow celebration. "All the guests are part of our family." See the section, "Give It To Them," in "Sharing the Gifts" for a brief discussion of some of these inclusions. Membership in the Schitsu'umsh family is based as much on a personal adherence to and expression of certain attitudes, i.e., the teachings, as it is on birth.

Among Salish speakers (such as the Kalispel and Spokane and the Schitsu'umsh), the term generally used to refer to whites is *Suuyapi*. While less frequently heard, the specific Schitsu'umsh term for "the white tribe" or "white people" is *Suuyepmsh,* sometimes shortened to *Suuyepi.*

11. However, there is not a complete absence of Coyote (e.g., in his many disguises) among the Schitsu'umsh family. Coyote may appear in an instance of some comic relief at a Powwow, when teasing, or in a practical joke played out against an older sister or brother. Coyote may also appear in the "Jeopardy"-like (as in the television game show) language games that pit various Coeur d'Alene language study groups in "friendly competition," helping to motivate young and old to learn the language. Certainly a good telling of a Coyote story can add a smile or laugh to an otherwise mundane day. And, most important (as will be discussed subsequently), the lessons found within Coyote's stories are to be taken seriously. Not only does Coyote establish a model for *how to* behave toward a potential opponent, but in the examples of his many failed schemes are the moral lessons on *how not to* behave toward one's kinsmen. Coyote's self-serving actions are the antithesis of proper familial behavior.

While additional research is suggested, I suspect a form of the "principle of segmentation" (Evans-Pritchard 1940:143) may also be at work within the boundaries of the Schitsu'umsh "family." Depending upon the circumstances of specific social, economic, and/or religious needs, there can occur a shifting and intensifying of "kinship" affiliations to meet various specific tasks. The result is a series of situationally defined kinship boundaries radiating out from an individual household to the extended family, to the band, to the tribe, and finally to Salish "relatives," for example. While an ethic of sharing would characterize relations within each shifting segment, outside each segment a competitive, though far less belligerent and self-serving,

Coyote might occasionally participate in these "friendly" relations with other Schitsu'umsh.

12. Refer to "Appendix A. Research Considerations" for a discussion of the intended use of vignettes in this book. In particular, note the example set forth by the Bitterroot Salish elder and storyteller Agnes Vanderburg. Also refer to "Appendix A" for a discussion of anonymity in the vignettes that draw upon quoted interviews.

SINCE TIME IMMEMORIAL

1. For a more complete view of Schitsu'umsh society during the precontact period, refer to the important work of James Teit (1930). Gary Palmer (1998) offers a concise cultural and historical overview of Schitsu'umsh society. Jerome Peltier's Schitsu'umsh consultants provide interesting ethnographic points (1975). This chapter is based primarily on the works of Teit (1930) and Verne Ray (1942), supplemented by specific information referenced here and by the interviews I conducted.

The term "since time immemorial" is often used by elders to note that the Schitsu'umsh have occupied and traveled their landscape since the beginning of time.

2. The Plateau region extends from the Cascade Mountains in the west to the Rocky Mountains in the east, encompassing the Columbia River basin. The Fraser River valley marks the northern boundary, and the Klamath, Columbia, and Salmon rivers mark the southern reaches of the Plateau.

3. Joseph Joset, S. J., born in 1810, served as one of the priests at the Sacred Heart Mission (while located at Cataldo and later DeSmet) from 1844 until his death in 1900.

4. This method of hunting is also described in great detail in Teit (1930:102).

5. This precontact population estimate is based on the research of Teit (1930:39) and is corroborated by Roderick Sprague (1996:31).

6. Besides offering an excellent overview of Plateau social organization and kinship, Lillian Ackerman (1994) argues convincingly for a "nonunilinear descent group" structure for the Plateau, including the Schitsu'umsh.

7. Teit reports the opposite, stating that "separation between husband and wife was uncommon" (1930:172).

8. What is referred to in this chapter as a "shaman" is today generally termed a "medicine man" by the Schitsu'umsh.

9. For descriptions of the Sweat House and Jump Dance ceremonies, and many of the burial rituals, see the discussions in the chapter "Sharing the Gifts." The ritual procedures for both the Sweat House and Jump Dance ceremonies have remained relatively unchanged into the present. The Jump Dance is also referred to as the Winter Spirit Dances (Ray 1942:248–53) and the Medicine Dances (Teit 1930:186–87).

WINDS OF CHANGE

1. I am using the analytical construct "history" to refer to the marking of events on a linear time line, from past to present. As such, past events are necessarily only remembered events, no longer events participated in. This Euro-American concept contrasts with the Schitsu'umsh understanding of the possibility of *participation* in past events. As will be discussed, in the act of storytelling, the creation time is made immediate and the listener allowed to become part of it. Similarly, in the act of singing

and dancing during a Jump Dance, there is a sense that the dancer has become his *suumesh* animal spirit, transcending his temporal and spatial immediacy. What might be considered a past event is thus made an immediate event. With this consideration in mind, "Coeur d'Alene history" necessarily begins when the Euro-American concept of "history" was imposed on the Schitsu'umsh experience.

While "history" may have doubtful application to an aboriginal Schitsu'umsh society, this is not to suggest that prior to Euro-American contact Schitsu'umsh society was somehow changeless through time. Regular contact with other tribal groups resulted not only in the exchange of trade goods and spouses but certainly in the diffusion of material culture as well as ideas about culture. For example, the artistic appreciation and use of dentalium and abalone—shells not native to the area—must have originated via the exchange of ideas and objects with neighbors linked to the Pacific coast. Such intertribal contact, coupled with internal innovation, resulted in a *dynamic* Schitsu'umsh society. This dynamism did not approach the pace or the pervasive nature of change that ensued after Euro-American contact; nor did the pre-contact dynamism engender events with such catastrophic consequences. My concern here is to suggest that the participatory manner in which temporal dynamics were (and are) conceptualized by the Schitsu'umsh is fundamentally distinct from the linear, nonparticipatory conceptualization of time held by Europeans and Americans. Thus the concept of history must be used cautiously.

As part of a history of a particular people's landscape, my intention in this chapter is nevertheless to convey how the Schitsu'umsh have reaffirmed, as well as redefined, the meaning of landscape, given the influences of Euro-American contact and assimilation on their society. The portrayal of Indian-white history has been far too often represented only by the voice of the instigator, and not the recipient, of the contact. Despite severe threats to their economic viability and political sovereignty, the Schitsu'umsh have continued to give voice and definition to their landscape. It is the Schitsu'umsh perspective on their own landscape history that I seek to convey.

For additional discussion of Coeur d'Alene history, consult Fahey (1997), Kowrach and Connolly (1990), and Peltier (1981). Along with Fahey and Kowrach and Connolly, and other specific published works and interviews cited below, Hart (1996) and Sprague (1996) were also drawn upon in the writing of this chapter.

2. Isaac Stevens, governor of the newly established Washington Territory, provided population figures for regional tribes in his report to the Commissioner of Indian Affairs in 1854.

3. This hypothetical example must be placed in its demographic context. Precontact Schi'tsu'umsh society was likely characterized by a relatively high infant-mortality rate, but, once infancy was survived, it was not unusual for individuals to live past sixty-five years.

4. Lawrence Aripa added, in reference to "Smallpox and the Five People", "It's a story that is away from the Coyote stories. It's different. But yet it has a lesson. It is tragic, but it is something we must all think about. Don't say anything bad about your neighbor. It may be bad for them and it could be bad for yourself. Anyone who we may slander may become a greater person." Lawrence was told this story by Bill Meshell, who had learned it from his grandfather, a small boy at the time the events occurred.

5. See Gary Palmer (1998:325) for a more complete discussion of the root of the name "Coeur d'Alene."

6. Stellam—translated as Thunder but called Twisted Earth by his father—was the eldest son of Circling Raven and head chief probably as early as 1760 (Kowrach and Connolly 1990:13) but certainly by 1820 (Teit 1930:153), and he continued in that capacity until 1844. It was Stellam's sister's son, Vincent, "a man of wisdom and courage," who succeeded him as head chief in 1844, and who served until at least 1865. Teit did not list Vincent as a head chief, stating that Andrew Seltice followed Stellam as head chief upon the latter's death in 1844 (1930:153).

7. Gary Palmer (2001) offers an excellent review of the historical forces that prompted the Jesuits to relocate the mission to DeSmet.

8. Compare this text with that "remembered" by Diomedi himself (1978:68). Peone may have learned this speech from Peter Moctelme.

9. In 1913 a flood broke the dikes of the impoundment areas, causing mine tailings from the silver mines located upriver to pollute the Cataldo area severely, rendering the land useless for farming.

10. Morris Antelope's head chief chronology differed from Teit (1930:154), who recorded that Wildshoe became head chief and Moctelme "second chief" in 1902, and with Wildshoe's death in 1907, Moctelme then became head chief. Teit's order of head chiefs was corroborated by Kowrach and Connolly (1990:13). I date Antelope's undated letter "around 1907," since he stated that he began writing business letters for the tribe in 1907, the year Wildshoe died (*Coeur d'Alene Teepee* 1[8]:17; 1981:158).

11. See Gary Palmer (1981b) for an excellent overview of Schitsu'umsh farming from 1842 to 1876.

12. This high level of production might be expected, if, following the traditional patterns of food distribution (as exemplified by the actions of the designated hunters), the high-yield production of some families was redistributed to less-successful farming families. However, I have not found historical evidence that supports such a scenario.

13. The teachings of the Jesuits had, and continue to have, a tremendous effect on the Schitsu'umsh. The comments provided here primarily address those Jesuit influences that directly affected the Schitsu'umsh view of, and relationship to, their landscape.

14. Two noted artists accompanied Isaac Stevens on his 1853 Northern Pacific Railroad survey: New York–born John Mix Stanley and the German Gustavus Sohon. Eight of Stanley's lithographs are included in this book. Stevens served out his four-year term as territorial governor (1853–57) and later became a major general during the Civil War, only to be killed in 1862 at the Battle of Chantilly.

15. John Mullan later became a "true friend of the Coeur d'Alene," acted as their attorney in Washington, D.C., and has descendants on the modern reservation.

16. Having served as head chief since 1844, Vincent, also known as Bassa, was followed in 1865 by Andrew Seltice. Selected because of his "wealth and intelligence," Andrew Seltice served as head chief until his death in 1902. Peter Wildshoe followed in that capacity from 1902 until his death in 1907. Peter Moctelme was head chief from 1907 until 1932, and died in 1934. And Andrew Seltice's son, Joseph, "elected by the tribe," served as head chief from 1932 until his death in 1949. Joseph Seltice was the last "traditional head chief" of the Schitsu'umsh.

17. The intent of this section is not to demonstrate the extent and severity of ecological damage in the Coeur d'Alene River basin brought on by mining. It is rather to clarify the consequences of such activities for the Schitsu'umsh landscape.

18. Joseph Garry began serving as Chairman in 1948 and continued almost uninterrupted until 1967. Oswald "Ozzie" George served as Chairman from 1967 to 1970. Bernard "Happy" LaSarte served as Chairman from 1970 to 1971, from 1974 to 1981, and in 1985.

19. Henry SiJohn served on the Tribal Council until his death in 1999; Alfred Nomee is the Director of Natural Resources for Coeur d'Alene Tribe.

PREPARING THE WORLD

1. It is important to note that while working among the Schitsu'umsh during the second half of the nineteenth century, Father Joset maintained that the Indians had "no idea of a supreme being, . . .of a soul, of a spirit hereafter," "no original word for . . . spirit," and "the idea of creation is by no means represented in the language" (1838–77:JP 69). But he also reports how the Schitsu'umsh sought and relied upon "somesh" (*suumesh*), seeking it in the mountains, prayed before the hunt, had "medicine lodges," and used medicine men when sick.

2. Additional accounts of the First Peoples can be found in narrative texts recorded by James Teit (1917), Gladys Reichard (1947), and myself (1995).

3. The specific text of "Rabbit and Jackrabbit" is based on the Julia Nicodemus narrative (undated) and on the Dorothy Nicodemus text as recorded in Reichard (1947:192–93). The translation of the Dorothy Nicodemus story from Schitsu'umsh into English was assisted by her daughter-in-law, Julia Antelope Nicodemus, and then published in free-translation by Reichard (1947). The use of "cousin" by Julia Nicodemus and "relatives" by Dorothy Nicodemus to characterize the relationship between Rabbit and Jackrabbit, as opposed to "brothers," for example, suggests that while each is related, they are not closely related.

While the story line and plots of all these narratives remain intact, I have slightly modified the style of the presentation to include elements I have come to associate with Schitsu'umsh storytelling. I seek to convey a better sense of their oral nuance in this literacy-based format. These elements are discussed below in the chapter "Sharing the Gifts."

4. For additional general background on Coyote, consult Bright (1993), Frey (1995), and Ramsey (1977).

5. The "Coyote and the Salmon" text is based upon, and is a continuation of, the "Crane and Coyote" narrative told by Dorothy Nicodemus in Reichard (1946:5–26; 1947:101–5). The story of the salmon release is widespread, but unique among the Schitsu'umsh when combined with the Crane story.

6. The "Coyote and Woodtick" narrative is based upon Reichard (1946:241–249; 1947:135–38).

7. Compare this version of "Coyote and the Rock Monster" with one, told by Aripa, appearing in Frey (1995:71–75). As with the other two narratives, each originally appeared in *Me-y-mi-ym: Oral Literature of the Coeur d'Alene People* (1994), and had been approved for dissemination by the Coeur d'Alene Tribal Cultural Committee.

8. Compare this version of the "Coyote and the Gobbler Monster" narrative with Dorothy Nicodemus's account in Reichard (1947:68–72). As with the vignette "Indian

Uprising on the St. Joe," this text is based upon an audiotape recording made by Jane Fritz as part of an Idaho Mythweaver project, funded by the Idaho Humanities Council in 1991, and upon my own witnessing of Lawrence Aripa telling the story at that time.

9. In telling the "Coyote and the Gobbler Monster" story, and upon saying, "And that's where the Spokanes came from," Lawrence typically adds the phrase, "They are poor!" It was not stated during this particular rendition, but added to the text. It should be noted the Lawrence's maternal grandmother, Mattie Garry, was Spokane.

10. Compare this version of "Coyote and the Green Spot" with the version, told by Lawrence Aripa, appearing in Frey (1995:162–67).

11. Comparisons are based upon the extensive recording of Thompson, Lillooet, and Sanpoil oral traditions by James Teit and Verne Ray. See Reichard (1947:63–68) for citations to these sources.

12. In Reichard's unpublished "Coeur d'Alene Texts" (1946), the specific term "Chief Child of the Root" is not actually used, but appears in her free-translation (1947).

13. The "Chief Child of the Yellow Root" narrative is abbreviated and based upon Reichard (1946:173–201; 1947:57–68).

14. As noted by Reichard, those who addressed the hero as "Chief" would be helped, but those who called him "Chief Child of the Yellow Root" would be "insulted" and "overcome" (1947:58).

RECEIVING THE GIFTS

1. As with the other plants and animals listed in this study, this is only a partial inventory of species traditionally relied upon by the Schitsu'umsh. See Teit (1930: 88–91) and Palmer, Kinkade and Turner (1996) for more complete listings.

2. The Schitsu'umsh today typically refer to spiritual power, or "medicine," as "*suumesh*," though the specific term is attributed to the Spokane (Nicodemus 1975 [1]:245). *Suumesh* is, in fact, the generally used term among the various Salish peoples throughout the Plateau, including the Colville, Flathead, Kalispel, Lake, Sanpoil, Southern Okanogan, and Spokane (Grim 1992; Ray 1937). It is important to note that both Father Joset (1838–77:JP 69) and Father Diomedi (1978:77), in the mid-to-late nineteenth century, referred to an "invisible power" and "spirit" as "somesh," thus establishing its affinity with the currently used term *suumesh*.

3. The terms *meymiym q'esp schint* and *meymiym łu' schint*, and their translations, were provided by Francis SiJohn, and reflect the Schitsu'umsh spoken in the "mountain country" north of the Cataldo region (Frey 1995:xvii). The terms mean, literally, "learning about the people of long ago" and "learning about those people," respectively (personal communication, Gary Palmer, October 1999).

SHARING THE GIFTS

1. In conversation with the storyteller, I became confident that the story of "Coyote losing his eyes" was as true to form and content as it had been when this twenty-year-old storyteller first heard it from his grandmother. With the exception of its being told in English, this 1997 retelling was also virtually identical to the story conveyed in 1927 by Dorothy Nicodemus to Gladys Reichard (1947:89–95).

2. Dennis Tedlock (1972) has developed a formatting technique that greatly helps in conveying different voice-stress patterns used by raconteurs in storytelling.

3. The narrative "Little Muskrat and Otter" is based upon Reichard's interlinear transcriptions of the story (1938:694–707) and is supplemented by her free-translation of it (1947:185–87).

4. The term *hoi hinxuxʷa'tpalqs* (using Reichard's orthography) is probably derived from the term *snła'palqs*, meaning, literally, "end of the trail" (Nicodemus 1975 [2]:199).

5. The narrative "Chipmunk and Snake" is derived from Reichard (1947:189–90). Lacking an interlinear text to work from, my placement of the added deictics is based upon "educated conjecture."

6. The expression "*u ya ha ya ha*" can been translated to mean "calm weather."

7. While it is nice that the words of Chipmunk won out over Snake's, we must still take care in the words we speak aloud.

8. See Frey (1995:171–77) for additional discussion on the "purposes" of the Schitsu'umsh oral traditions.

9. Compare this version of the "Coyote Devours His Children" narrative with Reichard (1947:86–89).

10. The Coeur d' Alene Tribal Wildlife Manager has estimated the total number of "primary" designated hunters at about forty, with an additional hundred or more individuals who may at some point be called on to hunt on behalf of someone else. This figure is only a guess, as the Wildlife Manager currently has no mechanism in place to record the actual number of Schitsu'umsh hunters.

11. While it is very difficult to estimate the total number of deer and elk killed on the Coeur d'Alene Reservation, as well as that obtained in the ceded territory just north and east of the reservation boundaries, extending to the lower end of Pend Oreille Lake and the Clearwater Mountains to the south, the Coeur d'Alene Tribal Wildlife Manager suggests that up to a "total of three to five hundred deer and elk along with twenty or thirty bear" are taken each year. However, many hunters do not wish to report the results of their hunt, making such estimates more difficult.

12. The ceremonies of the Sweat House and Jump Dance inevitably involve personal and intense expressions of Schitsu'umsh spirituality. Recognizing the private character of much of what transpires during these ceremonies, the comments that follow are only broad outlines of the processes and significances of the Sweat House and Jump Dance. With the exception of the particular vignettes included here, which the interviewees specifically wanted to have included, I have sought to avoid elaborating on the more personal nature as well as esoteric qualities of the Sweat House and Jump Dance.

13. Teit also provides a description of the Sweat House, the structure of which was similar to that "used by all the plateau tribes" (1930:62).

14. For additional background on the Salish Jump Dance, see Grim (1992) and Ray (1937, 1939). What Teit refers to as the "Medicine Dance" (1930:186–87) and Ray refers to as the "Winter Spirit Dance" (1939:111; 1942:248–53) is what the Schitsu'umsh today typically refer to as the Jump Dance. Elders use this term to refer both to the contemporary and the precontact expressions of this winter dance. Actual use of the name Jump Dance by the Schitsu'umsh may have come about only during the mid-twentieth century, derived from Kalispel or Flathead influences. In his important comparative study of the Plateau, Ray stated, "The Winter Guardian Spirit Dance is the

major religious ceremony of the Plateau, dwarfing all other rituals by comparison" (1939:102).

15. While James Teit failed to mention the Blue Jay specifically, or what could be identified as the "Blue Jay complex," Verne Ray documented its aboriginal presence among the Schitsu'umsh (1937:598–99; 1939:116; 1942:251–52). Ray observed most of the same defining attributes as are identified here in the relatively contemporary expression.

16. Note that a complete understanding of the contemporary Schitsu'umsh wake, funeral, and burial ceremony cannot be fully appreciated without consideration of the Catholic ritual elements and doctrines integrated within them, such as the practice and inclusion of the rosary, communion, and mass, and the use of holy water.

17. I use the word "remarkably" since much of the Schitsu'umsh funeral has been, and continues to be, officiated by local Catholic priests. Nonetheless, a number of traditional customs continue to be expressed.

18. The notion of "reunion with the dead" was also noted by Teit, who suggested it may have "been learned from the priests" (1930:183). However, I suggest that this understanding is indigenous to the Schitsu'umsh, though not always fully articulated by individuals. The notion of "preparing the way" makes implicit reference to the actions of the First Peoples as established in the oral literature.

IT'S HOME

1. In this context, it is instructive to note the name of a small lake near Cheney, Washington, just west of Hangman Creek. It is referred to as *Sile'* (Palmer, Nicodemus, and Felsman 1987:80), the term for one's maternal grandfather.

APPENDIX A. RESEARCH CONSIDERATIONS

1. My use of "landscape" is consistent with that employed by anthropologist Keith Basso in his study of the Western Apache (1997). See Hirsch and O'Hanlon (1995) for additional discussion of the concept of landscape.

2. For a presentation of the "linguistic geography" of the Schitsu'umsh landscape, see Palmer, Nicodemus, and Felsman (1987). This insightful work provides the Schitsu'umsh terms for many of the specific features in their landscape, as well as some valuable historical notes.

3. Palmer, Nicodemus, and Connolly (1987:41) offer a brief biographical sketch of Lawrence Nicodemus.

4. Morris Antelope offered a brief "self history" in the *Coeur d'Alene Teepee* (1[8]:17–18; reprinted 1981:158–59).

5. For a brief biographical introduction to Lawrence Aripa, see Frey (1995:31–34). Lawrence's great-grandfather, Rufinus Shi'itsin, had three sons, Louis, Andrew, and Stanislaw (Stanislas), and a daughter, Mary Madeline. The eldest son, Louis Aripa, was one of the signers of the 1889 Agreement, and the youngest son, Stanislaw, was Lawrence's grandfather and Felix Aripa's father. Rufinus Shi'itsin was given the Latin name "Alberti," after Saint Albert, by the Jesuit priests. "Difficult to pronounce by the Indians," over time Alberti became "Aripa."

6. In Schitsu'umsh society, no one typically "retires" from active involvement in the oral and ceremonial traditions. While one may no longer hunt deer, his voice would

continue to instruct a grandson in how to track deer. The grandfather's voice would also continue to be heard around the Powwow drum and in prayer offered in the Sweat House.

7. Following the example set by Agnes Vanderburg, I had actually contemplated not initially identifying the five key teachings, as I have done in the introductory chapter. The teachings would be discovered as the reader engaged the story texts, and then only confirmed at the conclusion of the book. But given the desire to establish unambiguously the Schitsu'umsh perspective on their landscape from the onset of the discussion, I elected to identify the five key teachings. Nevertheless, there remains much to be discovered by individual readers in the oral traditions and vignettes included in this book.

8. For some background on Tom Yellowtail, see Frey (1995:34–37).

9. Lewis-Clark State College's main campus is located in Lewiston, Idaho, with the city of Coeur d'Alene the site of its largest outreach campus. LCSC's North Idaho Program numbers more than 300 students, with baccalaureate majors in Communication Arts, Interdisciplinary Studies, Justice Studies, Management, Nursing, and Social Work. I served as Director from 1987 through 1998, as well as Professor of Social Sciences. North Idaho College, a two-year community college located in Coeur d'Alene, joined the partnership in 1997.

Bibliography

Ackerman, Lillian

1994   "Nonunilinear Descent Groups in the Plateau Culture Area," *American Ethnologist* 21(2):286–309.

Antelope, Morris

1938   "History of Morris Antelope of the Coeur d'Alenes," *Coeur d'Alene Teepee* 1 (8):17–18. Reprinted in 1981 by Serento Press, Plummer, ID.

n.d.   "Letter to Commissioner of Indian Affairs." Written around 1907 and signed by Thomas Prosper, Paul Polotkeun, John Louie, Neas Louie, Peter Joseph, Jasper, Tamiel, Louie Sam, Andrew, Bill Piliph, and Morris Antelope. California Province Archives, Society of Jesus, Gonzaga University, Spokane.

Basso, Keith

1997   *Wisdom Sites in Places: Landscape and Language among the Western Apache.* Albuquerque: University of New Mexico Press.

Bennett, Earl, Peter Siems, and James Constantopoulos

1989   "The Geology and History of the Coeur d'Alene Mining District, Idaho." In "Guide to the Geology of Northern and Western Idaho and Surrounding Area," *Idaho Geological Survey Bulletin* 28:137–56.

Bright, William

1993   *The Coyote Reader.* Berkeley: University of California Press.

Burns, Robert Ignatius, S. J.

1947   "Pere Joset's Account of the Indian War of 1858," *Pacific Northwest Quarterly* 38(4):285–314.

Chalfant, Stuart, and William Bischoff

1974   *Interior Salish and Eastern Washington Indians, I.* Commission findings. New York: Garland Publishing.

Chittenden, H. M., and A. T. Richardson, eds.

1905   *Life, Letters and Travels of Father Pierre-Jean DeSmet, S. J., 1801–1873.* New York: Harper.

Coeur d'Alene Teepee

1937–   Volumes 1–3. Reprinted in 1981 by Serento Press, Plummer, ID.
40

Commissioner of Indian Affairs

1892–   *Report of the Commissioner of Indian Affairs to the Secretary of the Interior.*
1924   Washington, D.C.

Connolly, Thomas, S. J.

1990   "A Coeur d'Alene Indian Story." (Young tribal member Reno Stensgar learns about Coeur d'Alene history, legends, and customs from his grandmother, Keena.) Centennial publication of the Coeur d'Alene Tribe in conjunction with the Idaho Indian Centennial Committee, 1890–1990. Fairfield, WA: Ye Galleon Press.

1997   "The Shift of Coeur d'Alene Tribal Dependency from Hunting-Fishing-Gathering to Dependency upon Agricultural Pursuits in the Palouse." Sacred Heart Mission, DeSmet, ID.

Cox, Thomas

n.d.   "Changing Patterns of Land Use among the Coeur d'Alene: An Environmental Ethnohistory." Manuscript.

Diomedi, Alexander, S. J.

1978   *Sketches of Indian Life in the Pacific Northwest.* Edited by Edward Kowrach. Fairfield: Ye Galleon Press.

Doak, Ivy

1991   "Coeur d'Alene Rhetorical Structure," *Texas Linguistic Forum* 32: 43–70. University of Texas Austin, Department of Linguistics and Center for Cognitive Science.

Dozier, Jack

n.d.   "History of the Coeur d'Alene Indians to 1900." M.A. thesis. University of Idaho, Moscow.

Elliott, T. C.

1920   "David Thompson and Beginnings in Idaho," *Oregon Historical Quarterly* 21(1):49–61.

Evans-Pritchard, E. E.

1940   *The Nuer: A Description of the Modes of Livelihood and Political Institutions of a Nilotic People.* New York: Oxford University Press.

Fahey, John

1997   "The Lake, the Odyssey, the Legacy and the Tribe," *Coeur d'Alene Council Fires*, series 2, 11 (2–7).

Frey, Rodney

1987   *The World of the Crow Indians: As Driftwood Lodges.* Norman: University of Oklahoma Press.

Frey, Rodney (translation with commentary)

1994   *Me-y-mi-ym: Oral Literature of the Coeur d'Alene People.* Idaho Humanities Council. (Text and videotape).

1995   *Stories That Make the World: Oral Literature of the Indian Peoples of the*

Inland Northwest As Told by Lawrence Aripa, Tom Yellowtail and Other Elders. Norman: University of Oklahoma Press.

Frey, Rodney, and Dell Hymes

1998   "Mythology." In *Smithsonian Handbook of North American Indians: Plateau*, Vol. 14. Edited by Deward Walker. Washington, D.C.: Smithsonian Institution Press.

Geertz, Clifford

1973   *The Interpretation of Cultures*. New York: Basic Books.

George, Paschal

1938   "The Sweat House," *Coeur d'Alene Teepee* 1 (9):16–17. Reprinted in 1981 by Serento Press, Plummer, ID.

Geyer, Charles

1846   "Notes on Vegetation and General Character of the Missouri and Oregon Territories, Made during a Botanical Journey from the State of Missouri: Across the South-pass of the Rocky Mountains, to the Pacific, during the Years 1843 and 1844." Transcript copied from *London Journal of Botany* 4:479–524. Washington State University, Pullman. (Referred to in Palmer 1981b.)

Grim, John

1992   "Cosmogony and the Winter Dance: Native American Ethics in Transition," *Journal of Religious Ethics* 20:389–413.

Hart, E. Richard

1996   "A History of the Coeur d'Alene Tribe's Claim to Lake Coeur d'Alene." Manuscript.

Hirsch, Eric, and Michael O'Hanlon, eds.

1995   *The Anthropology of Landscape: Perspectives on Place and Space*. Oxford: Clarendon Press.

Jacobs, Melville

1959   *The Content and Style of an Oral Literature: Clackamas Chinook Myths and Tales*. Chicago: University of Chicago Press.

Joset, Joseph, S.J.

1838–   Joset Papers. Manuscripts. Oregon Province Archives, Society of Jesus,
77   Gonzaga University, Spokane. Calendared in Burns (1947:307–14). File numbers converted from roman numerals. Partial list of titles of Coeur d'Alene materials:

JP 36: "The Coeur d'Alene"
JP 39: "R. F. DeSmet, foundateur de ces missions"
JP 41: "Ethnology and Primitive Religion of Coeur d'Alenes"
JP 42: "Notes on Mythology, Mores, and History of Coeur d'Alenes"
JP 48: "Comparative Ethnology of Rocky Mountain Tribes"
JP 69: "A Quarter of a Century among the Savages"

Kowrach, Edward, and Thomas Connolly, eds.

1990 *Saga of the Coeur d'Alene Indians: An Account of Chief Joseph Seltice.* Fairfield, WA: Ye Galleon Press.

Matheson, David

2001 *Red Thunder.* Portland, OR: Media Weavers.

McCarl, Robert

1993 "Spatial Analysis of Coeur d'Alene Traditional Literature: Aquatic Culture and Cultural Survival Through Narrative." Manuscript.

Mock, L. Bryd

1980 "The Lucerne of America," *Idaho Yesterday* 24(2):18–23.

Morning Dove

1990 *Coyote Stories.* Edited by Heister Dean Guie, with notes by L. V. McWhorter. Introduction and notes by Jay Miller. Lincoln: University of Nebraska Press. (Originally published in 1933.)

Nicodemus, Julia

n.d. "Jack Rabbit and Cotton-tail Rabbit." Mimeograph.

Nicodemus, Lawrence

1975 *Snchitsuumshtsn: The Coeur d'Alene Language.* 2 volumes. Volume 1: *Grammar, Coeur d'Alene-English Dictionary.* Volume 2: *English-Coeur d'Alene Dictionary.* Coeur d'Alene Tribal Council, Plummer, Idaho.

Nicodemus, Lawrence, Reva Hess, Jill Maria Wagner, Wanda Matt, Gary Sobbing, and Dianne Allen

2000a *Snchitsu'umshtsn: Coeur d'Alene Workbook.* 2 vols. Coeur d'Alene Tribe Department of Education, DeSmet, ID.

2000b *Snchitsu'umshtsn: Coeur d'Alene Reference Book.* Coeur d'Alene Tribe Department of Education, DeSmet, ID.

Occhi, Debra, Gary Palmer, and Roy Ogawa

1993 "Like Hair, or Trees: Semantic Analysis of the Coeur d'Alene Prefix *ne' 'amidst'.*" University of Nevada, Las Vegas. Manuscript.

Palmer, Gary

1980 "Chief Vincent's Descendants after Allotment: The Joseph Family, part I." Manuscript.

1981a "Indian Pioneers: Migration to *Ni'lukhwalqw* (DeSmet)." Paper presented at the 80th Annual Meeting of the American Anthropological Association, Los Angeles, California.

1981b "Indian Pioneers: Coeur d'Alene Mission Farming from 1842 to 1876," *Papers in Anthropology* 22(1):65–92. Department of Anthropology, University of Oklahoma.

1989 "The Gobbler: Destructive Creations in the Americas," *The World and I* (March):652–59.

1998 "Coeur d'Alene." In *Smithsonian Handbook of North American Indians:*

Plateau. Vol. 14. Edited by Deward Walker. Washington, D.C.: Smithsonian Institution Press.

2001   "Indian Pioneers: The settlement of *Ni'lukhwalqw* (upper Hangman Creek, Idaho) by the *Schitsu'umsh:* (Coeur d'Alene Indians)." *Oregon Historical Quarterly* 102(1): 22–47.

n.d.   "The Farm of Peter Vincent (Pierre Basa)." Manuscript.

Palmer, Gary, M. Dale Kinkade, and Nancy Turner

1996   "Coeur d'Alene Ethnobotany, with Comparative Notes on Spokan and other Interior Salish Languages." Manuscript.

Palmer, Gary, Lawrence Nicodemus, and Thomas Connolly

1987   *Khwi Khwe Guł Schitsu'umsh: These Are the Coeur d'Alene People.* Coeur d'Alene Tribe, Plummer, ID.

Palmer, Gary, Lawrence Nicodemus, and Lavinia Felsman

1987   *Khwi' Khwe Hntmikhw'lumkhw: This is My Land.* Coeur d'Alene Tribe, Plummer, ID.

Peltier, Jerome

1975   *Manners and Customs of the Coeur d'Alene Indians.* Spokane, WA: Peltier Publications.

1981   *A Brief History of the Coeur d'Alene Indians: 1806–1909.* Fairfield, WA: Ye Galleon Press.

Peone, Basil

1938   "An Indian Herodotus: Chief Peter Moctelme (from the Memoirs of Basil Peone)," *Coeur d' Alene Teepee* March 1(5):14, April 1(6):17, and May 1 (7):17. Reprinted in 1981 by Serento Press, Plummer, ID.

Peterson, Jacqueline

1993   *Sacred Encounters: Father DeSmet and the Indians of the Rocky Mountain West.* DeSmet Project, Washington State University. Norman: University of Oklahoma Press.

Phinney, Archie

1934   "Nez Perce Text," *Columbia University Contributions to Anthropology* 25.

Point, Nicolas, S. J.

1967   *Wilderness Kingdom. Indian Life in the Rocky Mountains: 1840–1847. The Journal and Paintings of Nicolas Point, S. J.* Translated by Joseph Donnelly. New York: Holt, Rinehart and Winston.

Ramsey, Jarold

1977   *Coyote Was Going There: Indian Literature of the Oregon Country.* Seattle: University of Washington Press.

Ray, Verne

1933   "Sanpoil Folk Tales," *Journal of the American Folk-Lore Society* 46(180): 129–87.

1937   "The Bluejay Character in the Plateau Spirit Dance," *American Anthropologist* 39(4, pt.1):593–601.

1939   *Cultural Relations in the Plateau of Northwestern America.* Publications of the Frederick Webb Hodge Anniversary Publication Fund, 3. Southwestern Museum, Los Angeles.

1942   "Culture Element Distributions: XXII Plateau," *University of California Anthropological Records* 8(2):99–262.

Reichard, Gladys

1938   "Coeur d'Alene." In *Handbook of American Indian Languages*, Vol. 3, pp. 517–707. Edited by Franz Boaz. New York: J. J. Augustin.

1946   "Coeur d'Alene Texts," part 2, xvii–xxiv. Archives of Languages of the World, University of Indiana, Bloomington. (Manuscript of interlinear transcription of texts that subsequently became the basis for "An Analysis of Coeur d'Alene Indian Myths.")

1947   "An Analysis of Coeur d'Alene Indian Myths, *Memoirs of the American Folk-Lore Society* 41. Philadelphia. Reprinted in 1969 by Kraus Reprint, New York.

Richards, Kent

1996   "United States Indian Policy and the Coeur d'Alene Tribe, 1842–1909." Manuscript.

Sprague, Roderick

1996   "An Anthropological Summary of the Coeur d'Alene Tribe's Occupation of the Lake Area." Manuscript.

Stevens, Isaac

1854   *Annual Report of the Commissioner of Indian Affairs.* Report no. 86, 33rd Cong. 2nd sess. Sen. Exec. Doc., vol. 1, no. 1 (serial set no. 746). Washington, D.C.

1855–   *Narrative and Final Report of Expeditions for a Route for a Pacific Railroad*
 60   *Near the Forty-Seventh and Forty-Ninth Parallels of North Latitude from St. Paul to Puget Sound 1855.* War Department, Washington, D.C.

Tedlock, Dennis

1972   *Finding the Center: Narrative Poetry of the Zuni Indians.* Lincoln: University of Nebraska Press.

Teit, James, and Franz Boas, eds.

1900   "The Thompson Indians of British Columbia," *Memoirs of the American Museum of Natural History*, 2; Anthropology 1(4). Publications of the Jesup North Pacific Expedition 1(4). New York.

1917   "Folk-Tales of Salish and Sahaptin Tribes," *Memoirs of the American Folk-Lore Society*, 11. Lancaster, Pennsylvania.

1930   "The Salish Tribes of the Western Plateaus," *Forty-Fifth Annual Report of the Bureau of American Ethnology for 1927–28*, pp. 23–396. Washington, D.C.: Smithsonian Institution.

Thwaites, Reuben Gold, ed.

1904–   *Original Journals of the Lewis and Clark Expedition, 1804–1806.* New York:

05   Dodd, Mead. Reprinted in 1959, Antiquarian Press, New York. Reprinted in 1969, Arno Press, New York.

Toelken, Barre, and Tacheeni Scott

1981   "Poetic Retranslation and the 'Pretty Language' of Yellowman." In *Traditional Literature of the American Indian*. Edited by Karl Kroeber, 65–116. Lincoln: University of Nebraska Press.

Winther, Oscar

1945   "Early Commercial Importance of the Mullan Road," *Oregon Historical Quarterly* (March) 46:22–35.

Wright, George

1859   "Topographic Memoirs and Map of Colonel Wright's Late Campaign against the Indians in Oregon and Washington Territories," 62. In *Report of the Secretary of War for 1858*. 35th Cong. 2d sess. Sen. Exec. Doc., vol. 10, no. 32 (serial set no. 984) and House Exec. Doc., no. 2 (serial set no. 998), pp. 346–48, 408–10. Washington, D.C.

Index

Abalone shells: as trade item, 23

Abraham, John, **158**; as consultant, 279; as reviewer, 286

Abraham, Vicki: as consultant, 279

Ackerman, Lillian: on social organization, 297*n*6

Afterlife, 249–50, 300*n*1; precontact notion of, 303*n*18. *See also* Memorial Giveaway; Religion

Agreements. *See* Legal agreements and decisions

Agusta: on move to DeSmet, 67, 68; Peone's description of, 68

Alcohol consumption, 61, 230

Allen, Dianne, 289; and language preservation, 106

Allgood, Tiffany, 291

Allotment Act. *See* Legal agreements and decisions

Amelia Wheaton (steamboat), 97

American Indian Art Institute, 105

Amǫtqn. See Creator

Ancestors. *See* Spiritual Beings

Anglican missionary activity, 62. *See also* Catholic missionary activity

Animal Peoples. *See* First Peoples

Antelope, Julia. *See* Nicodemus, Julia Antelope

Antelope, Louis, 273

Antelope, Mary Catherine, 273

Antelope, Morris, 303; as consultant for Ray, 273, 274; letter to Superintendent, 71–72, 299*n*10

Antelope, Susan, 273; and camas baking, 160–61

Apache Indians, 203, 303*n*1

Aripa (Rufinus Shi'itsin; "of the St. Maries clan"), 275, 303*n*5; on move to DeSmet, 67; and uprising on the St. Joe, 91–92

Aripa, Andrew, 303*n*5

Aripa, Felix, 44, **276**, 303*n*5; on berrying, 26–27; on consequences of Allotment, 95; as consultant, 279; on farming success, 75; on meaning of Lake Coeur d'Alene, 257–58; on move to DeSmet, 67; on name *Aɬkwɑri't* (Harrison), 70; recipient of camas, 211; as reviewer, 287; on war, 80; on water potato, 157, 159; on "white man's greed," 78

Aripa, Lawrence, ix, **194**, 303*n*5; assisted in Natural Resource Damage Assessment, 291; as consultant, 275, 279, 282, 288, 289; and Coyote, 119, 126, 290; funeral of, 292; on journeying to buffalo country, 53; on moral qualities of chief, 44–45; opening prayer at Powwow, 215; as reviewer, 287; as storyteller, 193, 196, 203, 284, 285, 286; on "Smallpox and the Five People," 298*n*4; on water potato, 157, 159

Aripa, Louis, 92, 303*n*5

Aripa, Mary Madeline, 303*n*5

Aripa, Stanislaw (Stanislas), 303*n*5; on move to DeSmet, 67

Bags: flat, 28; twined round, 28
Basil Blue Steer (Kui-kui-sto-lem): on move to DeSmet, 67
Baskets, 28–29; birch bark, 28; cedar bark, 28; cedar root, 28
Basso, Keith: on concept of landscape, 203, 303*n*1
Beauty Bay, 120
Benewah Market, 103
Benewah Medical Center, 103; and ethic of sharing, 254
Bernah (Bernard), Isadore: on move to DeSmet, 67
Berrying: ceremony associated with, 34; influence of Jump Dance on, 240; locations for, 34, 67, 170, 187; variety gathered during, 34; when ready, 26–27, 172. *See also* Plants; Subsistence
Big Bend country, 112; as root gathering area, 7
Birds: bustard, 26; Canada goose (*Branta canadensis*), 164; cinnamon teal (*Anas cyanoptera*), 26, 164; crane, 26; crow, 26; eagle, 26; fishing bird, 26; grouse (*Bonasa umbellus*; "pool hen"), 164, 173; hawk, 26, 36; heron (bittern), 26; magpie, 26; mallard duck (*Anas pletrhynchos*), 26, 164; osprey (calumet bird), 26; pelican, 26; robin (*Turdus migratorius*), 164; snipe, 26; Steller's jay, 237; swan, 26; swallow, 26; thrush, 26; turtledove, 26; woodpecker, 26. *See also* First Peoples
Bitterroot (*Lewisia rediviva*), 28, 155; description of, 156–57; gathering technique, 156–57; locations of, 7, 112, 156; preparation of, 156, 172; Rabbit and Jackrabbit provide, 112; as trade item, 22; when gathered, 156. *See also* Gathering; Plants
Bitterroot Valley, Montana, 63
Blackfeet Indians, 25, 56; Coyote's creation of, 119, 133; reaction to priests among, 75; warfare with, 12, 53
Black Robes. *See* Catholic missionary activity

Boas, Franz, 110
Bonners Ferry, Idaho, 25
Brinkman, Raymond, 106
Buffalo, 7, 25, 54, 56; distribution of meat, 206; last hunt, 56, 67; and move to DeSmet, 67; techniques of hunting, 51, 56; tribal hunts of, 55; "water," 30, 31
Bunker Hill mine, 97, 98
Bureau of Indian Affairs, 77, 103
Burial and funeral practices: Catholic influences on, 242, 243, 245, 303*n*16, 303*n*17; extended mourning, 246; ghosts associated with, 48; location of, 242, 245; meals during, 244; prayer leaders, 243; role and significance of, 242, 245; songs, 243–44; wake, 242–45; use of camas and bitterroots, 156, 244. *See also* Memorial Giveaway
Burke, Idaho: Hecla mine near, 98
Bush, George, Sr., 105–6
Byrne, Cornelius, S.J.: encouraged culture and arts, 77, 101. *See also* Catholic missionary activity

Camas (*Camassia quamash*; *sqha'w-lutqhwe'*), 6, 154, 155, 172; description of, 159; given in hospital, 154–55; locations of, 11, 27, 67, 73, 112, 159, 174; preparation of, 28, 160–61; Rabbit and Jackrabbit provide, 112; served at family gatherings, 156; sharing, 161, 170; technique of gathering, 159–60, 174–75. *See also* Gathering; Plants
Camel, Theresa, 154
Canoes: birch bark, 30; in burial, 48; cedar bark, 26, 30; in oral tradition, 41; "sturgeon-nosed," 26, 30; tule reed rafts, 30; used by Chief Child of the Yellow Root, 149; used in hunting, 36; used in travel, 26, 30; white-pine bark, 26, 30
Caruana, Joseph, S.J.: policies of, 71–72. *See also* Catholic missionary activity
Cataldo Mission (Old Mission; Mission of the Sacred Heart near the Coeur

served at family gatherings, 166; as trade item, 22, 36; Woodtick (First People) "calling in," 125. *See also* First Peoples; Hunting; Mammals
Dentalium: as trade item, 23
Departments, tribal. *See* Political organization
Designated hunter. *See* Hunting
DeSmet, Pierre-Jean, S.J., 63; observations on farming, 73. *See also* Catholic missionary activity
DeSmet, Idaho (*'L'lkhwi'lus*), 64, 112, 229; early years of, 75; first horse observed near, 50; meaning of *'L'lkhwi'lus*, 70; naming of settlement, 65
DeSmet Mission (Mission of the Sacred Heart near Hangman Creek), 64, 65; mission burns, 65; and move to Hangman Creek area, 65–68, 73; wakes and burials at, 242, 245. *See also* Cataldo Mission; Catholic missionary activity
Diet: balanced, 29; buffalo added to, 53; composition of, 41. *See also* Berrying; Fishing; Gathering; Hunting; Mammals; Plants; Subsistence
Digging stick (*pitse'*), 28, 156, 159
Diomedi, Alexander, S.J.: on *Amotqn*, 110; on move to DeSmet, 66–67, 299*n*8; oversees relocation of mission to DeSmet, 65; on spirits, 33. *See also* Catholic missionary activity
Diseases. *See* Smallpox
Doak, Ivy, 106

Economy: and economic development, 101, 103–4, 105, 108; and gaming operation, 104–5; and tribal employment, 106; and tribal farm, 104. *See also* Coeur d'Alene Casino; Subsistence
Education: boarding school (Convent of Mary Immaculate), 65; Coeur d'Alene Tribal School, 103, 105, 205; ethic of sharing demonstrated, 254; Lewis-Clark State College, 254, 289, 304*n*9; North Idaho College, 105, 254, 304*n*9; Red River School, 62; University of Idaho, 291–92. *See also* Rites of passage
Environmental Action Plan, 291

Fahey, John, 297–98*n*1
Family. *See* Social organization
Farming, 17, 67, 73, 74, 75, 76; location of early farms, 74; potato cultivation prior to arrival of priests, 73; success in, 74–75; and types of crops, 75
Felician: guide to Diomedi, 33, 110
Finlay, Jaco: establishes Spokane House, 60
Finley, Lucy, ix, 219; as consultant, 279, 282; on gathering water potatoes, 181; receives water potatoes, 292; as reviewer, 287
First fruits ceremonies, 204–11 passim; for deer hunting, 204; for first hunt, 13, 205–6; for fishing, 30; for gathering berries and roots, 34, 152, 204; purposes of, 13, 34. *See also* Religion; Shamans; *Suumesh*
First Peoples (Animal Peoples; Guardian Spirits), 3, 111–51 passim, 185–86; Animal Peoples becoming Guardian Spirits, 32–33, 176–80 passim; Ant, 228; Badger, 115, 117, 185; Bear, 26, 36, 113, 115, 185, 190, 191; Beaver, 36, 228; Bird, 182, 246; Blue Jay, 117; bring back to life, 116, 141–43; characteristics of, 111, 185; Chipmunk, 3–4, 10, 114, 183, 197, 198–99; Cougar, 178–79; Deer, 10, 26, 113, 153, 190, 197; Dove, 117, 176; Eagle, 33, 113–17, 153, 197, 257; Elk, 33, 113, 190, 197; Fish, 113, 185; Fox, 123, 131–32; Goats, 190; Hawk, 33, 113–17, 197, 228; Grizzly Bear, 41; Groundhog, 239; Jackrabbit, 111, 112, 153, 183, 300*n*3; Little Muskrat, 174, 193–96; Little Squirrel, 3–4, 10, 183; Mink, 195; Mole (Mrs.), 111, 115–16, 136–37, 141–43, 183, 191, 196; Muskrat, 11, 257; Osprey, 26; Otter, 174, 193–96; prepare the world for Human Peoples, 8–9, 110, 113, 116,

Made in the USA
Middletown, DE
18 August 2018